## COPYRIGHT REVERSION

Copyright law is meant to promote access to knowledge and culture and reward creators. But around the world, publishers, record labels and other investors continue to hoover up the rights and rewards due to creators and leave masses of creativity locked away from the public. This book shows why this bargain is broken, and how reverting copyright to creators can help redress it – allowing them to revitalise old works, turbocharged by technological advances that are providing more opportunities to do so than ever before. With cutting-edge empirical and doctrinal analysis of dominant reversion models from the United States, the Commonwealth and the EU, the book provides policymakers and academics with best-practice principles for designing reversion mechanisms that can help copyright laws do a better job of supporting the public interest in access while helping artists get paid. This title is also available as open access on Cambridge Core.

Joshua Yuvaraj is Senior Lecturer in the Faculty of Law, University of Auckland, and co-director of the New Zealand Centre for Intellectual Property. In 2021 he won the Mollie Holman Award for best doctoral law thesis at Monash University.

Rebecca Giblin is Professor and ARC Future Fellow at Melbourne Law School. She is the author of *Chokepoint Capitalism* (with Cory Doctorow, 2022).

CAMBRIDGE INTELLECTUAL PROPERTY AND INFORMATION LAW

As its economic potential has rapidly expanded, intellectual property has become a subject of front-rank legal importance. Cambridge Intellectual Property and Information Law is a series of monograph studies of major current issues in intellectual property. Each volume contains a mix of international, European, comparative and national law, making this a highly significant series for practitioners, judges and academic researchers in many countries.



A list of books in the series can be found at the end of this volume.

*For Tiffany, and for Levi.*

*For the artists, authors and performers whose efforts render bearable the human condition.*

# Contents

# Acknowledgements

**This book and the research within it have been supported with funding from:**

The Australian Research Council, via FT17010001 ('The Author's Interest Project') and LP160100387 ('The eLending Project')

The University of Melbourne

Monash University

The University of Auckland Research Development Fund

The Australian Government via a Research Training Program Scholarship

The funders of *Untapped: The Literary Heritage Project* (i.e. state and territory libraries from around Australia, plus contributions from a small number of private philanthropists)

## INCORPORATION OF PRIOR WORK

This book is the culmination of research conducted between 2017 and 2024. With the permission of the copyright holders, it incorporates some material from the following publications:

Joshua Yuvaraj, 'Implementing Copyright Revocation in Ireland and Malta: Lessons for Lawmakers' (2023) 18(7) *Journal of Intellectual Property Law & Practice* 528.

Joshua Yuvaraj, 'Back to the Start: Re-envisioning the Role of Copyright Reversion in Australia and Other Common Law Countries' (PhD Thesis, Monash University, 2021).

Joshua Yuvaraj, Rebecca Giblin, Daniel Russo-Batterham and Genevieve Grant, 'U.S. Copyright Termination Notices 1977–2020: Introducing New Datasets' (2022) 19(1) *Journal of Empirical Legal Studies* 250

Rebecca Giblin, 'A New Copyright Bargain? Reclaiming Lost Culture and Getting Authors Paid' (2018) 41 *Columbia Journal of Law & the Arts* 369–411.

Joshua Yuvaraj and Rebecca Giblin, 'Are Contracts Enough? An Empirical Study of Australian Publishing Agreements' (2021) 44(1) *Melbourne University Law Review* 380.

Joshua Yuvaraj and Rebecca Giblin, 'Why Were Commonwealth Reversionary Rights Abolished (and What Can We Learn Where They Remain)?' (2019) 41(4) *European Intellectual Property Review* 232

Rebecca Giblin and Cory Doctorow, *Chokepoint Capitalism* (Beacon Press, 2022).

## INDIVIDUAL ACKNOWLEDGEMENTS

We're grateful to academic colleagues from around the world for generously contributing their knowledge and expertise to the project, particularly Jane Ginsburg, Sam Ricketson, Martin Kretschmer, Séverine Dusollier, Ula Furgal, Paul Heald, and Paul Crosby.

We also thank the marvellous research assistants who have assisted us in pulling the book together: Anders Furze, Tessa Barrington, Joseph Zivny and Sian Vaughan-Jones, as well as Kirsty Wilson from Melbourne Law School's academic research service. Thanks to Fiona Rotstein for assisting with formatting and footnotes. Thanks also to An Hertogen and Maude Loutsch for invaluable assistance with French-language materials.

Thanks lastly to friends, family and colleagues who helped to sense-check draft chapters and who provided friendship and support throughout the writing process, particularly Brad Williams, Rachel Goh, Jeremy Yuvaraj, Joanne Yuvaraj, Yuvaraj Malaipan, Mui Mui Tan, Treasa Dunworth, Julia Tolmie, Lucy Holloway, Andrew Godwin, Jodi Gardner, Alexandra Allen-Franks, Craig Elliffe, and Daniel Gilbert. A special mention goes to Muntaha Khan, without whose dedication, support and encouragement this book would not exist.

# 1

# Reversion's Potential

## INTRODUCTION

Madeleine St John's novel *The Women in Black* is a rare peek into the post-war lives of Sydney's working women, including migrants who fled Europe in search of a better life and found themselves in a sunny, alien world. It went out of print quickly after its debut in 1993, despite another of St John's novels being shortlisted for the 1997 Booker Prize, but was rediscovered and republished in 2012 by a leading independent publisher. This time the world was ready: the new edition sold over 100,000 copies in physical and digital forms, the story was developed into a musical and a feature length film, and the book was translated into German, Italian, French and Hebrew.[1]

Republishing lost books is made possible by the fact that publishing contracts typically contain 'out-of-print' clauses that allow authors to reclaim their copyright if their book goes off the market. All kinds of creative workers can be obliged to license or assign their copyrights to cultural investors to get their works produced and distributed to audiences (including book authors and illustrators, recording artists, composers and screenwriters) and the process of reclaiming those rights is called 'reversion'. Research by the UK Authors' Licensing and Collecting Society has found that 63 per cent of authors who exercised a contractual reversion clause went on to earn more money as a result.[2] But reversion rights aren't just found in contracts – more than half the world's nations have some kind of author-protective reversion right enshrined in statute.[3]

1 Text Publishing, *The Women in Black* <https://perma.cc/GM63-3BYJ>; Text Publishing, *Ladies in Black* <https://perma.cc/7XUF-CFWL>; Andrea Hanke, 'Editorial: Rising Stars', *Think Australian* (Books+Publishing, 15 November 2018) <https://perma.cc/KW25-6483>; email dated 18 November 2019 from Anne Beilby (Rights and Contracts Director, The Text Publishing Company).

2 Authors' Licensing and Collecting Society, 'Contracts and Rights' (Web Page) <https://www.alcs.co.uk/knowledge/contracts-and-rights/>.

3 Joshua Yuvaraj, 'Back to the Start: Re-envisioning the Role of Copyright Reversion in Australia and Other Common Law Countries' (PhD Thesis, Monash University, 2021) 90.

Reversion rights have a wide range of potential triggers, but the most common are time-based (like the US law that permits transfers to be terminated after 35 years), or use-based (like the 'use-it-or-lose-it' rights common in Europe).

Reversion has been around for as long as copyright law itself, with the first statutory reversion right appearing in the *Statute of Anne*, and the earliest contractual example we could find dating back to 1694.[4] In the digital era however they have far more potential than ever before. Consider books, for example. In the analogue world, high marginal costs of copying and distribution used to mean nearly all books quickly disappeared.[5] Although authors could often reclaim their rights to out-of-print titles, that meant little in practice unless another publisher was interested in making the substantial investments necessary to bring them back to market. Now, however, there are vastly more options for doing so. Digital printing makes smaller print runs financially feasible – right down to single copies via print-on-demand ('POD') – enabling books to be available in physical form for longer. Further, the marginal costs of digital production and global instantaneous delivery are virtually zero, which opens new opportunities for online sales, including in foreign markets, either via publishers or author-to-reader direct. Technological advances give rise to new licensing opportunities, too – for example, to public libraries for 'elending'. This has become big business, with market leader OverDrive facilitating more than half a billion ebook loans in 2023.[6]

Rapid improvements in AI technologies are creating new opportunities too. AI-powered translation is already reducing the costs of translating books for foreign-language markets.[7] In the audio realm, AI-powered text-to-speech technologies are already on the market,[8] and for those who still want a human reader, high-quality online home recording is drastically reducing the costs of audiobook production.[9]

Books are just one example: technological progress is driving new opportunities for building upon and exploiting all kinds of other works too, including video games and movies, songs, visual art and more.[10]

4 Rebecca Schoff Curtin, 'The Transactional Origins of Authors' Copyright' (2016) 40(2) *Columbia Journal of Law & the Arts* 175, 213.

5 Mark Twain's Testimony to the US Congress, 'Mark Twain on Copyright' <https://perma.cc/S6FR-SE23>.

6 'Libraries Achieve Record-Breaking Circulation of Digital Media in 2023', *OverDrive* (Blog Post, 4 January 2024) <https://company.overdrive.com/2024/01/04/libraries-achieve-record-breaking-circulation-of-digital-media-in-2023/>.

7 Joanna Penn, 'Tips for Self-Publishing in Translation: Adventures with AI and German', *The Creative Penn* (Web Page, 22 November 2019) <https://perma.cc/S85N-QRWN>.

8 E.g. AWS, *Amazon Polly* <https://perma.cc/R4EC-M8QL>; Google Cloud, *Cloud Text-to-Speech* <https://perma.cc/US8J-6HLS>.

9 E.g. the Findaway Voices service, which provides high-quality audiobook narration via at-home narrators: <https://perma.cc/KA2E-5LQR>.

10 See, e.g., Sarah E Needleman, 'How AI Is Building the Next Blockbuster Videogames', *The Wall Street Journal* (online, 17 April 2023) <https://www.wsj.com/articles/how-ai-is-building-the-next-blockbuster-videogames-6fefdd1c>; Veena McCoole, 'How AI Is Changing the Art Market', *Artsy* (online, 27 October 2023) <https://www.artsy.net/article/artsy-editorial-ai-changing-art-market>; Neil Sahota, 'The AI Takeover in Cinema: How Movie Studios Use

The availability of new exploitation opportunities should be a good thing. However, the mere fact one party holds the rights for a work does not mean that they will have the interest or capacity to fully exploit them in all the formats and markets where they have (or develop) value. If we want creators to better share in the benefits of their work, and the public to better benefit from widespread access to knowledge and culture, well-scoped reversion rights are a promising path to reform.

## 1.1 COPYRIGHT'S FAILED BARGAIN

We need to explore such possibilities because the current copyright bargain, at least in the Western nations that make up the world's most lucrative markets for knowledge and culture, is doing a poor job of achieving its aims. This becomes very clear when we compare what copyright is supposed to achieve against its real-world results.

### 1.1.1 *What Is Copyright Meant to Achieve?*

While copyright has a number of aims, it is primarily about *incentives* and *rewards*, which map to historical 'instrumentalist' and 'natural rights' justifications for copyright.[11] While the two rationales are more strongly associated with common law and civil law jurisdictions, respectively, it has been persuasively demonstrated that considerations traceable to both rationales widely coexist within both international treaties and domestic laws.[12] These rationales provide the primary justifications for

Artificial Intelligence', *Forbes* (online, 8 March 2024) <https://www.forbes.com/sites/neilsahota/2024/03/08/the-ai-takeover-in-cinema-how-movie-studios-use-artificial-intelligence/?sh = 784c81e34a3f>; Elias Leight and Kristin Robinson, '5 Ways AI Has Already Changed the Music Industry', *Billboard* (online, 4 August 2023) <https://www.billboard.com/lists/ways-ai-has-changed-music-industry-artificial-intelligence/revolutionizing-production/>.

11 Rebecca Giblin, 'A New Copyright Bargain? Reclaiming Lost Culture and Getting Authors Paid' (2018) 41 *Columbia Journal of Law & Arts* 369, 373.

12 See Rebecca Giblin and Kimberlee Weatherall, 'If We Redesigned Copyright from Scratch, What Might It Look Like?' in Rebecca Giblin and Kimberlee Weatherall (eds), *What If We Could Reimagine Copyright?* (ANU Press, 2017) 17; Peter Drahos, A *Philosophy of Intellectual Property* (ANU Press, 2016) 96–7. For broader discussions of how these aims have animated global copyright policymaking, see, e.g., Martin Senftleben, *Copyright, Limitations and the Three-Step Test: An Analysis of the Three-Step Test in International and EC Copyright Law* (PhD Thesis, Institute for Information Law, 2004) especially 6–10; Jane C Ginsburg, 'A Tale of Two Copyrights: Literary Property in Revolutionary France and America' (1990) 64 *Tulane Law Review* 991, 995; Alain Strowel, *Droit d'auteur et copyright, Divergences et Convergences* (Bruylant, 1993); Gillian Davies, *Copyright and the Public Interest* (Sweet & Maxwell, 2nd ed, 2002) 348–51; JH Reichman, 'Duration of Copyright and the Limits of Cultural Policy' (1996) 14 *Cardozo Arts & Entertainment Law Journal* 625, 643–4; Sam Ricketson, 'The Copyright Term' (1992) 23 *International Review of Intellectual Property and Competition Law* 753, 755; Alfred C Yen, 'Restoring the National Law: Copyright as Labor and Possession' (1990) 51 Ohio State Law Journal 517.

the monopoly copyright creates over knowledge and culture, making them the most appropriate measures on which to evaluate its success.

### 1.1.2 *Copyright's Incentives*

Copyright seeks to incentivise two distinct things: first, the production of new cultural works and, second, investments in keeping those works available. While the first of these may receive the most attention, the second has always been important. That is reflected in the very first words of the full title of the first modern copyright statute, the UK's *Statute of Anne* ('An Act for the Encouragement of Learning'[13]) and in the purpose of the US Constitution's intellectual property clause ('To promote the Progress of Science and useful Arts . . .').[14] The fulfilment of those aims relies not only on knowledge being *produced*, but on the public having *access*. The importance of availability is also manifest in the effectiveness of Macaulay's 1841 speech to the UK House of Commons: his argument that a proposed copyright term extension could result in the suppression of important books was taken so seriously that it resulted in new provisions to guard against that risk.[15]

Thus, copyright's incentives were never just about getting works produced, but rather aimed at achieving the broader social benefits that flow from widespread access to knowledge and culture. Although the modern copyright discourse more commonly considers access at the exceptions level,[16] it's also critical to the rationale for granting rights in the first place. Accordingly, copyright's twin incentive aims can be more accurately thought of as access aims, which is how we refer to them in this book.

### 1.1.3 *Copyright's Rewards*

On top of those incentives, copyright is supposed to grant *rewards*. As Ricketson explains, '[t]here is a strong moral argument . . . that as authors confer benefits on society through their creative activity – the provision of learning, instruction and entertainment – this contribution should be duly rewarded'.[17]

[13] Copyright Act 1710, 8 Ann c 21.

[14] Constitution of the United States of America: Analysis and Interpretation, 'Article I: Section 8 Enumerated Powers: Clause 8 Intellectual Property' (Web Page) <https://constitution.congress.gov/browse/article-1/section-8/clause-8/#:~:text=Clause%208%20Intellectual%20Property,C8>.

[15] Ronan Deazley, 'Commentary on *Copyright Amendment Act 1842*' in Lionel Bently and Martin Kretschmer, *Primary Sources on Copyright (1450–1900)* (Web Page, 2008) <www.copyrighthistory.org>.

[16] See, e.g., Australian Government, Department of Infrastructure, Transport, Regional Development, Communications and the Arts, *Copyright Access Reforms* (Web Page, 13 August 2020) <https://www.infrastructure.gov.au/media-centre/copyright-access-reforms>.

[17] Ricketson (n 12) 757.

This rewards motivation is reflected in the Berne Convention's adoption of terms based on the author's lifetime, which Ricketson described as 'represent[ing] the success of an idea, rooted in natural law concepts, that authors have a natural right to property in the fruits of their creative endeavours.'[18] Even the US, which boasts a copyright tradition firmly anchored on the instrumentalist side of the spectrum, is demonstrably influenced by creators' moral claims.[19] That has been reflected in various statutory and judicial interventions, including its current law entitling creators to terminate most copyright transfers after 35 years (something we examine in detail in Chapter 3). Fromer describes this as 'a powerful signal to authors that copyright law cares about the personhood, labor, and possessory interests they have in their work'.[20]

The power and significance of rewards rationales can be seen in how persistently authors' interests have been used to justify broader and longer terms of copyright protection. Again, this can be seen even in the US, where the rhetoric accompanying the 1998 US term extension focused on the desirability of '[a]uthors [being] able to pass along to their children and grandchildren the financial benefits of their works.'[21] Such arguments dominated lobbying efforts even though the beneficiary of the resulting extension was, in almost all cases, the rightsholder at the time it was passed – very little was actually secured to the author or their heirs.[22]

Such rhetoric appeals to our inclinations to reward authors for their creative contributions, and they're effective because those moral claims have real power.[23]

Creators' moral claims to rewards are the leading justification for copyright terms that go beyond the amount necessary to incentivise initial production and promote ongoing availability of existing works: the public accepts that it's appropriate to grant additional rights because creators *deserve* some of the additional social surplus of their creations. If those rewards were captured by others instead, this justification would disappear.

[18] Ibid 783.

[19] Ginsburg (n 12).

[20] Jeanne C Fromer, 'Expressive Incentives in Intellectual Property' (2012) 98 *Virginia Law Review* 1745, 1806.

[21] House of Representatives, 105th Congress 2d Session, Report 105-452, Copyright Term Extension Act.

[22] See Copyright Term Extension Act of 1998, Pub L No 105-298, § 101, 112 Stat 2827, 2828 (1998) <https://perma.cc/58MK-GQBK>. The only exception was that the Extension Act did amend the Copyright Act to give authors and their heirs a termination right at the end of the original 75 years from first publication, but only if they hadn't exercised their prior termination right at the end of 56 years from first publication. See 17 USC § 304(c)–(d). See also William Patry, 'The Failure of the American Copyright System: Protecting the Idle Rich' (1997) 72 *Notre Dame Law Review* 907, 908.

[23] For a detailed tracing of the ways in which the concept of authorship has been used to promote particular positions in legal discourse, including in ways directly contrary to authors' interests, see Peter Jaszi, 'Toward a Theory of Copyright: The Metamorphoses of Authorship'(1991) *Duke Law Journal* 455; Rebecca Giblin, 'Should It Be Copyright's Role to Fill Houses with Books?' in Susy Frankel and Daniel Gervais (eds), *Intellectual Property and the Regulation of the Internet* (Victoria University Press, 2017) 18–19.

### 1.1.4 *How Well Is Copyright Achieving Its Aims?*

The copyright discourse typically blurs the distinction between incentives and rewards, talking about what investors *need* and what creators *deserve* without separating the one from the other.

When evaluating the extent to which copyright is achieving its aims, however, it is necessary to distinguish between them. Critically, we don't mind who gets copyright's incentive components: there, the public is simply interested in getting the works produced and available.[24] However, we *are* interested in who gets the rewards component. Since that is justified by authors' moral claims, it ought to be primarily captured by the person who actually creates the work.[25] This isn't to say that cultural investors don't play a vital role in the copyright ecosystem – of course they do. Authors, illustrators, photographers, screenwriters, recording artists, music composers, game developers and other creative workers partner with cultural investors to access the capital and services necessary to get their work produced and distributed, including services that they cannot or don't want to provide themselves. However, the importance of investors to creative ecosystems does not alter the fact that investors' interests and authors' interests are different, and need to be satisfied in different ways.

So how well is copyright achieving its aims? In a word – poorly.[26] There are any number of reasons for this of course, as we recognise below, including those arising from broader social, cultural and economic realities that are well outside the scope of this book.[27] The specific problem we're concerned with here lies in copyright's structural deficiencies around licensing and ownership. In sum, copyright rights are far longer and broader than what's necessary to incentivise initial production, but very often those rights are made alienable in a way that actually blocks investments in ongoing availability, and makes it harder for creators to appropriate rewards. This is the fundamental problem that reversion has such potential to help resolve.

#### 1.1.4.1 Current Copyright Grants Are Far Broader than What's Necessary to Incentivise Initial Production

Incentivising initial production is a purely economic aim, and the extent of rights necessary to do so is readily calculable. Two inputs are particularly significant to that

[24] 'Rebecca Giblin explains why authors and artists struggle to get paid' (*YouTube*, 2019) <https://www.youtube.com/watch?v=uaDIyE1UGt4>.

[25] Ibid.

[26] Our analysis below is drawn from Giblin's comprehensive evaluation of the extent to which existing approaches to copyright promote its incentives and rewards aims in 'A New Copyright Bargain', and we refer readers to that work if they wish to delve into greater detail on any of its points. See Giblin (n 11) 372–86.

[27] See the discussion about the limitations of our claims at Section 1.2.

calculus: the discounting necessary to reflect the time value of money, and rates of cultural depreciation.[28]

The 'time value of money' recognises that the further away in time a benefit will be received, the less it is currently worth. Thus, the promise of $100 next week is worth much more to us today than the promise of $100 in a decade's time. You do not have to be an economist to grasp this concept. Just imagine that you are interviewing housemates, and they offer the same amount in rent – but one would pay monthly in advance, and the other 10 years after they move out. One of those is obviously worth considerably more to you, right now, than the other.

The upshot of this principle is that the prospect of money to be received in the distant future will provide much less incentive than that you'll receive quickly. Assuming a real interest rate of 7 per cent, a dollar today is worth 93 cents if it's to be paid in a year, but just a fraction of a cent if it's going to take 80 years to end up in your pocket.[29]

Cultural depreciation also plays an important role in determining the incentives necessary to achieve the desired production. Like new cars and televisions, cultural works tend to lose commercial value over time. In the case of fiction books, sales become negligible within a single year.[30] Music takes a little longer, but a 2013 study out of the US Bureau of Economic Analysis found that most songs depreciate by 65 per cent in a year, making almost all their revenue in the first five years.[31] While the rise of streaming seems likely to extend lifespans, it's too new for there to be reliable data to measure its effects, and thus it's unlikely to be yet changing the assumptions on which businesses set the terms of their deals.[32]

Once the value of future earnings is discounted to their present value, and cultural depreciation is factored in, the consensus is that the period of exclusivity necessary to incentivise initial creation of even the most expensive works is about 25 years or less.[33]

28 Brief of George A Akerlof et al. as Amici Curiae in Support of Petitioners, *Eldred v Ashcroft*, 537 US 186 (2003) (No 01-618) 5–7.

29 Ibid.

30 Andrew Gowers, HM Treasury, *Gowers Review of Intellectual Property* (2006) 52 <https://perma.cc/78YV-RN3T>.

31 Rachel Soloveichik, *Music Originals as Capital Assets* 27 (Bureau of Econ. Analysis, Working Paper No WP2013–8, 2013) <https://www.bea.gov/system/files/papers/WP2013-8.pdf>.

32 From the data available to them in their 2019 study, Garcia and McCrary note that, while 'streaming may prolong the commercial viability of the average record', the resulting payments 'are so low that the economic benefit of this additional volume is unclear'. See Kristelia A Garcia and Justin McCrary, 'A Reconsideration of Copyright's Term' (2019) 71(2) *Alabama Law Review* 351, 380.

33 William M Landes and Richard A Posner, 'Indefinitely Renewable Copyright' (2003) 70 *University of Chicago Law Review* 471, 476 ('[T]he incremental incentive to create new works as a function of a longer term is likely to be very small (given discounting and depreciation) beyond a term of twenty-five years or so'). Rufus Pollock, 'Forever Minus a Day? Calculating Optimal Copyright Term' (2009) 6(1) *Review of Economic Research on Copyright Issues* 35, 56. Elsewhere, Kretschmer has argued for a still shorter initial term of 10 years, followed by

You can see these principles in action via sub-licensing practices between book publishers. Assume that a publisher who controls a book's rights across all languages decides to sub-licence the German rights. The German publisher will have virtually all the same costs of getting the original book to market, including editing, typesetting, distribution and so on, plus the cost of the translation to boot. If publishers really needed the full duration of copyright to incentivise such investments, that's how long those sub-licences would last. But when economist Paul Crosby and his team analysed over 9,000 international licensing deals, they found that publishers most commonly licensed translation rights for five-year terms (42.5 per cent), and that 62 per cent of deals were for a term of seven years or less.[34]

The fact that sub-licensees are willing to make such substantial investments in exchange for so much less than the full copyright term provides real-world confirmation that, even if publishers would *like* to have rights for the entire copyright term, they don't *need* them to incentivise their investments. We find similar evidence in the fact that record labels commonly write off bad debt after 20 years, indicating they don't expect copyrights to still generate value beyond that.[35]

This doesn't necessarily mean that it's problematic for copyright to last longer than that – it simply means that, to the extent copyright rights go beyond the amount necessary to incentivise initial production, they must be justified on other rationales. And copyrights nearly always last beyond this point: for works, treaties mandate minimums of the author's lifetime plus at least 50 years,[36] and often life plus 70.[37] Sound recordings and films must be protected for at least 20 and 50 years,

reversion to the author. See Martin Kretschmer, Copyright Term Reversion and the 'Use-It-or-Lose-It' Principle (2012) 1 *International Journal of Music Business Research* 44, 44–53.

34 For details of that project see Paul Crosby et al, *Success Story – International Rights Sales of Australian-Authored Books* (Macquarie University, 2019). The data around sub-licensing deals was not separately broken out in the results that have been published so far, but were provided by email: email from Paul Crosby to Rebecca Giblin, 9 May 2024.

35 Digital, Culture, Media and Sport Committee, *Economics of Music Streaming* (House of Commons Paper No 50, Session 2021–22) 34, 67.

36 See *Berne Convention for the Protection of Literary and Artistic Works*, opened for signature 9 September 1886, [1901] ATS 126 (entered into force 5 December 1887), as last revised by the *Paris Act relating to the Berne Convention for the Protection of Literary and Artistic Works*, signed 24 July 1971, 1161 UNTS 30 (entered into force 15 December 1972), and as amended by the *Amendments to Articles 22 and 23 of the Paris Act of 14 July 1971 of the Berne Convention for the Protection of Literary and Artistic Works*, signed 28 September 1979, [1984] ATS 40 (entered into force 19 November 1984) art 7(1). See also *Marrakesh Agreement establishing the World Trade Organization*, opened for signature 15 April 1994, 1867 UNTS 3 (entered into force 1 January 1995) annex 1C ('*Agreement on Trade Related Aspects of Intellectual Property Rights*') art 12.

37 See Directive 2006/116/EC of the European Parliament and of the Council of 12 December 2006 on the term of protection of copyright and certain related rights (codified version) (OJ L 372, 27.12.2006, 12–18). In 2005 Australia ratified the Australia-US Free Trade Agreement which required Australia to amend its domestic copyright laws to extend copyright protection in most cases to 70 years after the death of the author. See *Copyright Act 1968* (Cth) s 33(2).

respectively, under the Rome and Berne conventions,[38] but are routinely given far longer terms: throughout the EU, for example, thanks to an extension we return to in Chapter 4, copyright over sound recordings lasts for 70 years.[39]

#### 1.1.4.2 Copyright Makes Valuable Culture Disappear

One key rationale for terms that exceed what's necessary to elicit initial investment is that it is necessary to persuade rightsholders to invest in making works available ongoing.[40] In other words, achieving copyright's second access aim requires additional rights on top of what was necessary to achieve the first aim of getting them produced in the first place.

As we saw above, the core aim behind promoting ongoing access to knowledge and culture is to facilitate learning and progress.[41] Of course, this doesn't require making *all* works available ongoing – far from it. Many (perhaps most) works have no informational or cultural value, no audience and no justification for further investment. However, if we were to take this aim to its furthest point, it might suggest that all people with the time and inclination to benefit from past work would be able to access it.

In reality of course, there are numerous barriers to that ideal, including discovering such work exists in the first place, getting to the physical place necessary to experience it (or having the technology to do so) and the costs associated with all the above. Granting longer copyright rights can't help with any of those, but the promise is that those additional rights will nonetheless improve access by encouraging rightsholders to make investments in ongoing availability that they otherwise wouldn't.

The clearest example of the power of this aim comes from the project to extend the US copyright term in the 1990s. The then US Register of Copyrights testified to Congress in 1995 that a 'lack of copyright protection … restrains dissemination of the work, since publishers and other users cannot risk investing in the work unless assured of exclusive rights'.[42] Others, including the Coalition of Creators and

[38] Regarding sound recordings, see *International Convention for the Protection of Performers, Producers of Phonograms and Broadcasting Organisations*, opened for signature 26 October 1961, 496 UNTS 43 (entered into force 18 May 1964) art 14(a); *Convention for the Protection of Producers of Phonograms Against Unauthorized Duplication of their Phonograms*, opened for signature 29 October 1971, 866 UNTS 67 (entered into force 18 April 1973) art 4. Regarding films, see (n 36).

[39] See Chapter 4, Section 4.2.1.3.

[40] See Jacob Flynn, Rebecca Giblin and François Petitjean, 'What Happens When Books Enter the Public Domain? Testing Copyright's Underuse Hypothesis Across Australia, New Zealand, the United States and Canada' (2019) 42(4) *University of New South Wales Law Journal* 1215, 1219–22.

[41] See Section 1.1.2.

[42] Evidence to Subcommittee on Courts and Intellectual Property of the Committee on the Judiciary, House of Representatives, United States Congress, Washington, 13 July 1995, 171 (Statement of Marybeth Peters, Register of Copyrights and Associate Librarian for Copyright Services, Library of Congress).

Copyright Owners and the US Commissioner of Patents and Trademarks made similar claims.[43] Although none cited any empirical evidence in support of this argument, it was explicitly accepted by the US House of Representatives in its report recommending the copyright term be extended,[44] and by the Supreme Court upholding its constitutionality.[45] The close attention paid to these arguments throughout the process confirms the importance of ongoing access to works as a justification for copyright.

The reason none of its proponents provided evidence in support was that this claim had not yet been empirically tested. However, in the succeeding decades it has been (at least in Western, English-language, nations), and the resulting evidence overwhelmingly shows that the opposite is actually true: that works are subject to more investment, and become more available, when they enter the public domain.[46]

One striking finding emerged from a study by Paul Heald examining the availability of books by age on Amazon, which found availability drops sharply soon after publication, then spikes again as their copyright expires. The effect was so marked that there were more books from the 1880s available than from the 1980s.[47] This indicates there's appetite to invest in making older titles available, but that it's being stymied because rights are controlled by those with no wish to do so.

Another study carried out by Giblin's team investigated how commercial investment in books differed depending on copyright status. In *What happens when books enter the public domain?* the team used current editions of the Oxford Companions to English, Australian, New Zealand, American and Canadian Literature to identify authors with ongoing cultural significance, selecting all those who had died between 1962 and 1967. They then examined the relative availability of their books for libraries to license in digital form across New Zealand, Canada, Australia and the

43 Flynn et al (n 40) 1220–1.

44 Its report recommending the extension stated, among other reasons, that it would 'provide copyright owners generally with the incentive to restore older works and further disseminate them to the public'. House of Representatives Committee on the Judiciary, United States Congress, Copyright Term Extension Act (Report No 105-452, 18 March 1998) 4.

45 *Eldred* (n 28) 207 (Ginsburg J for Rehnquist CJ, Ginsburg, O'Connor, Scalia, Kennedy, Souter and Thomas JJ).

46 See, e.g., Paul J Heald, 'Property Rights and the Efficient Exploitation of Copyrighted Works: An Empirical Analysis of Public Domain and Copyrighted Fiction Bestsellers' (2008) 92(4) *Minnesota Law Review* 1031; Paul J Heald, 'How Copyright Keeps Works Disappeared' (2014) 11(4) *Journal of Empirical Legal Studies* 829; Tim Brooks, Council on Library and Information Resources and Library of Congress, *Survey of Reissues of US Recordings* (Report, August 2005); Christopher Buccafusco and Paul J Heald, 'Do Bad Things Happen When Works Enter the Public Domain?: Empirical Tests of Copyright Term Extension' (2013) 28(1) *Berkeley Technology Law Journal* 1; Flynn et al (n 40). But cf. B Zorina Khan, *Does Copyright Piracy Pay? The Effects of US International Copyright Laws on the Market for Books, 1790–1920* (Working Paper No 10271, National Bureau of Economic Research, January 2004) <https://www.nber.org/papers/w10271>.

47 Heald (n 46) 843.

US. All of these texts were in the public domain in New Zealand and Canada and under copyright in Australia. In the US, where they could have either status depending on whether their copyrights had been renewed, we coded each book as being in or out of copyright.[48] Since none of these books was natively digital, digitising the texts indicated some genuine investment by publishers. After controlling for other factors, they found that commercial publishers were investing in digitising and licensing culturally important older books at substantially higher rates in countries where they had entered the public domain compared to where they were still under copyright.[49] This again suggests that, during the copyright term, controlling exclusive rights didn't persuade the rightsholder to invest – but they *did* block other publishers from doing so.

This new evidence demonstrates that, just because an investor controls rights, that doesn't mean they'll actually exploit them.

Of course, not all copyrighted material has value (economic, social or cultural), and as we saw above, even that which does is unlikely to have it for long.[50] We're certainly not suggesting that *all* copyrighted material should be made available ongoing: doing so would waste resources that could be better used elsewhere, while doing nothing to further the underlying aim of promoting access to knowledge and culture. However, if copyright is to be justified as promoting investments in ongoing availability, it should actually do so. Where ongoing value does exist, where there is appetite to make those investments, and where the creator is eager to make it happen, copyright should help, rather than hinder.

The problem, in our view, stems from the ease with which investors can extract rights when combined with the absence of effective obligations (under the law or contracts) to actually use them.[51] Of course, it's perfectly rational for cultural investors to insist on taking broad rights, because at the time most copyright contracts are signed, nobody has a clear idea of what the work will be worth.[52] As noted above, investors play a critical role in cultural production, often by fronting the cost of getting works produced and available to audiences. That role is especially important given the notorious difficulty of predicting in advance which works will become hits – copyright markets are 'winner takes all', with investors taking a risk on a number of projects knowing that most will never make back the initial investment, but betting that one or more will pay off to such a degree that the overall enterprise turns a profit.[53]

[48] Flynn et al (n 40) 1227–32.

[49] Flynn et al (n 40) 1239.

[50] See Section 1.1.4.1.

[51] As we discuss at Chapter 4, the evidence suggests 'use-it-or-lose-it' provisions in various European countries have had little impact on creators' positions.

[52] Giblin (n 11) 384.

[53] Garcia and McCrary (n 32) 386.

These realities were already factored into the above analysis of the rights necessary to incentivise initial investments,[54] but they also help explain why cultural investors typically take the broadest rights they can. Those broad rights are necessary in case *this* one turns out to be a mega blockbuster that's worth exploiting in all possible formats and in all possible territories. If they can manage it (and they often can), they'll take rights for the entire term of copyright, which might be a hundred years or more.[55] Some contracts even extract upfront the benefit of any future rights that might accrue to the author later on – such as additional years of copyright protection, if lawmakers extend its term. Since at least 1919, the standard language in contracts between US music publishers and songwriters has delivered the benefit of any and all future term extensions to investors,[56] and our own empirical work has seen this happen in book publishing, too.[57]

Of course, very few works do become blockbusters, so most of the rights that are taken are never actually exploited. And even those that *are* aren't necessarily used for long, thanks largely to those high cultural depreciation rates we discussed above. For example, 87 per cent of video games released before 2010 were not available for purchase in the US by 2023.[58] But it means rights over an extraordinary number of creative works are locked up in the vaults of rightsholders who have no interest in exploiting them (or lack the capacity to do so). That becomes particularly problematic where the creator (independently or in partnership with a new investor) has the appetite to do so, but is blocked by a previous assignment.

There is widespread evidence that a great deal of culture with enduring value (which we define as unmet public appetite) is controlled by rightsholders who have no interest in exploiting them, or cannot adequately do so.[59] Very often, those

[54] See Section 1.1.2. For a more detailed treatment of the argument that additional rights are necessary to incentivise production in other cultural works, see Giblin (n 11) 376–7.

[55] See, e.g., Joshua Yuvaraj and Rebecca Giblin, 'Are Contacts Enough? An Empirical Study of Author Rights in Australian Publishing Agreements' (2021) 44(1) *Melbourne University Law Review* 380, 402–3.

[56] See William F Patry, 'The Copyright Term Extension Act of 1995: Or How Publishers Managed to Steal the Bread from Authors' (1996) 14 *Cardozo Arts and Entertainment Law Journal* 661, 675–6.

[57] Yuvaraj and Giblin (n 55). See also Alexander Lindey and Michael Landau, 'Lindey on Entertainment, Publishing and the Arts', *Thomson Reuters* (online, 11 April 2024) § 5:14, cl 1; Hugh Jones and Christopher Benson, *Publishing Law* (Routledge, 3rd ed, 2006) 77.

[58] Phil Salvador, *Survey of the Video Game Reissue Market in the United States* (July 2023, study for Video Game History Foundation and the Software Preservation Network in collaboration with the University of Washington Information School GAME Research Group) 2.

[59] United States Copyright Office, *Report on Orphan Works: A Report of the Register of Copyrights* (Report, January 2006) <https://www.copyright.gov/orphan/orphan-report.pdf>. In the US context, for example, the Copyright Office reports unmet demand from creators seeking to incorporate existing material into new works (at 36); institutions seeking to make material available to the public (at 37) and enthusiasts looking to make niche content available on a 'limited basis' (at 38). This demand is blocked due to inabilities to identify the owner (at 23, 26); or obtain the necessary permission, for example because the rightsholder does not respond (at 34).

owners cannot even be found: a UK regulatory impact assessment estimated rates of orphaning for works held by British cultural organisations (a proxy for ongoing public value) at up to 25 per cent for visual art, 10 per cent for sound recordings, 30 per cent for written material and 90 per cent for archive photographs.[60] A 2006 US Copyright Office report found that there is real demand for a wide variety of orphaned works, including from creators wishing to build upon them in new works, enthusiasts and public institutions.[61] Without provisions for appropriately promoting such uses, copyright terms that outlast their owners' interest in works can get in the way of desired access without any corresponding benefit.

But the problem of unmet demand is by no means limited to works with unlocatable owners. There are plenty of instances where rightsholders know they control rights that have some cultural or economic value, but choose not to exploit them anyway.

First-hand evidence of this was generated via *Untapped: The Australian Literary Heritage Project*, spawning from the Author's Interest Project and also headed up by Giblin. That project was influenced by concerns that most of Australia's literary heritage was out of print, and unavailable to the public. A preliminary scoping survey by Giblin investigating the availability of former winners of the Miles Franklin, Australia's most prestigious literary prize, which is awarded annually to 'a novel which is of the highest literary merit and presents Australian life in any of its phases', found that 37 per cent of former winners were not available as ebooks, 65 per cent were not available as audiobooks, and 16 per cent were unavailable to Australian audiences in any form at all.[62] Given the lack of investment in these well-famed books, you can readily imagine how many other stories were being lost: local histories and memoirs, beloved children's titles, the books that tell the story of a country and its people. That begged the question: were Australia's books being lost because there was no interest in them?

A collaboration between a multidisciplinary research team (including Giblin, economist Paul Crosby and literary sociologist Airlie Lawson), the Australian Society of Authors, a publishing partner (Matt Rubinstein of Ligature Press) and library partners from all around Australia, *Untapped* sought to answer that and other questions.

An independent, nationwide panel of library collections experts identified culturally important lost books to be targeted for inclusion in the project. After the team worked with writers, literary agents and heirs to help them navigate their contractual

60 Regulatory Policy Committee, *Orphan Works* (Impact Assessment, 15 June 2012) 11 <https://webarchive.nationalarchives.gov.uk/ukgwa/20140603093549/http:/www.ipo.gov.uk/consult-ia-bis1063-20120702.pdf>.

61 United States Copyright Office (n 59) 36–8.

62 Rebecca Giblin, 'The Availability of Miles Franklin Winners as eBooks, Audiobooks and in Print', *The Author's Interest* (Blog Post, 17 March 2020) <https://authorsinterest.org/2020/03/17/the-availability-of-miles-franklin-winners-as-ebooks-audiobooks-and-in-print/>.

out-of-print rights and re-license their books for publication in digital form, in December 2021 the Untapped imprint eventually republished 161 previously lost titles.[63] For the next year, the team gathered data to evaluate the extent of unmet demand for this neglected subset of Australia's literary heritage. That demand was higher than anyone had expected: during the data collection period covering the first year of availability, 5,923 copies were sold on retail platforms, and libraries lent out the ebooks almost 16,000 times. Although the team originally expected to be able to make them available only in digital form, the eventual collection was so strong that the team succeeded in selling the print rights as well. As a result, 148 *Untapped* titles also returned to physical shelves.[64]

Participating authors benefited from royalties on sales and loans and an advance of almost $500 on each print title, with some reporting that the return to availability had generated additional economic opportunities as well, including speaking fees, international translations and negotiations for film and television rights.

Why would publishers leave this value on the table? That's easy: it wasn't worth scooping up. Thompson's comprehensive history of trade publishing shows how the largest trade publishers came to adopt a deliberate strategy of maximising profits by reducing both the number of titles they publish, and the number of workers needed to support them.[65] Eventually, they downsized their sales teams to the point they could only support a quarter of the new titles being published.[66] While this obviously left money on the table, their reduced costs and the fact they weren't splitting the revenues from megasellers across a bigger range of books meant this still generated the best returns for their investors.

These principles scale to smaller publishers as well. As we showed, *Untapped* demonstrated substantial unmet demand for culturally important works, and when the rights were freed up to enable that new exploitation, it generated a small but welcome amount of new revenue for authors. However, the surplus generated across all titles was certainly less than what a publisher would make from publishing an equivalent number of quality new books. In those circumstances, it is perfectly rational for them to invest their limited resources elsewhere, despite controlling rights that still have value – to their authors, and to the broader public.

Such practices are much less problematic in circumstances where creators can easily get their rights back and exploit their works elsewhere. As we will explain in Chapter 5, this wasn't always the case for participants in *Untapped*. And it's not the case for

[63] For more about the project see 'Untapped: The Australian Literary Heritage Project' <untapped.org.au>; see also James Shackell, "Most of Australia's Literary Heritage Is Out of Print": The Fight to Rescue a Nation's Lost Books', *The Guardian* (online, 24 June 2021) <https://www.theguardian.com/books/2021/jun/24/most-of-australias-literary-heritage-is-out-of-print-the-fight-to-rescue-a-nations-lost-books>.

[64] 'Untapped' (n 63).

[65] John Thompson, *Merchants of Culture: The Publishing Business in the Twenty-First Century* (Wiley, 2nd ed, 2012) 189–90.

[66] Ibid.

creators in other fields who similarly experience rightsholder neglect of their work, but who lack the benefit of appropriate and enforceable rights to reclaim them.

Unmet public demand for knowledge and culture products exists well beyond the sphere of books.[67] In the context of sound recordings, this was evidenced by a clever 2005 study on behalf of the National Recording Preservation Board at the US Library of Congress that examined the exploitation of sound recordings during that medium's first 75 years of existence. At the time of the study, virtually all sound recordings ever made were still restricted by copyright in the US, with one of the key rationales being that it would incentivise rightsholders to invest in making those older recordings available to the public.[68] In other countries, however, older recordings had fallen into the public domain. That gave rise to a natural experiment: if it was true that works are under-exploited in the absence of copyright, those older recordings should have been made more available by their owners, who are not only likely to have the best access to master copies, but greater incentives to produce them thanks to their ongoing monopoly rights. However, the study found that, on average, just 14 per cent of sound recordings published between 1890 and 1964 had been re-released by rightsholders on compact disc. Over 50 per cent more recordings were re-issued by investors where they were in the public domain.[69] The sizeable investments needed to manufacture and distribute new physical versions makes these investments a good proxy for unmet public demand: record labels were unlikely to take that risk if they did not believe there was a market for those works. These results also provide further evidence that the mere control of rights translates poorly to investments in ongoing availability.

Many critically acclaimed television shows are unavailable despite public demand as well.[70] Often, this seems due to the copyright owner's unwillingness to make the investments necessary to clear the rights for incorporated works such as the music in their soundtracks. Barry Levinson was an executive producer for *Homicide: Life on the Street*, a multi-Emmy-award-winning drama which ran for seven seasons, but has lamented the unavailability of that work on streaming platforms:

> For the last four years, I've tried to get an answer for why we're not on streaming. No one, I mean no one, has been able to give me an answer. There's money to be made. You can't figure out how to handle whatever rights issues that may come up? You're talking over 120-some episodes. And somehow no one can figure out how to handle the rights? That doesn't make sense.[71]

[67] See our discussion on lost cultural value above in this section.

[68] 'One consideration by Congress in extending copyright protection to owners for such a long period was to give those owners an incentive to reissue, and thereby preserve, older recordings.' Tim Brooks, *Survey of Reissues of U.S. Recordings* <https://perma.cc/4ZX2-SSW8>.

[69] Ibid 7–8.

[70] See, e.g., Brian Tallerico, '11 Great Shows You Can't Find Streaming Anywhere (and Why)', *Vulture* (online, 17 April 2024) <https://www.vulture.com/article/best-shows-not-streaming-why.html>.

[71] 'When "Homicide" Hit Its Stride', *The New York Times* (online, 11 May 2023) <https://www.nytimes.com/2023/05/11/arts/television/homicide-life-on-the-street.html>.

In such cases, although copyrights are supposed to incentivise investments in ongoing availability, there are no consequences for studios failing to make them available. And the shift to a subscriber-only model of access to audiovisual content has curtailed *consumers*' ability to preserve that content (e.g. through purchasing DVDs and VCR recordings).[72] When physical, or permanent digital, copies of that content are not available for purchase, that culture is just 'gone'.[73]

While allowing corporations to take broad rights without any obligation to use them may be effective at driving their profits, this analysis suggests that it does not maximally promote the broader public interest in ongoing access to valuable knowledge and culture. If we really wish copyright to promote investments in ongoing availability, we need to design it in ways that facilitate the flow of rights to those who will actually make those investments – rather than making it so easy for them to languish with those who won't.

#### 1.1.4.3 Current Approaches to Copyright Divert Rewards Away from Creators

We demonstrated above that copyright grants are far broader than what's necessary to incentivise investments, but that, at least when they're awarded as a lump sum that can be easily extracted from creators upfront, those additional rights don't translate to investments in ongoing availability the way the public was promised they would. In fact, the evidence shows that they can actually hinder rather than help such investments. We'll now show that this lump sum approach also makes it harder for creators to share in copyright's rewards component – the amount above and beyond what is necessary to achieve copyright's incentives aims.

As we saw above, copyright's rewards component is justified by the moral claims of creators. For this to actually support that additional grant then, creators must be its primary beneficiaries.[74] In practice however, the evidence shows that this value is very often largely captured by investors instead. When this occurs, it is once again largely attributable to the way in which they can, very often, extract broad and long rights from creators via contracts.

We could choose countless stories to illustrate the way contracts can divert copyright's rewards away from creators, but we'll lead with one involving a cultural icon most people will know: Superman. Jerry and Joe Schuster came up with the

[72] See further Kathryn VanArendonk, 'TV Has Always Disappeared. This Feels Different', *Vulture* (online, 14 December 2022) <https://www.vulture.com/article/hbo-max-warner-cancelations-disappearing-tv-streaming-future.html>.

[73] Ibid.

[74] See discussion in *YouTube* (n 24).

character in the 1930s, and assigned all rights to DC Comics for a lump sum of US$130.[75] Their creation went on to generate billions of dollars for other people during the succeeding decades, but, having signed away their rights via contract, its progenitors were virtually 'destitute'.[76] It was only after the media publicised this injustice that Warner Brothers finally agreed, almost 40 years after the initial grant, to provide Superman's first creators with health insurance, a modest annual annuity, and attribution. Warner Brothers described itself as under a 'moral obligation' to do so,[77] which is undoubtedly true – and makes it even more damning that it took public shaming, decades after that obligation arose, before they would do even the minimum necessary to put things right.

While this story is particularly egregious, it's reflective of a broader pattern. Copyright rights have expanded considerably over the last few decades, and that additional value correlates with an increase in the equity value of the major firms that exploit them.[78] Over the same period, however, creator wages have stagnated or fallen.[79]

[75] *Siegel v Warner Bros. Entertainment, Inc*, 542 F Supp 2d 1098 (CD Cal, 2008) 1107; Barbara Goldberg, 'Check That Bought Superman Rights for $130 Sells for $160,000', *Reuters* (online, 17 April 2012) <https://www.reuters.com/article/idUSBRE83G02F/>.

[76] Anthony Cheng, 'Lex Luthor Wins: How the Termination Right Threatens to Tear the Man of Steel in Two' (2011) 34(2) *Columbia Journal of Law & the Arts* 261, 273, referring to *Siegel* (n 75) 1112 (citing Mary Brested, 'Superman's Creators, Nearly Destitute, Invoke His Spirit', *New York Times*, 22 November 1975, 62).

[77] See *Siegel* (n 75) 1107, 1112–13.

[78] Matthew J Baker and Brendan M Cunningham, 'Court Decisions and Equity Markets: Estimating the Value of Copyright Protection' (2006) 49 *The Journal of Law and Economics* 567.

[79] For more on creator incomes, see, e.g., Amy Thomas, Michele Battisti and Martin Kretschmer, 'UK Authors' Earnings and Contracts 2022: A Survey of 60,000 Writers' (CREATe, 2022) 7; Paul Crosby, David Throsby and Jan Zwar, '2022 National Survey of Australian Book Authors' (2022) 21; Thomas, Battisti and Kretschmer, 'UK Authors' Earnings', 2022, pp. 26–31; Jan Zwar, Paul Crosby and David Throsby, '2022 National Survey of Australian Book Authors' Industry Brief No. 3: Authors' Income' (Macquarie University, 2022) 7–8 <https://doi.org/10.25949/C63Y-XQ77>; Craig Butt, 'Average Income Interactive: How Authors Take on Extra Jobs to Make Ends Meet', *The Sydney Morning Herald* (online, 2 June 2017) <https://www.smh.com.au/entertainment/books/average-income-interactive-how-authors-take-on-extra-jobs-to-make-ends-meet-20170531-gwh7ug.html>. Economics of Music Streaming (Second Report) 31; see generally George Morgan and Julian Wood, 'Creative Accommodations: The Fractured Transitions and Precarious Lives of Young Musicians' (2014) 7(1) *Journal of Cultural Economy* 64; David Arditi, 'Precarious Labour in COVID Times: The Case of Musicians' (2021) 18(1) *Fast Capitalism* 13, 18; Bill Mesce, *Artists on the Art of Survival: Observations on Frustration, Perspiration, and Inspiration for the Young Artist* (University Press of America, 2004) 19; Joseph Darlington, 'The Writer's Action Group (WAG) and the Fight for Public Lending Right (PLR)' (2021) 13 *Angles* [33]; Ann-Mari Jordens, 'Assisting Australian Writers: Recording the History of the Public Lending Right and Educational Lending Right Schemes' (2005) 2(2) *History Australia* 47-1, 47-5; 'Devaluing Creators, Endangering Creativity. Doing More and Making Less: Writers' Incomes Today', The Writers' Union of Canada (2015) 5 <https://www.writersunion.ca/sites/all/files/DevaluingCreatorsEndangeringCreativity_0.pdf#overlay-context=news/canadian-writers-working-harder-while-earning-less>.

This contrast is particularly stark in the recorded music business, which more than doubled its revenue between 2015 and 2023 thanks to the surging market for music streaming.[80] By 2023, some 84 per cent of recorded music revenues came from streaming.[81] Streaming costs labels considerably less than other forms of music distribution because it has none of the manufacturing costs associated with physical media, and is much cheaper to distribute.[82] Thus, the music industry isn't just bigger now – it's more profitable than ever before.[83]

But while Sony Music CEO Rob Stringer happily boasts of its 'excellent' margins',[84] artists hear a different song. The structure of recording and songwriting deals means little of those rewards flow through to the people who actually make the music. In part, that's attributable to record industry recoupment practices, which require artists to repay most of the label's production and distribution costs from their share of royalties before being credited with any income. Under this system, a band signed in the 1970s with a $150,000 recoupment debt and earning a 5 per cent royalty would need their music to generate three million dollars before their 5 per cent (still just $5 out of every hundred generated) would be credited to their bank account rather than their label's.[85] There's no transparency around the number of artists who manage to recoup, but it's vanishingly small: expert Richard Burgess estimates it to be fewer than 5 per cent of all acts signed to major labels.[86]

This helps explain why, when two thirds of all UK recorded music revenue came from streaming in 2019,[87] streaming royalties made up just 6 per cent of artists' music-related income.[88] Even the few that have big commercial hits can end up earning almost nothing – like songwriter Fiona Bevan, who made just £100 from her hit track 'Unstoppable', co-written with and performed by Kylie Minogue

80 Mark Mulligan, 'Global Recorded Music Revenues Grows by 9.8% in 2023', *MIDiA* (Blog Post, 18 March 2024) <https://www.midiaresearch.com/blog/global-recorded-music-revenues-grew-by-98-in-2023>.

81 RIAA, *Year-End 2023 RIAA Revenue Statistics* <https://www.riaa.com/wp-content/uploads/2024/03/2023-Year-End-Revenue-Statistics.pdf>.

82 Competition and Markets Authority, *Music and Streaming* (Final Report, 29 November 2022) 34 <https://assets.publishing.service.gov.uk/media/6384f43ee90e077898ccb48e/Music_and_streaming_final_report.pdf>; Will Page, Submission to Digital, Culture, Media and Sport Committee, *Economics of Music Streaming* (16 November 2020) 26 <https://committees.parliament.uk/writtenevidence/15367/pdf/>.

83 Digital, Culture, Media and Sport Committee, *Economics of Music Streaming: Second Report of Session 2021–22* (House of Commons Paper No 50, Session 2021–22) 26 <https://committees.parliament.uk/publications/6739/documents/72525/default/>.

84 Tim Ingham, 'Rob Stringer Talks Sony's Strategy, Tencent/Universal … And Why Music Is Worth More than "2 Minutes of Someone Snoring in Lapland"', *Music Business Worldwide* (online, 26 September 2019) <https://www.musicbusinessworldwide.com/rob-stringer-talks-strategy-tencent-and-why-sonys-music-is-worth-more-than-2-minutes-of-someone-snoring-in-lapland/>.

85 Rebecca Giblin and Cory Doctorow, *Chokepoint Capitalism* (Beacon Press, 2023) 53–4.

86 Richard James Burgess, *The History of Music Production* (New York: Oxford University Press, 2014) 41.

87 Competition and Markets Authority (n 82) 13, fig 1.1.

88 Report Commissioned by the IPO (2021), *Music Creators' Earnings in the Digital Era* 171.

on an album that topped the British charts.[89] Songwriters like Bevan have been particularly hard-hit by the shift to streaming, to the point many are being forced to leave the industry.[90] The dismal financial picture for songwriters may also be influenced by the recoupment practices we identified above. The Big Three record labels control almost 70 per cent of the global market for recorded music, and they own the three music publishers that control almost 60 per cent of global song rights.[91] Since recording artists tend to have much higher recoupment debts than songwriters, these labels enjoy higher profits where income is attributed to the former, incentivising them to resist reforms that would help composers secure a fairer share.[92]

Heritage artists are another group that is disproportionately harmed by the shift to streaming. It was not uncommon for 1970s-era artists to have royalty rates as low as 4 per cent, reflecting that era's high costs of recording, producing, manufacturing and distributing music.[93] Those costs have fallen drastically with the advent of digital, and acts signed today will commonly be on royalty rates of at least 25 per cent.[94] Since those earlier contracts were for the entire copyright term however, the musicians who pioneered R&B, disco, soul and hip-hop keep having their royalties calculated at the same paltry rate. Although copyright's beyond-incentive rewards are justified only by the moral claims of artists, their record labels have no obligation to pass it on, and the resulting windfall fattens the wallets of investors instead.

A recent UK parliamentary inquiry confirmed that 'the major music groups are disproportionately benefiting from music streaming relative to creators', with 'record high levels of income and profit growth and historic levels of profitability for the major labels' – all while performers' incomes averaged less than the median wage.[95] Why do they have so much power? As Giblin and Doctorow explain in *Chokepoint Capitalism*, it's in part because they have been able to accumulate such huge portfolios of copyright rights, which they now use to shape music markets in ways that benefit their shareholders over the artists they claim to represent.[96]

That control over catalogue gave them the power to shape the music streaming market, which they quite understandably wielded to maximise their own profits at

89 Digital, Culture, Media and Sport Committee (n 83) 45.

90 MIDiA Research, *Rebalancing the Song Economy* (2021) <https://www.midiaresearch.com/free-report/rebalancing-the-song-economy>; Annie Reuter, 'Evolution of the Nashville Songwriter: From Solo Writes to Songwriting Apps', *Forbes* (online, 16 May 2020) <https://www.forbes.com/sites/anniereuter/2020/05/16/evolution-of-the-nashville-songwriter-from-solo-writes-to-songwriting-apps/?sh = 65b42d5145a3>.

91 Giblin and Doctorow (n 85) 56.

92 Ibid 69–70.

93 Ibid 59.

94 Ibid 58.

95 Digital, Culture, Media and Sport Committee (n 83) 63.

96 Giblin and Doctorow (n 85) chs 4 and 5.

the cost of artists.[97] As journalist and music commentator Pelly observes, streaming 'was shaped *by* the majors *for* the majors.'[98]

As generative AI technologies hit the market, these same dynamics are playing out. The majors have recently been in negotiations to license rights to YouTube for an AI tool that will use existing works to generate new music using the voices of existing artists.[99] If it makes commercial sense to license their catalogues in ways that conflict with artist interests to the benefit of their shareholders, they'll do so: since they already hold broad rights for the entire term of copyright, there is little to discipline them into treating their artists well.

There are other reasons too why creators so often end up transferring so much of copyright's rewards to others in the cultural value chain, as we explore below, including a chronic oversupply of creative workers and willingness to provide creative labour for less than other forms of work.[100] Here, however, it's sufficient to say that these combined realities mean that, when copyright laws are structured to enable investors to extract broad and long rights upfront, they make it harder, not easier, for creators to benefit from the rewards component that is justified as being especially for them.

### 1.1.5 *Is Any of This a Problem?*

The rationales for copyright are important because they justify why the public ought to agree to monopolies over knowledge and culture that, prima facie, make it more expensive and difficult to access.[101] The copyright bargain promises that these broad and long grants of rights will incentivise initial cultural production, promote ongoing access to the knowledge and culture that has enduring value, and ensure that the creators who come up with the works that add to human enlightenment and joy are fairly rewarded.

But as our above evaluation shows, the public is getting a poor deal. Allowing investors to take broad and long rights upfront, at least in the developed Western nations that are the subject of the empirical evaluations available to us, can actually act as a barrier to investments in the ongoing availability of works that have cultural and/or economic value that their current rightsholder has no interesting in exploiting.

97 Ibid ch 5.
98 Ibid 67.
99 Cait Stoddard, 'YouTube Negotiates Licensing Agreements with Major Record Labels for Forthcoming AI Tool' (online, 19 October 2023) <https://music.mxdwn.com/2023/10/19/news/youtube-negotiates-licensing-agreements-with-major-record-labels-for-forthcoming-ai-tool/>.
100 See Section 1.3.1.
101 See Deazley (n 15); Simone Schroff, 'The Purpose of Copyright – Moving beyond the Theory' (2021) 16(11) *Journal of Intellectual Property Law & Practice* 1262; Jane C Ginsburg and John M Kernochan, 'One Hundred and Two Years Later: The U.S. Joins the Berne Convention' (1988) *The Columbia Journal of Law & the Arts* 1.

Such practices simultaneously make it harder for creators to benefit from copyright's rewards component – something that's particularly problematic given the extent to which copyright's beyond-incentive grants are justified by their moral claims.

Drahos and Braithwaite have advanced a third distinct justification for copyright which sits outside the traditional incentives and rewards rationales. Dubbed 'financier's copyright', it 'rests on the view that copyright must serve the financier of copyright works by guaranteeing rights of exploitation in whichever markets the financier chooses to operate.' In this conception, 'Copyright becomes the servant of the financier rather than the author of the public welfare.'[102]

If we were evaluating copyright's performance against this rationale, the results would be much more favourable: the evidence above demonstrates that allowing investors to extract broad and long rights upfront is highly effective at prioritising their interests over both the public's interest in ongoing access and creators' interests in sharing fairly in the rewards of their work. However, cultural investors do not ground their claims in such terms – perhaps because they understand them to be much less sympathetic than those based on public access and creator rewards – and that's not the bargain the public has agreed to. If we really *are* motivated to achieve its public aims, consideration must be given to how we can design it to do a better job.

## 1.2 HOW REVERSION RIGHTS CAN HELP

Since 2018 we've been working on the Author's Interest Project, an Australian Research Council-funded project focused on authors' rights. While there are various ways to reframe copyright to help creators, including the EU's recently mandated rights to fair remuneration and transparency,[103] we focused on reversion rights because of their potential to address copyright's two failed aims at the same time: that is, to not only help creators get paid, but to simultaneously support investments in making works available ongoing.

We investigated reversion from a number of different angles. Using a range of historical, comparative and empirical methods, members of the project team have investigated how statutory reversion rights have been implemented around the globe,[104] the way rightsholder lobbying has affected their development,[105] how

[102] Peter Drahos and John Braithwaite, *Information Feudalism: Who Owns the Knowledge Economy* (Earthscan, 2002) 176.

[103] Directive (EU) 2019/790 of the European Parliament and of the Council of 17 April 2019 on copyright and related rights in the Digital Single Market and amending Directives 96/9/EC and 2001/29/EC, arts 18–20 <https://eurlex.europa.eu/eli/dir/2019/790/oj>.

[104] Joshua Yuvaraj, 'Data for Legal Mapping Study into Copyright Reversion Laws Applicable to Book Publishing Contracts (up to March 2019)', *Bridges* (Monash University) <https://doi.org/10.26180/16416747.v3>; Yuvaraj (n 3) ch 5; Ula Furgal, *Reversion Rights in the European Union Member States* (CREATe Working Paper 2020/11).

[105] Joshua Yuvaraj and Rebecca Giblin, Why Were Commonwealth Reversionary Rights Abolished (and What Can We Learn Where They Remain)? (2019) 41(4) *European Intellectual Property Review* 232.

real-world publishing contracts deal with reversion and how those practices have evolved over time[106] and how the US termination rights are actually being used.[107] We've generated new empirical evidence showing how current approaches cause culture to be lost,[108] and identifying the practical obstacles authors face when they attempt to exercise their rights.[109] We have also conducted theoretical work proving even quite radical approaches to reversion can be implemented without breaching the outdated, virtually unamendable treaties that stand in the way of some other promising reform pathways.[110]

And of course, as introduced above, we've experienced what reversion can achieve up close, via *Untapped: The Australian Literary Heritage Project*. As well as generating evidence about the unmet public demand for culturally important but neglected books, this project enabled us to study the challenges authors and their heirs experience when attempting to enforce contractual reversion rights,[111] and the economic and non-economic benefits that flowed from republication.

The results of the above program have convinced us that well-executed reversion rights are a promising tool for reshaping the copyright bargain in a way that better achieves its aims. This book seeks to persuade you of that, too.

Of course, there are limits to the scope of our claims. We're not claiming that reversion rights (no matter how well-framed!) are the solution to all of copyright's failures: among other things they need to be complemented by appropriately drawn rights and exceptions, effective enforcement mechanisms and effective interventions to help creators secure fair remuneration and transparency around use of their works.

Further, we acknowledge that they are an explicit response to Western common law philosophies of copyright, and do little to address the focus on individual authorship (rather than collaborative and iterative contributions over time) and individual ownership (as distinct from communal custodianship) that make the resulting colonial frameworks so inappropriate for protecting traditional cultural expressions.[112]

[106] Joshua Yuvaraj and Rebecca Giblin, 'Are Contracts Enough? An Empirical Study of Author Rights in Australian Publishing Agreements' (2021) 44(1) *Melbourne University Law Review* 380.

[107] Joshua Yuvaraj et al, 'U.S. Copyright Termination Notices 1977–2020: Introducing New Datasets' (2022) 19(1) *Journal of Empirical Legal Studies* 250.

[108] Flynn et al (n 40).

[109] See Chapter 5, Section 5.2.4.

[110] Giblin (n 11); Rebecca Giblin, 'A Future of International Copyright? Berne and the Front Door Out' in Graeme Austin et al (eds), *Across Intellectual Property: Essays in Honour of Sam Ricketson* (Cambridge University Press, 2020).

[111] Paul Crosby, Tessa Barrington, Airlie Lawson and Rebecca Giblin, 'Untapped Potential: Results from the Australian Literary Heritage Project' (October 2024) <https://law.unimelb.edu.au/__data/assets/pdf_file/0007/5096446/Untapped-Research-Report_v4.pdf>.

[112] For more on importing Western conceptions of copyright, and/or its underlying values, outside Western contexts, see, e.g., Alpana Roy, 'Copyright: A Colonial Doctrine in a Postcolonial Age' (2008) 26(4) *Copyright Reporter* 112; Akalemwa Ngenda, 'The Nature of the International

Our claims are further limited by the sources we have been able to access. Our investigations of Commonwealth and European reversion rights (populating Chapters 2 and 4) drew upon contributions from local scholars where possible, plus machine translation, but for the most part we have been obliged to rely largely on English-language materials and databases. The result is admittedly but unavoidably Western-centric, on everything from philosophies of copyright to the nature of creativity to practices around cultural production and distribution.

Finally, our work does not address the broader social, economic and legal contexts that have contributed substantially to the dire economic fortunes of today's creative workers, or indeed the growing inequality affecting the broader publics both in the Western nations we've focused on and beyond. Those structural realities have obvious impacts on our ability to achieve copyright's aims no matter how well those laws are framed, but as well outside the scope of this book.

Against the context of these limitations, this book's thesis is modest but important: that, where licensing and distribution practices result in copyrights being allocated in ways that are inconsistent with the rationales for awarding them in the first place, ensuring that creators have appropriately scoped reversion rights could do a great deal to improve outcomes.

## 1.3 CRITICISMS OF REVERSION

Unsurprisingly, not everyone agrees that reversion rights are a good idea. Below, we briefly canvass the dominant arguments against mandatory reversion rights, together with our responses. There are three main ones: that they unjustifiably interfere with freedom of contract, that they're insulting to authors, and that they might actually reduce the amount creators are paid for their work.

### 1.3.1 *What about Freedom of Contract?*

Perhaps the most common argument against statutory rights reversion mechanisms is that they would interfere with freedom of contract,[113] a key tenet of 'laissez-faire' capitalism.[114]

Intellectual Property System: Universal Norms and Values or Western Chauvinism?' (2005) 14(1) *Information & Communications Technology Law* 59.

[113] For examples of such arguments, see responses of music publishers in Richard Osborne and Hyojung Sun, 'Rights Reversion and Contract Adjustment' (UK Intellectual Property Office, 2023) 69 <https://papers.ssrn.com/sol3/papers.cfm?abstract_id=4443144>: '[I]t's an industry based on good faith conduct and relationships and to start interfering in ways which can't be anticipated is probably not taking account of that. It makes an assumption around unfairness which we view as unfair.'; it's 'quite unreasonable when you have a willing buyer and a willing seller to then subsequently several years after the fact introduce a change which says I know you signed this contract willingly, but now it no longer says what you say it says.'

[114] See Richard A Epstein, 'Free Bargaining and Formalism' in FH Buckley (ed), *The Fall and Rise of Freedom of Contract* (Duke University Press 1999) 29–30.

At its core, freedom of contract rests on the belief that individuals are best able to determine their own interests, and then bargain for the conditions that best achieve them. In this conceptualisation, the law is there to ensure the bargain is voluntary and then enforce it – not to determine its terms.[115]

Proponents assume that, if reversion rights were in fact necessary to a deal's proper functioning, the parties would ensure that they were appropriately included in the contract, and there would be no need for external intervention.[116]

From the beginning, the principle was couched in romantic terms – that courts would 'hold sacred' contracts that had been entered into 'freely and voluntarily'.[117] In its nineteenth-century heyday, the principle was given so much deference that courts permitted contracts to override worker protection statutes[118] and provide legal imprimatur to the activities of trade cartels.[119]

Not surprisingly, it soon became clear that prioritising freedom of contract above all else had seriously harmful effects. Freedom of contract relies upon relative equality of bargaining power between the parties to achieve the 'voluntariness' that is at its heart.[120] In the absence of that, the will of the stronger party will simply be imposed on the weaker. In response to this reality, even the most economically liberal countries soon introduced broad limits on contractual freedom, justified on both economic and public interest grounds.[121]

For example, employees are commonly granted statutory protections that employers cannot derogate from, like mandatory annual and sick leave, parental leave, and protections against discrimination and job loss.[122] In many jurisdictions, consumers can similarly rely on guarantees that sellers cannot bypass, for example that goods

[115] Arthur Chrenkoff, 'Freedom of Contract: A New Look at the History and Future of the Idea' (1996) *Australian Journal of Legal Philosophy* 1, 37.

[116] See, e.g., 'Statutory Review of the Copyright Act: Report of the Standing Committee on Industry, Science and Technology' (Chair: Dan Ruimy), 42nd Parliament, 1st Session, June 2019, 36–7; 'Review of the Copyright Act 1994: Submission by the International Publishers Association' (4 April 2019) 7 <https://www.mbie.govt.nz/dmsdocument/6707-international-publishers-association-review-of-copyright-act-1994-issues-paper-submission-pdf>; 'Submission on Review of the Copyright Act 1994: Issues Paper', Publishers Association of New Zealand, 9 <https://www.mbie.govt.nz/dmsdocument/6753-publishers-association-of-new-zealand-review-of-copyright-act-1994-issues-paper-submission-pdf>.

[117] *Printing and Numerical Registering Company v Sampson* (1875) LR 19 Eq 462, 465.

[118] *Lochner v New York*, 198 US 45 (1905).

[119] PS Atiyah, *The Rise and Fall of Freedom of Contract* (Oxford University Press, 1985) 697–703.

[120] See generally Carl Renner and Michael Zollner, 'Contracts and Humanity: How Freedom and Fairness of Contract Can Be Secured in the Digital Age' in Kai Jacob, Dierk Schindler and Roger Strathausen (eds), *Liquid Legal – Humanization and the Law* (Springer, 2022) 343.

[121] Hugh Collins, 'Theories of Rights as Justifications for Labour Law' in Guy Davidov and Biran Langille (eds), *The Idea of Labour Law* (Oxford Academic, 2011); Atiyah (n 119) 703–8.

[122] See, e.g., *Fair Work Act 2009* (Cth) ss 87, 70, 119–22; *Cap 57 Employment Ordinance* (Hong Kong) 12, 15E, 41AA, 31B(1)(a); *Employment Rights Act 1996* (UK) ss 71–72, 76–77, 13-5-136; *Working Time Regulations* 1998 (UK) 13, 13A; *Canada Labour Code* (RSC, 1985, c L-2): 183–187.1, 204–206.1, 235(1).

will be of reasonable quality.[123] Many countries have introduced schemes by which standard form contracts between consumers and suppliers, and small businesses, can be declared unfair and unenforceable.[124] And some countries, recognising that companies can suffer from power imbalances too, even give small businesses special protections in their interactions with larger ones.[125] Each of these interventions recognises the need to protect the more vulnerable party.

This is relevant because creative workers are particularly vulnerable in their interactions with cultural investors. That vulnerability begins with the fact that creative labour markets are characterised by an oversupply of labour, caused by the fact that many individuals view creative work as more desirable than other jobs.[126] That then translates to lower wages: because many creators are driven by an intrinsic desire to create, they're willing to do this for less than what they'd charge to pore over spreadsheets.[127] The fact that unions like the Screen Actors' Guild try to stop their members from driving down their own wages by prohibiting them from taking work that does not comply with union minimums hints at the strength of the enticement to do so. As Johnson wryly puts it: 'the only way actors can overcome the temptation to work for below scale is to enter into a group pledge to punish one another for doing so'.[128]

This isn't to say that a desire to make a living is not also a powerful motivator,[129] but simply to point out that creators' vulnerability to exploitation is exacerbated by

[123] See, e.g., *Consumer Protection Act*, 2008 (South Africa) ss 55–56; *Consumer Protection Act 1999* (Malaysia) ss 30–65; *Consumer Protection (Fair Trading) Act 2003* (Singapore) ss 14–18; *Consumer Rights Act* (UK) ss 9–24; *Competition and Consumer Act 2010* (Cth) Sch 2, ss 51–64A; *Cap 26 Sale of Goods Ordinance* (Hong Kong) ss 15–16; *Consumer Guarantees Act* 1993 (NZ) ss 5–34.

[124] See, e.g., *Consumer Protection Act 2019* (Zimbabwe) ss 45–46; *Consumer Protection Act 68 of* 2008 (South Africa) s 48; 'Unfair Contract Terms and the Consequences Thereof under the CPA', *Dentons* (Web Page, 27 April 2016) <https://www.dentons.com/en/insights/newsletters/2016/april/27/south-africa-newsletter/south-africa-newsletter-april-edition/unfair-contract-terms-and-the-consequences-thereof-under-the-cpa>; *Competition and Consumer Act 2010* (Cth) Sch 2, ss 23–28; *Consumer Rights Act 2015* (UK) Part 2; *Unfair Contract Terms Act 1977* (UK); Cap 458 (Unconscionable Conduct Ordinance (Hong Kong) s 5(1); *Consumer Protection Act 1999* (Malaysia) s 24G; Sophie Bienenstock, 'The Deterrent Effect of French Liability Law: The Example of Abusive Contract Terms' (2019) 129(2) *Revue D'Économie Politique* 205, [20]–[22]; 'Unfair Contract Terms', *European Commission* <https://commission.europa.eu/document/download/dcofbc69–185d-4f69-a095-f1dfaa4f3a4d_en?filename = Unfair%20contract%20terms_2023.pdf>; *Unfair Contract Terms Act BE 2540* (1997) (Thailand).

[125] See, e.g., *Competition and Consumer Act 2010* (Cth) Sch 2, ss 21–23.

[126] See Giblin (n 11) 382–3.

[127] See Ruth Towse, *Creativity, Incentive and Reward* (Edward Elgar, 2001) 53–8; Charles David Throsby and BJ Thompson, 'But What Do You Do for a Living? A New Economic Study of Australian Artists' (1994) (reporting on an extensive study of Australian artists demonstrating that artists often worked in non-arts jobs, but only to the extent necessary to support their artistic occupation).

[128] Eric E Johnson, *Intellectual Property and the Incentive Fallacy* (2012) 39 *Florida State University Law Review* 623, 668–9.

[129] See, e.g., TJ Stiles, 'Among the Digital Luddites' (2015) 38 *The Columbia Journal of Law & the Arts* 293.

their having motivations that go beyond the purely economic. As Boyle muses, there seems to be some 'innate human love of creation that continually drives us to create new things even when homo economicus would be at home in bed, mumbling about public goods problems'.[130] Leading cultural economist Ruth Towse sums up the result: '[f]irms in the creative industries are able to "free-ride" on the willingness of artists to create and the structure of artists' labor markets, characterized by short term working practices and oversupply, mak[ing] it hard for artists to appropriate rewards'.[131]

That oversupply of labour can also contribute to creator fears that, if they attempt to negotiate the terms they're offered, the deal might simply be transferred to the next person in line – something we'll talk about in more detail in Chapter 5.[132] These fears are exacerbated now that decades of corporate consolidation have dramatically reduced the number of buyers available for many kinds of cultural work. We already saw that three record labels control almost 70 per cent of the global market for recorded music, and they own the three music publishers that control almost 60 per cent of global song rights, but that's just the tip of the iceberg. The music streaming market is controlled by Spotify and a few companies owned by Big Tech; Amazon has a stranglehold on large markets for physical, digital and audio books; and if you're watching music videos, you're almost certainly doing it on YouTube.[133] Live Nation Entertainment controls concert promotion and ticketing, Disney takes 35 per cent of the US box office, and Google and Facebook have a lock on the digital ads that are wrapped around online music, videos and news.[134] Even the video game market has become massively consolidated.[135] Investors can offer terms on a take-it-or-leave-it basis knowing there is a bottomless pool of exciting prospects, while creators know that accepting that deal might be their only chance to break through.[136]

[130] James Boyle, 'The Second Enclosure Movement and the Construction of the Public Domain' (2003) 66 *Law and Contemporary Problems* 33, 45–6.

[131] Ruth Towse, 'Copyright and Cultural Policy for the Creative Industries' in Ove Granstrand (ed), *Economics, Law and Intellectual Property* (Springer 2003) 419, 427.

[132] See Chapter 5, Section 5.3.1.

[133] By way of disclosure Yuvaraj is an independent musician with music available for streaming and purchase on major platforms.

[134] Giblin and Doctorow (n 85) 2, 56.

[135] Lewis Gordon, 'The Great Consolidation of the Video Game Industry', *The Ringer* (online, 19 August 2022) <https://www.theringer.com/video-games/2022/8/19/23308468/video-games-acquisitions-mergers-microsoft-sony-tencent-embracer>.

[136] Theresa E Van Beveren, 'The Demise of the Long-Term Personal Services Contract in the Music Industry: Artistic Freedom Against Company Profit' (1996) 3 *UCLA Entertainment Law Review* 377, 384; see also Lauren K Turner, 'The Impact of Technology on Pre-Digital Recording Agreements: An Examination of *F.B.T. Productions, LL v. Aftermath Records*' (2011) 114(1) *West Virginia Law Review* 347, 351; Kate Darling, 'Contracting about the Future: Copyright and New Media' (2012) 10(7) *Northwestern Journal of Technology and Intellectual Property* 485, 502.

Since many creative workers have low incomes, that makes it harder for them to access expert advice on the terms they're offered[137] – something that's particularly problematic given how complex copyright contracts can get. It also further adds to the inequality between the parties, since the investor is usually the one to draft the contract, and is much more likely to have had the benefit of legal advice to do so. These relationships clearly lack the 'freedom' that freedom of contract relies on.

Cultural investors are themselves well aware of how unequal power can translate to poor outcomes from contracts. Consider the record industry for example, which has for years sought help from lawmakers in its campaign against the 'value gap' – the difference between the royalty rates the labels were able to negotiate with music streamers like Apple and Spotify, and the amount it had been able to persuade Google's YouTube to agree to.[138] YouTube's stranglehold over the video streaming market gave it the power to extract a better deal, similarly to how major labels use their hegemony to put the squeeze on artists. But of course, the record industry didn't respond to YouTube's tactics by acknowledging the sanctity of freedom of contract – rather, it begged for (and finally obtained) legal intervention.[139]

### 1.3.2 *Aren't Reversion Rights Insulting to Authors?*

Another argument against reversion rights is that they are insulting to creators. Justice Felix Frankfurter exemplified this in a US Supreme Court judgment we'll revisit in Chapter 3: 'While authors may have habits making for intermittent want, they may have no less a spirit of independence which would resent treatment of them as wards under guardianship of the law.'[140]

Rightsholder representatives resisting the push for meaningful US termination rights in the 1970s similarly claimed that mandatory reversion rights made authors out to be 'improvident', 'nincompoops' and 'fools'.[141] Around the same time, Barry Torno, a leading Canadian entertainment lawyer, argued that reversion laws 'perpetuate the stereotypical image of the author as the gifted but "congenitally irresponsible" artist who cannot be expected to assume full responsibility for the consequences of his actions and must be guarded against himself'. This was 'insulting', he argued, and 'do[ing] a disservice to authors'.[142]

[137] See, e.g., Séverine Dusollier, 'EU Contractual Protection of Creators' (2018) 41 *Columbia Journal of Law & Arts* 435, 474; *Arts Law Centre of Australia Annual Report 2017* (Report, 2017) 6–7.

[138] IFPI, *Global Music Report 2018: Annual State of the Industry*, ch 26 <https://perma.cc/sGZ3-PLhM>.

[139] See (n 103) art 17.

[140] *Fred Fisher Music Co v M Witmark & Sons*, 318 US 643, 657 (1943).

[141] Copyright Law Revision Part 3 (US Government Printing Office, 1964) 282, 285; Copyright Law Revision Part 4 (US Government Printing Office, 1964) 250, 275.

[142] Barry Torno, *Term of Copyright Protection in Canada: Present and Proposed* (Consumer and Corporate Affairs Canada, 1980) 39.

Such claims obviously fail to acknowledge the power imbalances between creative workers and the investors, discussed above, which are a much more compelling reason for introducing mandatory reversion protections than the idea that authors are stupid or uninformed. And they are further undermined by the fact that creators are themselves the staunchest advocates for mandatory reversion protections. During development of the 1976 US copyright law for example, authors made it clear that reversion rights were so important to them that they would oppose *any* amendment of the copyright law in the event they were not included. Karp explained the strong author support for reversion was because they were the *opposite* of improvident, nincompoop fools:

> Any prudent, provident author, bargaining to sell or lease rights to a motion picture company, doesn't want to give away his copyright forever. He wants to give a limited grant, because he knows that the value of his rights can't be adequately determined at the time the bargain is made. He knows that in thirty years the rights may be worth many times more. He knows that if he gives a limited grant the movie company could make the movie, distribute copies, and exploit their work. He knows that if he gets another crack at it he will then get the same chance that everybody else involved with the second remark of the movie gets – of being paid, according to latter-day standards, the value of what he contributes. And, as I say, he would never assign the copyright away unless he were forced to. The same holds true in book publishing, and music publishing, and every other kind of publishing. (Copyright Law Revision Part 3, 286)

As the following chapters will show, in the subsequent decades creative workers have lobbied strongly for reversion rights all around the globe. Given that they clearly don't find such rights paternalistic, arguments to the contrary have a disingenuous odour. It's the foxes arguing it's insulting to chickens to coop them at night.

### 1.3.3 *Wouldn't Reversion Reduce Creator Pay?*

Finally, reversion rights are sometimes resisted by arguing that they'll result in authors being paid even less than under current arrangements.[143] Such arguments can be powerful: creators struggling to survive on an already measly share are understandably fearful at the prospect of receiving still less.

But of course, whether or not any reversion right would put downward pressure on prices depends on factors like its design and the likelihood of its being successfully exercised. Entitlement for an author to reclaim rights that it's clear the investor

[143] See, e.g., Guy A Rub, 'Stronger than Kryptonite? Inalienable Profit-Sharing Schemes in Copyright Law' (2013) 2749, 97–8 (2013); Kate Darling, 'Occupy Copyright: A Law & Economic Analysis of U.S. Author Termination Rights' (2015) 63 *Buffalo Law Review* 147, 165–6; Amy Gilbert, 'Note, The Time Has Come: A Proposed Revision to 17 U.S.C. § 203' (2016) 66 *Case Western Reserve Law Review* 807, 810; AA Keyes and C Brunet, 'Copyright in Canada: Proposals for a Revision of the Law' (Consumer and Corporate Affairs Canada, 1977) 69 <https://publications.gc.ca/collections/collection_2021/isde-ised/RG43-41-1977-eng.pdf>.

is not going to exploit, for example, is likely to have minimal impact, since they rarely expect to use all the rights they take, and would have already had ample opportunity to exploit all those that turned out to have value.

In the case of time-based rights, their likelihood of reducing prices depends primarily on when they may be exercised. If a creator had a mandatory right to reclaim their copyrights after just a year, that could certainly be expected to depress the original price paid. However, longer periods of exclusivity are less likely to have any negative effect, as we saw in the above analysis of how the present value discounting and cultural depreciation impact investor incentives. That showed that, beyond a relatively short time horizon, the grant of additional years of exclusivity makes little or no difference to the value of those rights at the time the decision is made to invest. Given these realities, it's not surprising that there is no evidence that the US law entitling creators to terminate most copyright transfers after 35 years has had any downward impact on prices.[144] In fact, recent economic modelling suggests that, rather than making contracts riskier for authors, it might actually have a beneficial effect.[145]

We get another hint of the upside potential of time-based reversion rights in the practices around publisher sub-licensing deals, which as we saw commonly last just five years or less. By insisting that rights revert back after that, the head publisher puts themselves in a position to negotiate a subsequent, better deal in the event the translation is a commercial success (or a more modest continuation if it's not). If authors had the power to do the same, they might similarly increase their ability to share in their work's success.

Another problem with arguments that reversion rights will reduce creator incomes is that they assume the amounts paid are economically rational in the first place. As we saw above, however, the oversupply of creative labour, willingness to provide it for less than other forms of labour and fear of losing deals to the next artist in line all prevent this from being the case. In other words, the dynamics of creative labour markets mean that what rightsholders extract from creators can be largely divorced from both the cost of their investment and the work's ultimate commercial value. Indeed, as the UK's parliamentary streaming inquiry discovered, many recording artists and composers receive no upfront payment at all.[146]

In light of these realities, Litman has argued that giving creators a right to revert after, say, 10 years, may actually improve the initial terms on offer.[147] That's because

[144] Giblin (n 11) 397.

[145] Michael Karas and Roland Kirstein, 'Efficient Contracting under the U.S. Copyright Termination Law' (2018) 54(C) *International Review of Law and Economics* 39.

[146] See Digital, Culture, Media and Sport Committee (n 35) 31 citing All Party Parliamentary Jazz Appreciation Group, Submission to Digital, Culture, Media and Sport Committee, *Economics of Music Streaming* (15 November 2020) 6 (regarding recording artists); 47 (regarding song-writers) <https://committees.parliament.uk/writtenevidence/15360/pdf/>.

[147] Jessica Litman, 'Real Copyright Reform' (2010) 96 *Iowa Law Review* 1, 48.

intermediaries would be motivated to keep their creators happy to ensure they aren't tempted to leave the stable – a prospect they don't have to concern themselves much about under current arrangements. For the same reason, such rights could also rein in the kind of abuses the major labels engaged in when striking their deal with Spotify, and which have been up in the air again as providers of generative AI technologies seek licences of their own.[148] It would of course be vital to calibrate the duration of the initial term carefully to avoid interfering with the incentives for initial investment, but if copyright laws permitted, dissatisfied creators could take their rights elsewhere after that, it's well plausible that more of the wealth generated by creative labour would flow to those who actually do the work.

## 1.4 NAVIGATING THIS BOOK

This book makes the case that reversion rights have enormous potential as a mechanism for reworking the copyright bargain in a way that better achieves its ends. But if that's the case, why haven't they done so already? After all, as we pointed out right at the beginning, statutory reversion rights have been around for as long as copyright itself.

The answer will become clear in Chapters 2 and 3, which trace the histories of statutory reversion rights in the UK and US, and Chapter 4, which evaluates current approaches in Europe. That work will show that these reversion rights have not been effective because, despite their long history, they have not generally been implemented in a way that would meaningfully shift the balance of power between creators and cultural investors. In particular, we show there were remarkably few attempts to tailor reversion rights in ways that take advantage of the new exploitation opportunities facilitated by the shift to digital technologies and the internet.

The lack of meaningful reversion rights doesn't reflect a lack of appetite for them. We show how attempts in these jurisdictions to enact reversion rights in ways that could have actually made a meaningful difference to creators were derailed – both by poor design *and* by resistance from the same powerful corporations that were the primary beneficiaries of existing arrangements. That resistance should be viewed as evidence of reversion's potential: rightsholders would not have fought so hard (or so dirty) if they had not believed that reversion did not have the potential to retilt the playing field.

Chapter 5 then takes a closer look at copyright contracts, sharing results from our empirical studies investigating how reversion rights are incorporated into publishing

[148] See further Hibaq Farah, 'Google and Universal Music Working on Licensing Voices for AI-Generated Songs', *The Guardian* (online, 9 August 2023) <https://www.theguardian.com/technology/2023/aug/09/google-and-universal-music-working-on-licensing-voices-for-ai-generated-songs>; Chris Cooke, 'Sony Music Tells 700+ AI Companies to Respect Its Copyrights', *Complete Music Update* (online, 17 May 2024) <https://completemusicupdate.com/sony-music-tells-700-ai-companies-to-respect-its-copyrights/>.

contracts, and the challenges authors face when actually exercising those rights. That evidence builds on the observations in this chapter by identifying additional problems that make contracts an inappropriate repository for these important author rights.

Finally, Chapter 6 synthesises the key lessons learnt throughout the book in a series of best practice principles for advocates and lawmakers to consider as we move toward reform. The tremendous wealth and influence wielded by the Big Tech and Big Content companies that are the major beneficiaries of existing structures create obvious political barriers to any reforms that might redirect any meaningful amount of wealth, and in the current political environment they may well be insurmountable. However, as Giblin and Doctorow pointed out in *Chokepoint Capitalism*, it's important to have 'ideas lying around' that can be picked up and pressed into service once a system reaches crisis. The perilous state of creative labour markets suggests we might be close. When that point arrives, it's our hope that this contribution will help.

# 2

# Statutory Reversion Rights in the British Commonwealth

## INTRODUCTION

This chapter chronicles the history of statutory reversion rights in England and other Commonwealth countries.[1] While reversion was part of the copyright system since the *Statute of Anne*, and has appeared in various forms since, it has had remarkably little success in benefiting authors or their heirs. It's sometimes dismissed for that reason – the fact that reversion *hasn't* worked very well is offered as evidence that it *can't* work very well. But we show that these previous iterations were set up for failure, with every example having been implemented in ways that made it impossible to achieve their author-protective aims.

We contrast those failures with the shining success of the UK's 'Terms of Trade' reforms, which have massively increased British film and TV revenues along with the international reach of British stories. Though technically a restriction on what creators can be obliged to give away rather than a reversion right per se, they achieve the same end – and provide powerful real-world evidence of how interventions that centre creators can further copyright's access and rewards aims.

Finally, we briefly summarise the current state of play on reversion reform in South Africa, Canada and the UK. Although political realities continue to make it extremely difficult to enact reforms that would meaningfully shift money and power from investors to creators, recent developments show that reversion's potential to do so is beginning to be well and truly recognised.

[1] Some material in this chapter was first published by Sweet & Maxwell in the *European Intellectual Property Review*: Joshua Yuvaraj and Rebecca Giblin, 'Why Were Commonwealth Reversionary Rights Abolished (and What Can We Learn Where They Remain)?' (2019) 41(4) *European Intellectual Property Review* 232 and is reproduced by agreement with the Publishers.

## 2.1 1710: THE BIRTH OF STATUTORY COPYRIGHT AND REVERSION RIGHTS

Statutory reversion rights were born with the first modern copyright statute. The UK's *Statute of Anne* provided that rights to new works would last for 14 years, after which the 'sole right of printing or disposing of copies' would return to their authors, if still alive, for 14 years more.[2] If the authors did not survive the initial period, the copyright ended after that first 14-year term.

It's unclear exactly what Parliament meant to achieve via this dual-term framework,[3] but the consensus suggests the reversion right was intended to benefit authors by giving them the right to decide what happened to their books once the initial term expired. As Bently and Ginsburg explain, '[w]ere the objective otherwise ... there would be no point dividing the "sole right" into two periods, nor tying the second to the author's survival, much less designating the author as the person to whom the exclusive right shall "return"'.[4] The return of rights seems to have been intended to put authors in a position 'to grant rights anew from a stronger bargaining position should her work have earned a substantial audience',[5] particularly where the initial payment was insufficient in comparison to the book's subsequent popularity.[6]

In practice, however, authors rarely benefited from the second term. Sometimes this was because they died before it could accrue, or because their book stopped selling within the first 14 years. But even when they survived and their books kept their value, it was common practice for publishers to purport to take authors' renewal rights upfront, together with transfer of the initial term, and without payment of any fresh sum. As book historian Harry Ransom explains, '[t]he true intention of this proviso was ignored from the start: authors continued to sell their books outright'.[7] Or perhaps more accurately, considering the relative bargaining power of the various parties: publishers were powerful enough to insist on extracting both the initial and reversionary terms at the time of the initial contract, and so that's exactly what they did.

The text of the statute was ambiguous as to whether upfront takings of both terms would be valid, or whether publishers needed to wait until the second term to

2 Statute of Anne 1710 (UK).

3 For a detailed discussion and evaluation of the competing viewpoints see Lionel Bently and Jane C Ginsburg, '"The Sole Right ... Shall Return to the Authors": Anglo-American Authors' Reversion Rights from the Statute of Anne to Contemporary U.S. Copyright' (2010) 25(3) *Berkeley Technology Law Journal* 1475, 1482.

4 Ibid 1485.

5 Ibid 1479; Jane C Ginsburg, 'Copyright' in Rochelle Dreyfuss and Justine Pila (eds), *The Oxford Handbook of Intellectual Property Law* (Oxford University Press, 2017) 497.

6 Isabella Alexander, *Copyright Law and the Public Interest in the Nineteenth Century* (Hart, 2010) 25.

7 Harry H Ransom, *The First Copyright Statute: An Essay on an Act for the Encouragement of Learning, 1710* (University of Texas Press, 1956) 104.

bargain for the additional 14 years of rights.[8] Obviously though, if publishers could simply extract all rights upfront, the reversion right would only benefit those who had sufficient bargaining power to hold onto it – and in practice, that was very few.

Writers and their supporters sought to combat this practice via new reforms, and in 1737 a draft bill was advanced to limit what authors could be obliged to give away.[9] Though crafted almost 300 years ago, its framing of the problem (and potential solution) still feels timely. The bill recognised the information problem we introduced in Chapter 1, that comes about from the fact that most copyright contracts are signed before anyone knows what the work is worth: 'foreasmuch as the true Worth of Books and Writings is, in many Cases, not found out till a considerable time after the Publication thereof'. It also acknowledges that authors might be obliged to sign away the rights prematurely: 'Authors, who are in Necessity, may often be tempted absolutely to sell and alienate the Right . . . before the Value thereof is known.'

The 1737 bill would have extended copyright to last the author's lifetime plus 11 years, but simultaneously have limited grants during the author's lifetime to a maximum of 10 years at a time. Upon expiry of each term, authors and publishers could enter into fresh grants – now each equipped with much more knowledge about what the work was worth. It's worth taking a moment to consider how different the creative industries might look like today, had that been the model everything else was built on.

Obviously, that didn't happen. The bill failed to pass into law, with Deazley explaining that, '[f]rom the booksellers' point of view, [it] was anathema'.[10] His commentary suggests that it was the clauses limiting the booksellers' rights that prevented the bill from passing. 'The prospect of having to renegotiate contracts with the author every ten years must have made most of the metropolitan book trade baulk in disbelief.'[11]

Publishers continued asserting that their initial contracts with authors gave them rights not only for the full initial term, but also the entirety of the renewal.[12] In exchange, authors typically received a single lump sum payment – and not a penny more in the event they lived long enough to trigger the second term.[13]

8 William Cornish, 'The Statute of Anne 1709–1710: Its Historical Setting' in Lionel Bently, Uma Suthersanen and Paul Torremans (eds), *Global Copyright* (Edward Elgar, 2010) 23.

9 Bill for the better Encouragement of Learning, and for the more effectual securing the Copies of Printed Books to the Authors or Purchasers of such Copies, during the Times therein mentioned (1737).

10 Ronan Deazley, 'Commentary on the Booksellers' Bill (1737)' in Lionel Bently and Martin Kretschmer, *Primary Sources on Copyright (1450–1900)* (Web Page, 2008) [9] <www.copyrighthistory.org>. Note however Patterson's suggestion that booksellers influenced the drafting of this bill in an attempt to obtain perpetual copyright, and were not fazed by the 10-year limit: '. . . the language . . . indicates how little fear the booksellers had of the authors' interference with their monopoly; they were willing that an author should retain a control over his works, as they were interested only in the profits from publishing': Lyman Ray Patterson, *Copyright in Historical Perspective* (Vanderbilt University Press, 1968) 157.

11 Deazley (n 10).

12 For a detailed and nuanced analysis of contractual practice during the relevant period, see Bently and Ginsburg (n 3) 1494–508.

13 Ibid 1508.

The validity of publisher attempts to extract the renewal rights upfront was not much tested, and there was considerable uncertainty about the formalities that would need to be satisfied (if any) for their extraction to be valid as a matter of law.[14] However, an unreported 1765 decision indicated pre-vestiture assignments *could* be valid,[15] and in 1786 it was held that sufficiently broad language could indeed transfer the reversionary right before it vested, even in the absence of a deed.[16] The courts that reached these findings may have been influenced by notions of freedom of contract, mentioned in Chapter 1, which were enjoying primacy around this time.[17]

Even where the contracts did not expressly deal with the renewal term – and Bently and Ginsburg's historical research demonstrates that this was often the case[18] – authors were unlikely to have succeeded in publishing their books elsewhere. By the 1730s, control of book rights had come to be concentrated in the hands of a powerful bookseller syndicate known as the Conger.[19] As Patterson explains in his comprehensive history, 'there grew up a tacit understanding among the booksellers [publishers] of the eighteenth century that there should be no interference with each other's lapsed copyrights', with any who dared publish a competitor's title after its statutory copyright expired being bullied and shunned by their peers.[20] Such practices would no doubt have been applied with even more vigour to those who tried to recognise the author's reversionary right *during* that term.

Analysis of historical records shows that the *Statute of Anne* did little to improve the economic position of authors, with authors getting paid about the same under the system of statutory copyright as under the licensing system that preceded it.[21] The reversion right seems to have been particularly ineffective, with Bently and Ginsburg's historical research unearthing just four documents that even dealt with it explicitly – most notably and ironically the contract for Adam Smith's *Wealth of Nations*.[22] Smith had held onto the copyright after the work was published in 1776 before finally selling the copyright outright for £300 in 1788.[23] In 1790, when rights 'returned' to him under the statute, his publishers paid him that same amount again to renew their copyright for another 14 years.[24] Little else is known about the circumstances surrounding this transaction, but it's likely that the initial success of Smith's treatise gave him the

[14] Ibid 1514.
[15] *Millar & Dodsley v Taylor* C33/426 (Ch 1765). See Bently and Ginsburg (n 3) 1518–22 for a more comprehensive discussion of this decision and its significance.
[16] *Carnan v Bowles*, 2 Bro. C.C. 80 (1786).
[17] Cornish (n 8).
[18] Bently and Ginsburg (n 3) 1494–508.
[19] Patterson (n 10) 151–2.
[20] Patterson (n 10) 152 citing W Forbes Gray, 'Alexander Donaldson and His Fight for Cheap Books' (1926) 38(2) *Juridical Review* 180, 193.
[21] Deazley (n 10) [5].
[22] Bently and Ginsburg (n 3) 1539.
[23] Richard B Sher, *The Enlightenment and the Book* (University of Chicago Press, 2006) 236.
[24] Ibid.

bargaining power necessary to withhold the second term. Whatever the reason, this case shows the reversion right had the potential to provide direct economic benefits to authors where they were able to hold onto it until it vested. If improving the lot of authors had indeed been parliament's intention when it designed the dual term framework, its neglect in not appropriately securing the reversion right to those intended beneficiaries goes a long way to explaining why it failed.

## 2.2 1814: REVERSION RIGHTS EXTINGUISHED

With the *Statute of Anne*'s reversion right having been rendered all but useless by this combination of judicial interpretation and industry practice, it had few mourners when it was finally repealed by the British Parliament in 1814. Its replacement substituted *Anne*'s dual term with 28 years of protection, or the author's lifetime if they were still living after that.[25]

The new law was the result of spirited publisher lobbying. Although they had been successful in using contracts to wrest away all authors' rights upfront, *Anne*'s second 14 years wouldn't accrue unless the author was still alive at the expiry of the first. But rather than pointing out how this harmed their commercial interests, publishers instead argued the old system had been 'productive of great hardships to the families of authors'.[26] An anonymously published pamphlet purporting to represent the views of authors (but subsequently attributed to solicitor Sharon Turner, who had given evidence on behalf of the booksellers when the 1814 law was being debated[27]) emotionally evoked those hardships:

> The author's family loses all the profits of his labours at the very time when, from the event of his death, they are in the greatest need of them. It seems the dictate of reason and justice that authors should have at least the full twenty eight years, without any reference to the life of the author.[28]

Bently and Ginsburg describe this argument as 'tendentious to say the least', since so many publishing contracts purported to extract the full right upfront, and because even those few authors who held on to their copyrights initially still tended to sell them within the initial term.[29] As they point out, had the *real* intent been to benefit the families of deceased authors, the renewal term could have vested in them, as became the law in the US and Canada soon after.[30]

25 *Literary Copyright Act* 1814, 54 Geo 3, c 156.

26 Bently and Ginsburg (n 3) 1543 citing 24 PARL DEB, HC (1st ser) (1812) 308, 310 (UK).

27 Ibid 1546.

28 Ibid 1543 citing Sharon Turner, *Reasons for a Modification of the Act of Anne Respecting the Delivery of Books and Copyright* (Nichols, Son, and Bentley, 1813) 1.

29 Ibid 1544.

30 Ibid.

Thus, although the linkage between author's lifetime and copyright term appeared to be a victory for creators, in practice it was unlikely to serve them much better than the old regime: those additional rights could be (and were!) acquired in their entirety by publishers, often for a fixed sum rather than ongoing royalties.[31] Accordingly, Bently and Ginsburg describe it as 'of largely symbolic, rather than pecuniary, significance', before acidly noting the disconnect between rhetoric and practice:

> The amendment reflected the legal embodiment of what Bracha has called 'the ideology of authorship,' at the same moment that the law abandoned its attempt to intervene in the functioning of the book market to protect the interests of real, flesh-and-blood, writers.[32]

## 2.3 1911: REVERSION RIGHTS RETURN IN THE UK AND COMMONWEALTH

Statutory reversion rights next appeared almost a century later with the passage of the *Imperial Copyright Act* 1911 (UK) ('Imperial Act'), which applied throughout the British Empire,[33] and was adopted by self-governing dominions including Australia,[34] Canada[35] and New Zealand.[36]

That law extended copyright to the author's life plus 50 years, but with a wrinkle found in a proviso to section 5(2): authors could not assign or license their rights to

[31] Ibid 1548.

[32] Ibid citing Oren Bracha, 'The Ideology of Authorship Revisited: Authors, Markets, and Liberal Values in Early American Copyright' (2008) 118(2) *Yale Law Journal* 186.

[33] Uma Suthersanen, 'The First Global Copyright Act' in Uma Suthersanen and Ysolde Gendreau (eds), *A Shifting Empire: 100 Years of the Copyright Act 1911* (Edward Elgar Publishing, 2013) 18. See *Copyright Act 1911* (UK) 1 & 2 Geo 5, c 46, s 25(1) ('*Copyright Act 1911* (UK)'). These are 'believed to include the following: Anguilla, Antigua, Ascension Islands, Australia, Bahamas, Bangladesh, Barbados, Barbuda, Belize, Bermuda, Botswana, British Antarctic Territory, British Virgin Islands, Brunei, Canada, Cayman Islands, Central and Southern Line Islands, Channel Islands, Cyprus, Dominica, Falkland Islands, Federated Malay States, Gambia, Ghana, Gibraltar, Grenada, Guyana, Haiti, Hong Kong, India, Republic of Ireland, Isle of Man, Israel, Jamaica, Kenya, Kiribati, Lesotho, Malawi, Malaysia, Malta, Mauritius, Montserrat, New Zealand, Nigeria, North Borneo, Pakistan, Pitcairn Islands, Redonda, Republic of South Africa, Sarawak, Seychelles, Sierra Leone, Singapore, Solomon Islands, Somalia, South Georgia, South Sandwich Islands, Sri Lanka, St Helena, St Kitts-Nevis, St Lucia, St Vincent, Swaziland, Tanzania, Tonga, Trinidad and Tobago, Tristan de Cunha, Turks and Caicos Islands, Tuvalu, Uganda, United Kingdom, Zambia, Zimbabwe': Alter Kendrick Baron, 'Protecting Your Musical Copyrights', *Copyright Due Diligence*, 32 n 33 <https://akbllp.com/wp-content/uploads/Protecting-Your-Musical-Copyrights.pdf>.

[34] *Copyright Act 1912* (Cth), implementing the *Copyright Act 1911* (UK) (n 33). See also Sam Ricketson, 'The Imperial Copyright Act 1911 in Australia' in Uma Suthersanen and Ysolde Gendreau (eds), *100 Years of the Copyright Act 1911* (Edward Elgar Publishing, 2013) 52, 68–9; Benedict C Atkinson, *The True History of Copyright: The Australian Experience 1905 – 2005* (Sydney University Press, 2007) 94–5.

[35] *Copyright Act 1921* (Canada) RSC 1985, c C-42, s 11(2) ('*Copyright Act 1921* (Canada)').

[36] *Copyright Act 1913* (NZ) s 8(2).

anyone for longer than their lifetime plus 25 years. Once that time passed, rights would revert, automatically, to their heirs, regardless of any contract to the contrary.[37] The reversion right contained within the proviso applied to all instances where the author was the first owner of the copyright, except in cases involving collective works.

When we first wrote about this right back in 2018–19, we described its origin as something of a mystery.[38] The Committee commissioned to review Britain's copyright law in light of the 1908 Conference on the Berne Convention made no such recommendation, and even the contemporaneous legislative debates indicated confusion about its source.[39] Fortunately, copyright expert Dr Elena Cooper took that as invitation to fill the gap, and we are now able to draw on her historical research to better explain how it came to be.[40]

The Berne Convention's Berlin revision mandated that copyright terms be extended to life plus 50 years. For the UK, that was a substantial jump. Until it was implemented, literary copyrights lasted 42 years or 7 years after the author's death, whichever was longer.[41] Engravings and sculptures were covered by copyright for just 28 years from publication.[42]

As Cooper explains, that jump was controversial on two main grounds. First, it was criticised for favouring the interests of assignees over those of authors.[43] Like the emotive rhetoric that supported the removal of *Anne*'s reversionary term in favour of a single lump sum term, the rhetoric used to sell the term extension strongly emphasised the interest of authors in providing for their families after their passing. However, critics pointed out that it would do little to ensure that. Among them were Lord Courtney, debating the bill in the House of Lords:

> I believe that this change in the law will not be found to operate at all to the advantage of authors, speaking broadly. It will be found to operate to the advantage of publishers only, who will get an extended period of the copyright in the books which they publish.[44]

[37] *Copyright Act 1911* (UK) (n 33) s 5(2).

[38] Yuvaraj and Giblin (n 1) 233.

[39] Report of the Committee on the Law of Copyright (1909). See also, e.g., United Kingdom, *Parliamentary Debates*, House of Lords, 14 November 1911, vol 10, col 113–66, 15–18 per Lord Courtney: 'There is no convention at all leading up to [this provision] . . . I do not know how the proposal originated, and I do not know that it is found in the system of laws of any other country . . . it is an entirely novel proposition . . . for which there is no parallel elsewhere . . . That is, indeed, putting authors in leading strings, and treating them as persons who cannot take care of their own interests and who must be protected in this very unusual fashion.'

[40] Elena Cooper, 'Reverting to reversion rights? Reflections on the Copyright Act 1911' (2021) 43(5) *European Intellectual Property Review* 292.

[41] *Copyright Act 1842* (5 & 6 Vict c 45) s 3; Cooper (n 40) 294.

[42] Cooper (n 40) 294 n 22.

[43] Ibid 295–6.

[44] Ibid 295 citing United Kingdom, *Parliamentary Debates*, House of Lords, 31 October 1911, vol 10, col 49 (Lord Courtney).

The reversion right was ultimately proposed by the Solicitor-General as a way of addressing this controversy.[45] Alive to the possibility that an author would be obliged to contract away rights for the entirety of the copyright term (however long that might be), the amendment sought to ensure that their heirs would have an opportunity to benefit from the extension in some meaningful way. In other words, it sought to ensure the scope of rights better matched the rhetoric being relied upon to justify the extension.

The other key criticism of the term extension was that it would impede access to important knowledge and culture, both by reducing access to public domain works and keeping prices higher for longer.[46] These concerns were addressed via two compulsory licensing provisions. A proviso to what became section 3 in the Imperial Act gave any publisher the right to republish works 25 years after the author's death upon payment of a 10 per cent royalty. Section 4, which applied where copyright owners had withheld public access to works after the author's death, authorised the grant of compulsory licences for the purposes of republication. Parliament hoped that these provisions would prevent important books from being lost altogether, or being accessible only at a high price.[47]

The reversion right is sometimes called the 'Dickens' provision', a nod to the public outrage in the decades prior to its passage over publishers benefiting from the sale of Charles Dickens' books while his descendants were living in poverty.[48] While there's no direct link – Dickens' longest literary copyrights had expired by the time the 1911 Act came into operation – it's likely that scandal drove public and parliamentary support for meaningful protections for author heirs.

But, like the *Statute of Anne* before it, this law signally failed to improve the lot of authors or their heirs, with Copinger and Skone James describing 'the benefits to the author's family or dependants [as] somewhat illusory'.[49] The reasons are obvious with hindsight, and indeed should have been anticipated and addressed at the time of drafting. While the legislature learned from the previous failure by explicitly making it impossible for the author to transfer the reversionary right during their lifetime, it regrettably introduced new shortcomings that proved almost as detrimental.

45 Ibid, 296 n 52.

46 Ibid 294–5.

47 Ibid 295.

48 David Vaver and Pina D'Agostino, 'What the Dickens? Fact or Folklore?', *IPOsgoode* (Blog Post, 19 July 2021) <iposgoode.ca/2021/07/what-the-dickens-fact-or-folklore/>.

49 Walter A Copinger and EP Skone James, *Copinger and Skone James on Copyright: Including International Copyright, with the Statutes and Orders Relating Thereto and Forms and Precedents* (Sweet & Maxwell, 11th ed, 1971) 163; see also JM Cavendish, A *Handbook of Copyright in British Publishing Practice* (Cassell, 1974) 32: 'Few people today seem to know that this proviso exists, probably because it is seldom worth anyone's while to invoke it. To publishers it can only mean a loss; to an author's heirs, sorting out rights of inheritance via an estate 25 years old or more, it will usually mean legal expenses without any offsetting financial advantage.'

One of the most substantial arises from the way in which the law actually returns the rights. We have been discussing the 1911 right as being for the benefit of author heirs, but that's a convenient shorthand: technically, reverted rights vested in the author's 'legal personal representatives as part of his estate'. This can be contrasted with the US termination rights (discussed in Chapter 3), which vest directly in heirs. The Imperial right's structure is problematic because, by 25 years after the author's death, when the rights actually vested, few estates would still be open.[50] Assets that accrue so long after death can be a headache for executors. The available evidence suggests that few executors of author estates were even aware of their reversionary assets, and that those who were often sold it off cheaply soon after death so they could fully wind them up.[51]

Another reason for the lack of value is the way the reversion right interacted with section 3's compulsory licence. Recall that section 3 (the compulsory royalty) and section 5 (the reversion right) both applied from 25 years after the author's death. Their combined effect was to give heirs a fresh opportunity to benefit from their copyrights while capping the financial upside: after all, nobody would pay more than the 10 per cent royalty they could obtain under the compulsory licence, and the fact they could not be guaranteed the exclusive right to publish (since anyone could take advantage of the compulsory licence) further reduced the value.[52]

In practice, both the reversion right and compulsory licence were largely ignored from the get-go: '[p]ublication by former publishers of technically reverted works simply continued, and royalty payments continued to be made pursuant to and at the royalty rates contained in prior grants.'[53] The law worked so poorly that it might as well not have existed at all.

## 2.4 1956–1968: REVERSION REPEALED AGAIN

Countries were prompted to again re-evaluate their copyright laws following the 1948 Brussels Revision of the Berne Convention. In the UK, this process was led by the Gregory Committee. The compulsory licensing provisions in section 3 (entitling republication 25 years after the author's death upon payment of a royalty) and section 4 (covering cases where the copyright owner withheld access from the public) were justifiably challenged for interfering with the rights mandated by Berne, and the Gregory Committee recommended their repeal.

50 M William Krasilovsky, 'Reversion: The Sleeping Giant of British Copyright' (1979) 9(1) *Performing Art Review* 1, 2.

51 Copinger and Skone James (n 49) 163.

52 Ibid.

53 M William Krasilovsky and Robert S Meloni, 'Copyright Law as a Protection against Improvidence: Renewals, Reversions and Terminations' (1983) 5(4) *Communications and the Law* 3, 27.

However, it additionally recommended repealing section 5, the reversionary provision, due to a perceived link with the problematic section 3.[54] Remarkably, the Committee's linkage of section 5 (the reversion right) and section 3 (the provision for compulsory licence) seems to have come about simply because of that shared reference to a 25-year period after the author's death. That reasoning is woefully inadequate, especially since the two provisions had such distinct motivations. The contemporaneous parliamentary record, and subsequent judicial and academic commentators, agree the reversion right was intended to provide some protection to authors and their heirs where works had been subjected to term-long contracts that turned out to be disadvantageous.[55] The fact that the compulsory licensing provision was no longer possible did nothing to change the need for that protection. The Gregory Committee found it must be repealed regardless.

Its reasoning has been criticised, with neither the English Court of Appeal nor the authors of *Copinger and Skone James on Copyright* convinced of a link between the section 5(2) reversion right and the problematic section 3.[56] The Canadian committee tasked with post-Brussels review did not even consider whether the reversionary right was incompatible with Berne, suggesting it, too, was unconvinced by the Gregory analysis,[57] and the New Zealand review committee expressly disagreed that

[54] Great Britain Copyright Committee, *Report of the Copyright Committee* (Cmd 8662, 1952) 9 [23] ('Gregory Committee Report'). See also Paul Abel, 'The Brussels Copyright Convention and Its Influence on Domestic Copyright Legislation (in Particular in the United Kingdom and in Austria)' (1954) 3(2) *International & Comparative Law Quarterly* 880, 888.

[55] See, e.g., Gillian Davies, Nicholas Caddick and Gwilym Harbottle (eds), *Copinger and Skone James on Copyright* (Sweet & Maxwell, 17th ed, 2016) 5–118. See also Paul Torremans and Carmen Otero García Castrillón, 'Reversionary Copyright: A Ghost of the Past or a Current Trap to Assignments of Copyright?'(2012) 2 *Intellectual Property Quarterly* 77, 78; EJ Macgillivray, *The Copyright Act, 1911 Annotated* (Steven and Sons, 1912) 67; David Vaver, *Essentials of Canadian Law: Copyright Law* (Irwin Law, 2000) 110; Hugh Laddie et al, *The Modern Law of Copyright and Designs* (Butterworths, 3rd ed, 2000) 882; George Stuart Robertson, *The Law of Copyright* (Oxford University Press, 1912) 97; Charles Clark (ed), *Publishing Agreements: A Book of Precedents* (Unwin Hyman, 3rd ed, 1998) 191; *Chappell & Co Ltd and others v Redwood Music Ltd* [1980] 2 All ER 817, 825; *Redwood Music Ltd v Francis, Day & Hunter Ltd and Others* [1978] RPC 429, 450 (Goff J); *Crown Record Co Ltd v Eng Kin Film Co Ltd* [1992] HKCA 241 [17]; *Anne of Green Gables Licensing Authority Inc v Avonlea Traditions Inc* [2000] OJ No 740 [83]. See also Bernard Rudden, 'The Resurrection of Reversionary Copyright: Redwood Rides Again' (1981) 1(2) *Oxford Journal of Legal Studies* 296, 298; Helen Norman, *Intellectual Property Law Directions* (Oxford University Press, 2011) 444–5; United Kingdom, *Parliamentary Debates* (n 39) 159 (Viscount Haldane).

[56] *Novello and Co Ltd v Keith Prowse Music Publishing Co Ltd* [2004] EWCA Civ 1776 [41]; Davies et al (n 55) 5–120 n 98. Cf. *Novello & Co Ltd v Keith Prowse Music Publishing Co Ltd* [2004] EWHC 766 (Ch) [10], [22], in which the court approved the Gregory Committee's reasoning.

[57] Though note it referred to the Gregory Report elsewhere and did find the Canadian equivalents of the impugned compulsory licence provisions problematic: Edmond Cloutier, *Canadian Royal Commission on Patents, Copyright, Trade Marks and Industrial Designs* (Report on Copyright, 1957).

removing section 5(2) was a 'necessary corollary' to removing sections 3 and 4 of the Imperial Act.[58]

Australia's review committee ('the Spicer Committee') described the Berne compatibility of the reversion right as 'somewhat doubtful',[59] but provided no analysis or authority in support. That omission is particularly notable given its New Zealand counterpart had so recently reached the opposite conclusion. Proceeding from that view, the Spicer Committee observed that the reversion right could only be maintained if Australia refused to ratify Berne's Brussels revision, and found it was not sufficiently beneficial to authors' families to justify such drastic intervention.[60]

In this regard too, its analysis was lacking. The Spicer Committee cited *Copinger and Skone James on Copyright* as authority for the proposition that the reversionary right's benefits were limited, but seemingly failed to notice that *Copinger*'s criticisms of the limited benefits the reversionary right generated for heirs were inextricably entwined with the existence of section 3's compulsory licence provision.

As flagged above, *Copinger* argued publishers did not pay much for reversion rights because the compulsory licence provisions meant they could not acquire an exclusive right, and in any event had the right to publish so long as they paid a 10 per cent royalty.[61] But section 3's compulsory licence provision would have to be repealed to ratify the Brussels Act, and on *Copinger's* reasoning that would *increase* the value of the reversionary right – a reality the Committee seemed to overlook.

Ultimately, the Spicer Committee recommended that Australia repeal its reversionary provision.[62] To the best of our knowledge, that was the only provision in Australia's copyright law that directly secured benefits to authors or their heirs, as distinct from other assignees, making that cavalier disposal particularly worthy of note.

Had the Committee engaged in a fuller analysis of the treaty compatibility issue, the reversion right could have been kept – as was the case in Canada, and as was recommended in New Zealand. The New Zealand review committee had described removal as 'a retrograde step' that would benefit publishers or other assignees over authors' families,[63] and reasoning that the proviso should be retained since it 'can do no harm and may possibly do good'.[64] Unfortunately for authors, this point seems to

[58] New Zealand Copyright Committee, *Report of the Copyright Committee* (Appendix to the Journals of the House of Representatives of New Zealand H. 46, 1959) 35 [80] ('*Report of the New Zealand Copyright Committee*').

[59] Copyright Law Review Committee, Parliament of Australia, *Report of the Committee Appointed by the Attorney-General of the Commonwealth to Consider what Alterations are Desirable in the Copyright Law of the Commonwealth* (1959) [395] ('Spicer Committee Report') <https://static-copyright-comau.s3.amazonaws.com/uploads/2015/05/R00079-theSpicerReport.pdf>.

[60] Ibid.

[61] Davies et al (n 55) 5–126.

[62] *Spicer Committee Report* (n 59).

[63] *Report of the New Zealand Copyright Committee* (n 58) 24–5.

[64] Ibid 35 [80].

be one of the very few on which the New Zealand Parliament disagreed with the Copyright Committee – it repealed the right despite a strong recommendation to keep it.[65]

As well as being repealed in the UK, Australia and New Zealand, the Imperial reversion right has now also been abolished in nearly every other enacting country.[66]

The Berne Convention is supposed to protect the interests of authors (as distinct from those of assignees), and the moral claims of author heirs were central to the campaign to secure Berne's extension of rights to life plus 50 years. It's ironic then that compliance with that Convention was used to justify the removal of one of the only provisions that focused on precisely that.[67]

### 2.4.1 *The Imperial Reversion Right Could Benefit Author Heirs*

While none of the review committees identified any evidence about actual use of the reversionary interest by author heirs, two notable examples arising after the repeal suggest the New Zealand Committee's view was correct: that the reversionary right originating with the Imperial Act *could* achieve its aim of benefiting author heirs.[68] These cases, discussed below, demonstrate some of the real-world potential that could be unlocked were we to take reversion rights more seriously.

#### 2.4.1.1 Mbube: The Solomon Linda Story

In 1939, Solomon Linda recorded his song *Mbube* with the Gallo record label, in what was then the only recording studio in Africa. The third take was different to any version that had come before. 'He just opened his mouth and out it came, a haunting skein of fifteen notes that flowed down the wires and into a trembling stylus that cut tiny grooves into a spinning block of beeswax.'[69]

65 See mentions of the copyright term in New Zealand, *Parliamentary Debates*, House of Representatives, v 332, 24 October 1962, 2324; also see amendments to be read in, none of which involve the reversionary provision, in New Zealand, *Parliamentary Debates*, House of Representatives, v 333, 27 November 1962, 2970.

66 Canada still retains this law: *Copyright Act*, RSC 1985, c C-42, s 14(1).

67 Since 2013, the UK has had an additional reversion right applying in limited circumstances to performers in sound recordings, contained in section 191HA of the *Copyright, Designs and Patents Act* 1988. As this was mandated by an EU Directive, we discuss it in Chapter 4 instead.

68 There may be other cases of rights returning to heirs under the reversionary scheme elsewhere in the Commonwealth: see, e.g., *Newspapers Ltd v Ratna Shankar Prasad* AIR 1977 All 356 per R Misra and J Sinha (4 April 1977, Allahabad High Court, India). However, we focus on the *Mbube* and *Redwood* examples for their prominence in discourse about how the Imperial reversion right operated.

69 Rian Malan, 'Inside the Long, Hidden Genealogy of "The Lion Sleeps Tonight"', *Rolling Stone* (online, 14 May 2000) <https://www.rollingstone.com/feature/in-the-jungle-inside-the-long-hidden-genealogy-of-the-lion-sleeps-tonight-108274/>.

The saga that followed that moment of magic has been described as 'one of the most complicated and convoluted music publishing-songwriting stories ever',[70] and we don't have room here to fully unskein it. But here are the key points. The song became a huge hit – the first South African record to sell more than 100,000 copies. It soon caught the attention of American folk legend Pete Seeger, who meticulously transcribed it before releasing it as *Wimoweh* with his band, The Weavers, in 1952. Their music publisher, Folkways, registered the song's US copyright in January that year.

In May, Gallo registered its own US copyright claim telling Folkways the song was written by Linda but that it owned the rights. So it did – but the ink was barely dry on the transfer. Although the song had been recorded some 13 years earlier, the copyright was not formally assigned until April 1952, when Gallo called Linda into the office (he was working in a low-level job at their record pressing plant) and had him sign over the entirety of his rights to the song.[71] In exchange they paid him 10 shillings – about US$0.87.[72]

With the new exposure from the *Wimoweh* cover, Mbube's haunting melody quickly captured the imaginations of other musicians. More than 150 other versions came out.[73] Several were hits, but the song became part of the cultural zeitgeist with its appearance in Disney's *The Lion King* as 'The Lion Sleeps Tonight'.

While *Mbube* generated enormous wealth in its various forms, almost none of it went to Linda. He died in 1962 with just a few dollars to his name, his wife unable to afford a stone for his grave.[74] Indeed, even after *The Lion King* became a global phenomenon, Linda's family received only meagre royalties. It's not entirely clear, but it seems these came from Pete Seeger's share of *Wimoweh*, which he tried to secure to Linda once he discovered the tune was not a traditional Zulu song as he'd originally been told, but one by a living composer. However, it seems that even Seeger's minority share didn't always reach his family, which continued living in poverty: one daughter died of AIDS-related complications when her family couldn't afford the medicine that could have helped her,[75] and others worked as domestic servants.[76] While all this was happening, the powerful corporations who were

[70] Randy Lewis, 'Who Wrote "The Lion Sleeps Tonight"? A Netflix Film Seeks Answers, and Closure', *Los Angeles Times* (14 May 2019) <https://www.latimes.com/entertainment/music/la-et-ms-lion-sleeps-tonight-netflix-documentary-20190515-story.html>.

[71] *The Lion's Share* (ReMastered, Triage Entertainment, 2018) 0:26:00.

[72] Bill DeMain, 'The Lion Sleeps Tonight AKA "MBUBE" AND "WIMOWEH"' (2006) 14(95) *Performing Songwriter* 92.

[73] Ibid.

[74] Ibid.

[75] TraxpAdmin, 'The Lion King's Ransom: The Story of "Mbube", "The Lion Sleeps Tonight" and the 70 Years Struggle to Get the Writer, Solomon Linda Credited', *Traxploitation* (29 July 2019) <https://traxploitation.com/solomon-linda>, archived at <https://web.archive.org/web/20230130035313/https://traxploitation.com/solomon-linda>.

[76] Rory Carroll, 'Lion Takes on Mouse in Copyright Row', *The Guardian* (online, 3 July 2004) <https://www.theguardian.com/world/2004/jul/03/film.arts>.

benefiting most from the song strategised to keep it in their grasp, twice requiring Linda's heirs to freshly sign over any rights they may have had on top of what they'd already extracted from Linda himself.[77]

A spotlight was finally shone on the injustice in 2000, when South African journalist (and descendant of an apartheid-era prime minister) Rian Malan published an exposé in *Rolling Stone*.[78] The story captured global media attention, including a documentary. Leading South African copyright lawyer Owen Dean was approached by Gallo, now facing a PR nightmare for its role in the heist, and wondering what might be done.[79]

Dean initially thought it was hopeless given how broadly the contracts were worded, but then he remembered an obscure reversion provision he'd come across a few years before – the Imperial Act had been law in South Africa until 1965. The proviso to section 5 had been repealed in South Africa as in most other countries, but under the transitional arrangements, it still applied to this work. Linda died in 1962, so in 1989 the song rights had reverted. Without fresh licences, subsequent uses would be infringing.

As discussed above, reverted rights technically vested in the author's 'legal personal representatives as part of his estate'. That technicality usually made things more difficult for heirs, since estates are usually wound up long before that, but here it turned out to be the saving grace. The additional agreements Linda's wife and daughters had been obliged to sign extracted not only any rights they may have had at that time, but any they might obtain in the future. As Dean explains, 'The effect of the assignments they executed would be that, once copyright in *Mbube* became vested in them, those assignments would be activated and immediately deprive them of their copyright in favour of the assignees.'[80] To avoid that happening, he came up with the plan of having an executor appointed to the estate as Linda's legal representative. If successful, the *executor* would take ownership of the reverted rights.

Given the success of the song in its myriad forms, numerous individuals and companies could have been targeted by an infringement claim. The family's legal team decided to target the most formidable of them all: Disney. That caused Gallo to withdraw its offer to fund the case, knowing how hard the media giant would fight, and aware of its ability to harm the record label's own commercial interests. As one executive explained: 'If Disney had withheld all the rights that Gallo held at that time, it would have had a major impact on our earnings.'[81]

77 DeMain (n 72).
78 Malan (n 69).
79 See Owen Dean, *Awakening the Lion: The Case of the Lion Sleeps Tonight* (Tafelberg, 2013) ch 1.
80 Ibid ch 3.
81 *The Lion's Share* (n 71) 0:50:00.

That would have probably been the end of the fight, had Linda family's lawyers not persuaded the South African culture ministry to step in and fill the gap.[82] Once that was done, the underdogs obtained a big victory – an order attaching Disney's South African trade marks as security for any award made against the corporation, effectively putting Donald Duck and Mickey Mouse on the line.[83] Dean remembers the retribution being swift and savage, just as Gallo had anticipated. '[Disney] reacted like scalded cats, and brought their heavy artillery to bear on us and anything connected to us.'[84]

Despite that pressure, the parties eventually reached a confidential settlement acknowledging Linda as the original composer of what became 'The Lion Sleeps Tonight'. A trust was established to take ownership of the song rights (avoiding the trap that was waiting for any heir who took ownership in their own right), and the compensation for past infringement as well as future royalties as agreed under the settlement. Critically, the royalty obligation was not limited to uses in South Africa (which were minimal), but worldwide.[85] In achieving that result, the applicants may have been assisted by the fact that identical reversionary rights applied throughout the Commonwealth, meaning that similar actions could have been launched in the UK and other nations.

Disputes remain ongoing about whether the licensees are actually paying what's owed, and whether the settlement amount was fair.[86] However, as a result of the reversion right contained in the 1911 Act, Linda's heirs have now received far more than they would have without it.

#### 2.4.1.2 The Redwood Music Litigation

When he was 25, Fats Waller signed a contract assigning all rights in the ten songs from his Broadway musical *Connie's Hot Chocolates* for US$500.[87] His work went on to make a great deal of money for other people, making this assignment precisely the kind of 'improvident' transaction the British parliament intended the reversion right to guard against.

Miriam Stern, a passionate advocate for songwriters and former director of the American Guild of Authors and Composers, got wind of the inequity around the Waller transfer, as well as those affecting the estates of other composers including Sergei Rachmaninoff, and thought the British reversionary right might be able to

82 Ibid 0:51:00.

83 *Disney Enterprises, Inc. v S.G. Griesel*, High Court of South Africa [Transvaal Provincial Div.] Case No 12003/04 (2004).

84 *The Lion's Share* (n 71) 0:55:00.

85 Regarding the settlement generally, see Dean (n 79) ch 7.

86 *The Lion's Share* (n 71).

87 Mark Chilla, 'The Songs of Razaf and Waller', *Afterglow* (Web Page, 5 April 2019) <https://indianapublicmedia.org/afterglow/songs-razaf-waller.php>.

help. Though it had been repealed by the time she took up the cause, the UK law's transitional arrangements meant it still applied to works created before 1957.[88] Motivated by concern for the heirs of composers including Waller, who were often too poor to afford lawyers, she set up the Miriam Rose Stern Agency (MRSA) to help estates enforce their reversionary rights and bargain for a fairer share. The MRSA quickly came to represent 177 estates and up to 40,000 songs.[89]

Undaunted by the refusal of leading music publishers to negotiate with her agency, Stern initiated a series of test cases. The most critical issue concerned whether the assignment of the copyright in a song was the assignment of 'the copyright in a collective work', and thus excluded from the reversion right by the final sentence of the proviso to section 5(2). Most songs have lyrics written separately from the music, and the defendant music publishers strenuously argued that in such cases the reversion right did not apply.

At first instance Goff J agreed with the publishers, reasoning that songs comprising both music and lyrics (and thus both musical and literary copyrights) were indeed collective works.[90] Redwood had argued that songs were not collective works as conceptualised under the proviso to section 5(2), because that proviso only excluded assignments of the copyright in a collective work, and after all, the combination of the music and lyrics did not create a separate combined copyright.[91] But Goff J ruled such songs did fall within the scope of the exclusion, influenced not only by principles of statutory interpretation but also practical considerations: his Honour thought it would be highly inconvenient if ownership of different parts of a song were to change at different times.[92]

A second test case, this time involving a song with jointly authored music and lyrics – that is, written by two authors together, rather than separately – evoked a different result. The reversion right was held to apply notwithstanding the inconvenience that might bring about.[93]

The UK Court of Appeal had more good news for heirs, overturning the lower court ruling that reversion wouldn't apply to songs with separate authors for music and lyrics.[94] While songs with lyrics and music written by different authors were confirmed to be collective works, they were nevertheless not excluded from the scope of the reversion right because 'there is no separate and independent copyright in the song as a collective work'.[95] The only copyrights were those for the lyrics and music, and the reversion right applied to each.[96] Emphasising that the proviso's

88 *Redwood Music* (1978) (n 55) 434.
89 Ibid 433–7.
90 Ibid 455.
91 Ibid 451.
92 Ibid 450–3.
93 *Redwood Music Ltd v B Feldman & Co Ltd* [1979] RPC 385, 404–6 ('*Redwood Music* (1979)').
94 Ibid 403–3.
95 Ibid 402–3.
96 Ibid 400–3.

intention 'was to safeguard authors and their heirs', the House of Lords upheld that decision.[97]

This long battle translated to real benefits for songwriter heirs. In the case of the Fats Waller songs that began the whole saga, the previous music publisher acknowledged it no longer had any claim.[98] Within two years of the litigation finally ending, new deals entered into by Waller's sons had already secured them some US$12,500, with 'substantial additional sums expected' to follow from sources such as theatrical licence fees.[99]

#### 2.4.1.3 Lessons from the Canadian Experience

Although these examples show that the Imperial right could achieve its aim of benefiting author heirs, their scant number (relative to the literally millions of works covered by the right across the Commonwealth) says much more about the legislature's failure to achieve its aims. In Canada, where the equivalent right has so far survived both the wave of Berlin revision repeals, and multiple subsequent calls for its abolition,[100] we found just two reported examples where the Imperial right actually, or even potentially, benefited an heir.

The first Canadian example involved Theresia Winkler, the elderly former landlord of writer Thomas P Kelley Jr, and heir and executor of his estate. Kelley, who died in poverty in 1982, had been a prolific writer of pulp fiction – most notably two books loosely based on a vigilante murder which are estimated to have sold over

[97] *Chappell & Co Ltd v Redwood Music Ltd; Redwood Music Ltd v Francis, Day & Hunter Ltd* [1980] 2 All ER 817 (Viscount Dilhorne dissenting).

[98] Krasilovsky and Meloni (n 53) 36.

[99] Ibid.

[100] See, e.g., Laurent Carrière, 'Limitation Where Author Is First Owner of Copyright: Reversionary Interest in the Copyright', *Limitation Where Author Is First Owner of Copyright: Reversionary Interest in the Copyright – Some Comments on Section 14 of the Canadian Copyright Act* (Web Page, 1 January 2003) 10 <https://www.robic.ca/en/?publications=limitation-where-author-is-first-owner-of-copyright-reversionary-interest-in-the-copyright-some-comments-on-section-14-of-the-canadian-copyright-act> referring to Andrew A Keyes and C Brunet, *Copyright in Canada: Proposals for a Revision of the Law* (Consumer and Corporate Affairs Canada, 1977) 76 <https://publications.gc.ca/collections/collection_2021/isde-ised/RG43-41-1977-eng.pdf>; Judy Erola and Francis Fox, *From Gutenberg to Telidon: A White Paper on Copyright* (Consumer and Corporate Affairs Canada, 1984); Barry Torno, 'Term of Copyright Protection in Canada: Present and Proposed' (1980) 46 *Canadian Patent Report* (2d) 257. Two other government copyright reports were released between the Ilsley Report and the 1988 amendments, being the Report on Intellectual and Industrial Property (1971) and the Charter of Rights for Creators – Report of the Subcommittee on the Revision of Copyright (1985). Neither of these reports mention the reversionary provision. See also Douglas A Smith, 'Recent Proposals for Copyright Revision: An Evaluation' (1988) 14(2) *Canadian Public Policy/Analyse de Politiques* 175, 175; Linda Hansen, 'The Half-Circled "c": Canadian Copyright Legislation' (1992) 19(2) *Government Publications Review* 137, 144–8.

a million copies.[101] Winkler succeeded in obtaining a declaration that the publishing and film rights in those books would revert to her in 2007, 25 years after the author's death.[102] Subsequently, Darling Terrace Publishing, which appears to be run by John Winkler, republished Kindle editions of those books in 2019. This allows Kelley's heirs to keep benefiting from sales of these books, but also keeps a fascinating part of Canadian history available to the public.[103]

The second involved descendants of author LM Montgomery who, in the 1980s, discovered rights in the beloved (and highly lucrative) *Anne of Green Gables* series had reverted to them, and began licensing rights for the production of *Anne* merchandise, like dolls, clothing and souvenirs.[104] They terminated one of those licences for non-payment of royalties, and instituted legal action after the defendant – then the world's largest *Anne* merchandiser – continued to use the names and likenesses.[105]

The Court rejected the defendant's argument that the heirs did not own the rights, finding they had a valid copyright interest from the rights having reverted to them, either as a result of the Canadian iteration of the Imperial law or transitional arrangements covering works that pre-dated it.[106] The Court didn't have to decide which, because the heirs did not become aware of their interest until the mid-1980s – rendering the choice of avenue used to calculate the date the reversionary interest began immaterial. As a result, the heirs were able to benefit from their rights for only a few years before the *Anne* books entered the public domain.

#### 2.4.1.4 The Imperial Reversion Right's Illusory Promises

The fact that there was so little awareness around reversion even for such lucrative properties further demonstrates how poorly tailored this law was to the job at hand. Even in Canada, where it's still on the statute books, it is routinely ignored, with licensees continuing to exploit works even after the rights automatically revert.[107] They can get away with that because, as Tarantino explains, lack of awareness of the law means relatively few estates assert their rights.[108] That lack of awareness follows

[101] Paul Waldie, 'Fight over Black Donnellys Novels Settled', *The Globe and Mail* (online, 25 September 2002) <https://www.theglobeandmail.com/news/national/fight-over-black-donnellys-novels-settled/article1026530/>.

[102] *Winkler v Roy* [2002] FCT 950, [62].

[103] Joshua Yuvaraj, 'Back to the Start: Re-envisioning the Role of Copyright Reversion in Australia and Other Common Law Countries' (PhD Thesis, Monash University, 2021) 68–9, n 412.

[104] *Anne of Green Gables Licensing Authority Inc v Avonlea Traditions Inc* 2000 CanLII 22663 (ON SC) [87]; [2000] OJ No 740 (QL); 4 CPR (4th) 289.

[105] Ibid 4.

[106] Ibid at [87], [90].

[107] Bob Tarantino, 'Long Time Coming: Copyright Reversionary Interests in Canada' (2013) 375 *Développements récents en droit de la propriété intellectuelle* 3, 26 <https://ssrn.com/abstract=2368464>.

[108] Ibid.

from the fact that the right, overwhelmingly, has so little value. Since Canada repealed the compulsory licence provision, publishers can now be assured of exclusive rights during the reversionary term. However, their financial value is nonetheless impacted by the fact that rights don't revert until a full generation after death, and because they vest in estates that by then probably no longer exist, making ownership complicated and costly to assert.

The fact it takes so long to kick in also raises the transaction costs of complying by making it harder to identify the heirs.[109] The copyrights may have been left to multiple people, who may be difficult to track down (or may even have died themselves) by the time the rights transfer to them.

While these criticisms of the Imperial right are valid, others have less merit. For example, a 1977 report published by Canada's Department of Consumer and Corporate Affairs argues that the reversion right's limitation on what can be assigned would tend to reduce the prices paid.[110] However, as discussed in Chapter 1, the time value of money and cultural depreciation mean that, at the time of entry into the original contract, publishers are exceedingly unlikely to pay any more for life plus 50 years than they would for life plus 25 years. Thus, a reversion right that kicks in so late is unlikely to have any downward effect on prices.

The same report criticises the right for being 'defeatable by testamentary disposition'.[111] This is a reference to the fact that while the statute otherwise prohibits authors from disposing of the interest in their lifetime, it permits dispositions by will. In theory then, a rightsholder might subvert the intent of the statute by requiring an author to bequeath it the reversionary interest as well as their lifetime rights. The author might change their will later, but contracts involving transfer of property interests can survive death, so such circumstances might still give rise to a claim against the estate for breach of contract. Rather than being used to attack the case for reversion rights altogether, however, this risk could be managed by rendering void contracts bequeathing reversionary rights where the effective intent is to render those rights alienable, an option we examine further in Chapter 6.

Tarantino criticises the Canadian reversion right for creating uncertainty in publishers about when rights will revert,[112] but we don't find this argument convincing either: they should know when their authors die, at least because it will result in the entitlement to royalties transferring elsewhere, and after that time they still have 25 years – a full generation! – to plan for the handover.

Tarantino also argues 'exploiters will be disinclined to invest resources towards the exploitation of a work which is nearing the reversionary threshold, because they will be uncertain whether an author's estate/heirs will assert an ownership claim'.[113]

109 Ibid 25.
110 Keyes and Brunet (n 100) 69.
111 Ibid.
112 Tarantino (n 107) 25.
113 Ibid 26.

This argument is not persuasive either. The reversionary interest becomes assignable immediately upon death,[114] as Tarantino himself notes elsewhere,[115] and there's nothing stopping the rightsholder from negotiating with heirs to buy the interest then (or at any later point) to secure their future investments.

Finally, Tarantino argues that further uncertainty arises because publishers don't know 'whether an author's estate or heirs will be informed or savvy enough to become aware of the reversionary interest and assert ownership'.[116] But we don't consider it a relevant detriment that publishers must factor in uncertainty over whether they will be successful in heisting an interest that rightfully belongs to others! They could always manage that risk by doing what the original lawmakers intended, and negotiating a fresh deal with the author's heirs.

The real objection by rightsholders to Canada's reversion law seems to be that they would need to pay an additional amount for still valuable works after decades of benefit – even though that's precisely the bargain they struck.

## 2.5 OTHER COMMONWEALTH STATUTORY REVERSION RIGHTS

So far this chapter has focused exclusively on the reversion rights that originated in the UK. As we noted above, the Imperial right was widely exported throughout the Commonwealth. In addition to that, however, some nations have enacted additional rights. Language and resource restrictions prevent us from any comprehensive analysis, but we have summarised some of these provisions in Table 2.1.[117]

They include rights to revert where publishers are acquired, where they fail to publish a work within a specific time, or where a work goes out of print. Additionally, Malawi, Mauritius, Nauru, Tanzania and Zanzibar have a general 'use it or lose it right' entitling creators to reclaim their copyrights for lack of exploitation. Use-it-or-lose-it rights are more commonly found in European copyright laws, and the EU's 2019 Digital Single Market Directive mandated that all Member States provide mechanisms for authors and performers to reclaim their

[114] Copinger and Skone James (n 49) 110–11.

[115] Tarantino (n 107) 22–3.

[116] Ibid 26.

[117] These provisions are drawn from a study Yuvaraj undertook in 2019 into copyright reversion provisions applicable to all types of works and also specifically to book publishing contracts. For more information about the study's methodology please refer to Yuvaraj (n 103) ch 5. The dataset is available here: Joshua Yuvaraj, 'Data for Legal Mapping Study into Copyright Reversion Laws Applicable to Book Publishing Contracts (up to March 2019)', *Bridges* (Dataset, 24 August 2021) <https://doi.org/10.26180/16416747>. The provisions at Table 2.1 are current, as far as we can tell, as of March 2024. For consistency we used the list of countries on the official Commonwealth webpage: 'Member Countries', *The Commonwealth* (Web Page) <https://thecommonwealth.org/our-member-countries>. Further research into reversion provisions specific to recording artists, screenwriters and other types of creator would helpfully supplement this data.

TABLE 2.1 *Copyright reversion provisions in Commonwealth countries that are different from section 5(2) of the 1911* Imperial Copyright Act

| Country | Law | Description of provision |
|---|---|---|
| Pakistan | Copyright Ordinance, 1962, art 14(1) | No copyright assignment by an author can last for longer than 10 years 'except where the assignment is made in favour of a Government or an educational, charitable, religious or non-profit institution'. |
| Cameroon | Law No. 2000/011 of 19 December 2000 on Copyright and Neighbouring Rights, ss 46–47 | The author can end a publishing contract if the publisher's transfer of their business would 'seriously jeopardize the material and moral interests of the copyright holder' (s 46(2)). |
| | | The publishing contract will automatically end if the publisher destroys all copies of the work (s 47(1)). |
| | | The author can terminate the contract if the publisher fails to republish the work after the author gives notice, with a work being out of print if two 'requests for supply of copies sent to the publisher are not met within six months' (s 47(2)). |
| Mauritius | Copyright Act 2014, art 14 | The creator can revoke a grant of exclusive rights in a work if those rights are not exercised, or are exercised inadequately, in a way that is prejudicial to the creator's legitimate interests (art 14(1)). |
| | | The creator must allow a minimum of three years from the grant of the right or when they provided the work to the exploiter before attempting to revoke rights (art 14(3)). |
| | | The creator cannot revoke rights where the non-exploitation or inadequate exploitation is 'primarily due to circumstances which the author can be expected to remedy' (art 14(2)). |
| | | The use-it-or-lose-it right cannot 'be waived in advance' (art 14(4)). |
| Malawi | Copyright Act, 2016, art 55(5)–(7) | The creator can revoke a grant of exclusive rights in a work if those rights are not exercised in a way that is prejudicial to the creator's legitimate interests (art 55(5)). |

| Country | Law | Description of provision |
|---|---|---|
| | | The creator must allow a minimum of two years from the grant of the right or when they provided the work to the exploiter before attempting to revoke rights (art 55(6)).<br><br>To do so the creator must give the exploiter a reasonable time to exercise the right, failing which they can revoke the grant (art 55(7)). |
| Rwanda | Law No. 31/2009 of 26/10/2009 on the Protection of Intellectual Property, arts 235, 237 | A publishing contract will end if the publisher transfers their business and this is likely to harm the author's moral or economic interests *and* they are not equitably compensated for this (art 235).<br><br>The author can terminate the publishing contract when the edition is 'exhausted' and the publisher fails to reprint after two successive reprinting notices without reasonable grounds (art 237). |
| United Republic of Tanzania | The Copyright and Neighbouring Rights Act, 1999, s 20 which governs copyright law in mainland Tanzania and the Zanzibar Copyright Act, 2003, s 21(4)–(6) which covers copyright protection in Zanzibar. | **Copyright and Neighbouring Rights Act 1999**<br><br>The creator can revoke a grant of exclusive rights in a work where those rights are not used in a way that is 'prejudicial to [the creator's] . . . legitimate interests'. The creator can only exercise this right two years from the contract or when the work was delivered, and must give the exploiter a reasonable opportunity to exercise the right, 'except . . . where the exercise of the right by the [exploiter] . . . became impossible or he refused it.' The creator cannot 'waive . . . [this right] in advance' (s 20).<br><br>**Zanzibar Copyright Act 2003**<br><br>The creator can revoke a grant of exclusive rights in a work if those rights are not exercised, or are *inadequately exercised*, in a way that is prejudicial to the creator's legitimate interests (s 21(4)).<br><br>The creator must give the exploiter a reasonable time (s 21(6)), and cannot revoke rights where the non-exploitation |

(*continued*)

TABLE 2.1 (*continued*)

| Country | Law | Description of provision |
|---|---|---|
| | | or inadequate exploitation is 'primarily due to circumstances which the author can be expected to remedy' (s 21(5)). |
| Togo | Law No. 91-12 of June, 1991, on the Protection of Copyright, Folklore and Related Rights, art 56 | The author can terminate a contract if the publisher has failed to publish the work having been given a specific time in which to do so. |
| | | The author can terminate the contract if the publisher fails to republish the work after the author gives notice, with a work being out of print if two 'requests for delivery of copies addressed to the publisher have not been met within six months.' |
| | | The publishing contract will automatically end if the publisher destroys all copies of the work. |
| Nauru | Copyright Act 2019 (amended by the Revised Written Laws Act 2021), s 22 | The creator can revoke a grant of exclusive rights in a work if those rights are not exercised, or are *inadequately exercised*, in a way that is prejudicial to the creator's legitimate interests (s 22(1)). |
| | | The creator must wait at least two years from the grant or delivery of the work before revocation (s 22(2)). |
| | | The reversion right cannot 'be waived in advance' (s 22(3)). |

copyrights in cases of a 'lack of exploitation'.[118] As we will discuss in Chapter 4, that mandate has been largely implemented in a way that suggests rights can only be reclaimed where there is no exploitation at all.[119] The Malawian and Tanzanian laws are similarly narrow, but the others are scoped more broadly to entitle creators to take back inadequately exploited rights. Inquiry into the way those laws actually work in practice is beyond the scope of this book, but it's an interesting counterpoint to the restrictiveness of the EU's approach.

Nauru, Mauritius and Tanzania also prevent authors from transferring their use-it-or-lose-it rights via contract, which may reflect lessons learned from the failures we

[118] *Directive (EU) 2019/790 of the European Parliament and of the Council of 17 April 2019 on Copyright and Related Rights in the Digital Single Market and Amending Directives 96/9/EC and 2001/29/EC* [2019] OJ L 130/92, art 22.

[119] See Chapter 4, Section 4.4.4.

described at the beginning of this chapter. This is again a stricter approach than that taken by the EU, which as we will see did not require Member States to prohibit contracting out of its own use-it-or-lose-it right.[120]

## 2.6 RECENT DEVELOPMENTS

In the last few years, there are signs that the laissez-faire approach is losing currency even in Commonwealth strongholds, with the strongest pushes for reversion rights reform coming from Canada, South Africa and the UK.

### 2.6.1 *Canada*

Reversion rights became a hot topic in Canada in 2017 when singer-songwriter Bryan Adams and law professor Daniel Gervais argued before a Committee of the Canadian House of Commons that rights ought to revert 25 years after transfer rather than 25 years after the author's death.[121] One parliamentary standing committee subsequently recommended an amendment to that effect, while another proposed the introduction of an inalienable 25-year termination right bounded by certain additional restrictions.[122]

As we go to press, however, more than half a decade later, there are few signs that a more meaningful reversion right will actually pass into Canadian law. There was an ideal opportunity to do so in 2022, when Canada extended its copyright terms from life plus 50 years to life plus 70 years as mandated by the Canada-US-Mexico trade agreement, but it was ultimately passed without the recommended reversion reforms.[123]

However, the Canadian equivalent of the Imperial right – as unsatisfactory as it is – remains in force, and thanks to that term extension, heirs are now entitled to the final 45 years (rather than 25 years) of copyright. The publicity triggered by the reform effort may have raised awareness among executors and heirs about the potential value of their rights, and that this long-ignored feature may finally have a greater impact.

[120] See Chapter 4, Section 4.4.5.

[121] Canadian Parliament, Canadian Heritage Committee Meeting #118, 18 September 2018 per Bryan Adams at 11:25am <https://openparliament.ca/committees/canadian-heritage/42-1/118/bryan-adams-7/?page = 1>.

[122] Standing Committee on Canadian Heritage, Parliament of Canada, *Shifting Paradigms: Report of the Standing Committee on Canadian Heritage* (Report, 42nd Parliament, 1st Sess, May 2019); Standing Committee on Industry, Science and Technology, Parliament of Canada, *Statutory Review of the Copyright Act: Report of the Standing Committee on Industry, Science, and Technology* (Report, 42nd Parliament, 1st Sess, June 2019).

[123] Michael Geist, 'The Canadian Government Makes Its Choice: Implementation of Copyright Term Extension without Mitigating against the Harms', *Michael Geist* (Blog Post, 27 April 2022) <https://www.michaelgeist.ca/2022/04/the-canadian-government-makes-its-choice-implementation-of-copyright-term-extension-without-mitigating-against-the-harms/>.

### 2.6.2 *South Africa*

South Africa has also been considering reversion reform. But the proposal for such reform goes even further than those mooted in Canada, potentially giving authors one of the world's most powerful reversion rights: an automatic 25-year limit on all copyright assignments for literary and musical works.[124]

The Copyright Review Commission initially proposed this limit in 2011 to deal with musical artists not getting royalties because they had made poor initial assignments.[125] The initial bill, however, was considerably wider: it covered *all* copyright assignments.

This proposal garnered opposition, including from Owen Dean, despite his success with the Imperial provision in the *Mbube* case: 'There is no logic to this provision and it is completely arbitrary.'[126] Dean was concerned that non-authors would benefit because *all* assignments were limited, not just the ones authors made: so if the author assigned the rights to the publisher, who then assigned it to another publisher, the first publisher would benefit.[127] He also interpreted it as not allowing assignments *shorter* than 25 years, which was 'preposterous'.[128]

Other stakeholders continued to oppose reversion through Parliamentary committee discussions and consultations,[129] even though its scope was subsequently reduced to literary and musical works.[130] Lawmakers persisted with reversion,

[124] Copyright Amendment Bill B13F-2017 (South Africa) cl 25. This section adapts material from Yuvaraj (n 103) 76–8.

[125] Department of Trade and Industry Republic of South Africa, *Copyright Review Commission Report* (2011) 80 [10.12.10] <https://www.gov.za/documents/other/copyright-review-commission-report-2011-31-aug-2012>.

[126] Anton Mostert, *Commentary on the Copyright Amendment Bill 2015* (2015) 54('*Commentary on the Copyright Amendment Bill 2015*') <https://blogs.sun.ac.za/iplaw/files/2015/08/CIP-Formal-Comments-Copyright-Amendment-Bill-2015-Online1.pdf>.

[127] Ibid.

[128] Ibid.

[129] International Federation of the Phonographic Industry, *Submission to the Portfolio Committee on Trade and Industry of the Parliament of the Republic of South Africa on the Copyright Amendment Bill 2017* (22 February 2019) <https://www.asktheeu.org/en/request/7916/response/28127/attach/28/9%20EN%20annexe%20acte%20autonome%20nlw%20part1%20v1.pdf?cookie_passthrough=1>; Law Society of South Africa, *Submission to the Portfolio Committee on Trade and Industry of the Parliament of the Republic of South Africa on the Copyright Amendment Bill 2017* (16 May 2017) <https://www.lssa.org.za/wp-content/uploads/2020/01/LSSA-Submission-on-Copyrigt-Amendment-Bill-2.pdf>; Publishers Association of South Africa on the Copyright Amendment Bill, *Submission to the Portfolio Committee on Trade and Industry of the Parliament of the Republic of South Africa on the Copyright Amendment Bill 2017* (18 July 2018) <https://publishsa.co.za/wp-content/uploads/2021/07/Pasa-Submission-Copyright-Amendment-Bill-18-July-2018-1.pdf>.

[130] National Assembly Trade, Industry and Competition Committee, Parliament of the Republic of South Africa, *Copyright Amendment Bill: DTI Briefing on Bill and DAC & DTI Positions* (31 May 2018) <https://pmg.org.za/committee-meeting/26550/>; Copyright Amendment Bill B13B-2017 (South Africa) s 23(b).

though, and it looked like it would pass in 2019 when Parliament sent the Bill to President Cyril Ramaphosa for assent. However, the President refused, citing concerns over the Bill's constitutionality.[131]

Rightsholders were particularly vocal against reversion when the Bill came back to Parliament.[132] They argued that *creators* would be worse off by not being able to bargain away more than 25 years of rights,[133] that reversion unduly imposed on the parties' contractual freedom,[134] and that works would be lost to the public if joint authors/performers held up attempts to re-license works.[135] The Publishers' Association of South Africa expressed concern that other publishers or platforms could profit from all the work a first publisher had done in the initial 25-year

[131] Parliamentary Monitoring Group, 'Bill Returned to Parliament by the President', *That Week in Parliament* (Blog Post, 6 July 2020) <https://pmg.org.za/blog/BillReturnedtoParliamentbythePresident>.

[132] See, e.g., National Assembly Trade, Industry and Competition Committee, Parliament of the Republic of South Africa, *Copyright & Performers' Protection Amendment Remitted Bills: Further Public Hearings Day 2*, 12 August 2021 (Bertrand Moullier, Senior Advisor of the International Film Producers' Association Film Producers Worldwide); National Council of Provinces Trade & Industry, Economic Development, Small Business, Tourism, Employment & Labour Committee, Parliament of the Republic of South Africa, *Copyright Amendment Bill & Performers' Protection Amendment Bill: Public Hearings*, 21 February 2023 (Philippa Rafferty, Group Executive Legal and Business Affairs of eMedia Investments); National Council of Provinces Trade & Industry, Economic Development, Small Business, Tourism, Employment & Labour Committee, Parliament of the Republic of South Africa, *Copyright Amendment Bill & Performers' Protection Amendment Bill: Public Hearings*, 7 March 2023 (Stan McCoy, Motion Picture Association; Brian Wafawarowa, Publishers Association; and Danny Dohmen, Licensing Executives of South Africa); National Council of Provinces Trade & Industry, Economic Development, Small Business, Tourism, Employment & Labour Committee , Parliament of the Republic of South Africa, *Copyright Amendment Bill & Performers' Protection Amendment Bill: Public Hearings*, 14 March 2023 (Sipho Diamini and Pierre Rautenbach, Recording Industry of South Africa; Ziyanda Buthalezi-Ngcobo and Bradely Silver, Netflix; and Anne Kang and Lindi Vundla, Amazon).

[133] National Council of Provinces Trade & Industry, Economic Development, Small Business, Tourism, Employment & Labour Committee, Parliament of the Republic of South Africa, *Copyright Amendment Bill & Performers' Protection Amendment Bill: Public Hearings*, 7 March 2023 (Danny Dohmen and Brian Wafawarowa).

[134] National Assembly Trade, Industry and Competition Committee, Parliament of the Republic of South Africa, *Copyright & Performers' Protection Amendment Remitted Bills: Further Public Hearings Day 2*, 12 August 2021 (Bertrand Moullier, Senior Advisor of the International Film Producers' Association Film Producers Worldwide); National Council of Provinces Trade & Industry, Economic Development, Small Business, Tourism, Employment & Labour Committee, Parliament of the Republic of South Africa, *Copyright Amendment Bill & Performers' Protection Amendment Bill: Public Hearings*, 21 February 2023 (Philippa Rafferty, Group Executive Legal and Business Affairs of eMedia Investments).

[135] National Council of Provinces Trade & Industry, Economic Development, Small Business, Tourism, Employment & Labour Committee, Parliament of the Republic of South Africa, *Copyright Amendment Bill & Performers' Protection Amendment Bill: Public Hearings*, 14 March 2023 (Collen Dlamini and Pierre Rautenbach).

period: 'Amazon and others would reap where they have never sown, cherry picking and leaving the rest stranded like a ship in the Namib.'[136]

Parliament was undeterred, however, and passed the Bill without amending the reversion provision.[137] As we go to press, however, the Bill's future is uncertain: the President referred it to the Constitutional Court in October 2024 over constitutional concerns, though none in relation to the reversion provision.[138]

We find most of these arguments unpersuasive for reasons documented elsewhere in the book. However, we are concerned that the automatic operation of this provision may worsen the problem of orphan works. As we explain in Chapter 6, making reversion rights automatic can be an effective way of helping creators actually enforce them. But what if rights revert to creators or heirs who have no interest in them, or perhaps don't even realise they control them? To avoid such undesirable outcomes, we recommend automatic mechanisms be combined with appropriate safeguards to ensure they promote rather than hinder access.[139] Unfortunately, the South African law contains no such scaffolding.

It's also problematic in other ways. For example, it doesn't expressly bar publishers from signing multiple agreements for different 25-year blocks when initially negotiating the copyright grant with an author or composer, increasing the risk of its author-protective intent being undermined.[140] This kind of subversion is a real risk: as we explain in Chapter 4, publishers in Spain have attempted to contract around

[136] Publishers' Association of South Africa, *Submission to National Council of Provinces Select Committee on Trade and Industry, Economic Development, Small Business Development, Tourism, Employment and Labour* (27 January 2023) <https://publishsa.co.za/wp-content/uploads/2023/02/PASA-Submission-to-NCOP-Select-Committee-27Jan2023.pdf>; see also National Council of Provinces Trade & Industry, Economic Development, Small Business, Tourism, Employment & Labour Committee, Parliament of the Republic of South Africa, *Copyright Amendment Bill & Performers Protection Amendment Bill: Public Hearings* (7 March 2023) (Brian Wafawarowa).

[137] National Council of Provinces Committee on Trade and Industry, Economic Development, Small Business Development, Tourism, Employment and Labour, Parliament of the Republic of South Africa, *Copyright & Performers' Protection Amendment Bill: Voting on Negotiating Mandates (Continuation)*, 20 June 2023 (Meeting Minutes) <https://pmg.org.za/committee-meeting/37264/>; South Africa, *Parliamentary Debates*, National Council of Provinces, 26 September 2023 <https://pmg.org.za/hansard/37600/>.

[138] Matamela Cyril Ramaphosa, President of the Republic of South Africa, *Notice of Referral in Terms of Sections 79(4)(b) and 84(2)(c) of the Constitution of the Republic of South Africa, 1996: Copyright Amendment Bill [B13F – 2017] and Performers' Protection Amendment Bill [B24F – 2016]* (Letter to Constitutional Court, 10 October 2024) <https://static.pmg.org.za/Copyright_Bill_Notice_of_Referral.pdf>.

[139] See Chapter 6, Section 6.1.8.2. For a more detailed exploration of how such safeguards could be constructed to simultaneously generate rewards for creators and promote access for the public, see Rebecca Giblin, 'A New Copyright Bargain? Reclaiming Lost Culture and Getting Authors Paid' (2018) 41 *Columbia Journal of Law & Arts* 369.

[140] Owen Dean, 'Authors, You've Got a Friend?', *The Anton Mostert Chair of Intellectual Property* (Blog Post, 31 May 2021) <https://blogs.sun.ac.za/iplaw/2021/05/31/authors-youve-got-a-friend/>.

an analogous 15-year limit on publishing contracts by making them automatically renewable in 15-year blocks.[141]

Further, the provision doesn't address vital issues like what happens with joint authors and collective works, or commissioned works/works made in the course of employment. And Dean's initial criticism remains valid, too: it's unclear to us why it should apply to assignments made by those *other than* the author.

As we argue in Chapter 6, such issues *must* be appropriately dealt with for reversion rights to fully achieve their potential. We anticipate significant problems will emerge in the implementation of the forthcoming South African reversionary system precisely because it does not adequately address them.

### 2.6.3 *The UK*

Finally, the UK has also exhibited considerable renewed interest in reversion rights over the last few years.

#### 2.6.3.1 The 'Terms of Trade' Triumph

That new interest is contextualised by the success of the UK's independent film industry since 2004, when public service broadcasters like the BBC and Channel 4 ('PSBs') were required to implement new codes of conduct regulating the terms on which they commissioned independent productions.[142] These 'Terms of Trade' must cover matters such as licence duration, exclusivity of rights, and transparency around payment, and be approved by the regulator, OFCOM.[143]

The biggest effect of the change was to give independent film and television producers greater control over secondary rights to their content. Before this, independent film and television producers had little power to negotiate with PSBs, which are a powerful force in the UK market, and as a result were often obliged to license all or virtually all their rights in order to get their projects funded.[144] However, just as we've seen in other culture markets, that didn't mean the broadcasters actually actively exploited those rights, by (for example) licensing them into other territories: 'the PSBs had little or no interest in actively or even passively

[141] European Commission, Directorate-General for Communications Networks, Content and Technology, Olivia Salamanca and Lucie Guibault, *Remuneration of Authors of Books and Scientific Journals, Translators, Journalists and Visual Artists for the Use of Their Works* (2016) 115 <https://data.europa.eu/doi/10.2759/14126>.

[142] *Communications Act 2003* (UK) s 285(1).

[143] Ibid s 285(3).

[144] Oliver & Ohlbaum, *The Impact of Terms of Trade on the UK's Television Content Production Sector: A Report Prepared for the Canadian Media Producers Association (CMPA)* (2018) 2 <https://ised-isde.canada.ca/site/broadcasting-telecommunications-legislative-review/sites/default/files/attachments/968_CMPAAppendixC1.pdf>.

administered much of the content they controlled'.[145] This frustrated the production companies who had made the works and wanted them to be widely accessible, but because they'd been obliged to hand over the foreign rights, they were unable to exploit them themselves.[146]

Under the new regime, however, the producers retain control over those secondary rights. While they must share any proceeds with the commissioning broadcaster, the creators themselves get to decide where and how to monetise their projects overseas.[147] The change 'had a radical, sector-altering impact on television production in the UK'.[148] From 2004 to 2008, international income from UK TV rights grew an average of 22 per cent per year, and then continued to grow at around 7 per cent, while overall TV revenues increased from £1.5 billion in 2004 to more than £2.6 billion in just 13 years.[149]

Terms of Trade are limits on what creators can be obliged to give away, rather than reversion rights per se, but they achieve the same end: they help creators share fairly in the proceeds of their work by enabling them to negotiate additional deals once they have a better idea of what the work is worth, and help promote access to knowledge and culture by placing the exploitation rights in the hands of those most motivated to exploit them.

France now similarly regulates terms of trade for its film industry by limiting licence terms. Previously, streaming companies like Netflix insisted on buying out all rights on the shows it financed, but the new restrictions limit exclusive rights to a maximum of just three years.[150] Recognising the power of such interventions, creator organisations are advocating for them elsewhere, too.[151]

[145] CREATe, *Public Service Broadcasting, Streaming Services and the Future for "Terms of Trade": Response by CREATe (www.create.ac.uk) to the Parliamentary Inquiry by the Digital, Culture, Media and Sport Committee into 'The Future of Public Service Broadcasting'* (2020) 5 <https://committees.parliament.uk/writtenevidence/7077/pdf/>.

[146] Ibid 5–6.

[147] Ibid 5.

[148] Ibid 6.

[149] Oliver & Ohlbaum (n 144).

[150] Elsa Keslassy, 'Netflix, Amazon Must Invest 20–25% of French Revenues in Local Content, France Government Decrees' (online, 30 June 2021) <https://variety.com/2021/streaming/global/avms-france-netflix-new-rules-streamers-1235008364/>.

[151] See, e.g., Lateral Economics, *Taking Australian Stories and Skills to the World in the Age of Global Streaming: A Lateral Economics Discussion Paper Commissioned by Screen Producers Australia* (7 October 2021) <https://assets-us-01.kc-usercontent.com/89c218af-4a5a-00a2–9d83–3913048b3bc7/6d1aca76-d99a-4806-957a-38fecf032f73/Lateral%20Economics%20SPA%20Report%20Final%207%20October%2021.pdf>; Patrick Frater et al, 'Damming the Stream: Global Governments Try to Set Boundaries for Streaming Giants. Will They Work?' (online, 1 July 2019) <https://variety.com/2021/global/global/netflix-europe-avms-regulation-streamers-1235009148/>; and Oliver & Ohlbaum, *Supporting Local Content Investment: International Policy Approaches to VOD Services: A report for the ABC and Free TV Australia* (May 2021) <https://www.infrastructure.gov.au/sites/default/files/documents/mrgp-abc-attachment-b-oliver-and-ohlbaum.pdf>.

### 2.6.3.2 Recognising Reversion's Potential

British creator groups, most notably the Society of Authors, were among those pushing hardest for the inclusion of 'use-it-or-lose-it' rights in the European Digital Single Market Directive. Book authors often have reversion rights included in their publishing contracts, but that approach is far from satisfactory (as we demonstrate in Chapter 5), and they have long advocated for improved protections.[152] Although the campaign to incorporate these rights into the Directive succeeded, authors did not enjoy the fruits of that work in the UK, with Brexit torpedoing domestic implementation.[153]

Reversion rights stayed on the agenda, however, thanks to a UK parliamentary committee inquiry into the economics of music streaming. As we explained in Chapter 1, it found that the major record labels had become massively more profitable in the streaming era, but that those rewards were not being shared equitably with the recording artists and songwriters who actually make the music.[154]

In response, it recommended that creators be entitled to reclaim their rights 20 years after transfer, being after the point labels commonly write off bad debt, but likely still within the creator's working life.[155] This, in the Committee's view, 'would create a more dynamic market for rights and allow successful artists to go to the market to negotiate better terms for their rights'.[156] It also recommended adopting other creator-favouring interventions such as rights to equitable remuneration and contract adjustments to bring the UK in line with Europe.[157]

We revisit this proposal in our upcoming best practice analysis (Chapter 6). As we go to press, however, it remains unclear whether the inquiry's recommendation will translate to legislative reform. Giving musicians the right to reclaim rights after 20 years is the kind of intervention we think would make a real difference to their bargaining power, resulting in more profits going to artists and less to their labels. This would disproportionately affect the majors who control the bulk of catalogue, and whose record profit margins are being fattened by the contracts of heritage artists that pay much lower royalties than the going rate today. Given the power of those

[152] See, e.g., the 2015 CREATOR campaign, which called for reasonable contract terms including time limits and use-it-or-lose-it clauses: Society of Authors, 'C.R.E.A.T.O.R – Fair Contract Terms', *Where We Stand* (Web Page) <https://societyofauthors.org/Where-We-Stand/C-R-E-A-T-O-R-Campaign-for-Fair-Contracts>.

[153] Answer from Chris Skidmore, 'Copyright: EU Action: Question for Department for Business, Energy and Industrial Strategy', *UK Parliament Written Questions, Answers and Statements* (Web Page, 21 January 2020) <https://questions-statements.parliament.uk/written-questions/detail/2020-01-16/4371>.

[154] Digital, Culture, Media and Sport Committee, *Economics of Music Streaming* (House of Commons Paper No 50, Session 2021–22) 34, 63.

[155] Ibid 67.

[156] Ibid.

[157] Ibid.

labels, such an initiative would take real political courage. It may be that the UK's highly effective Terms of Trade reform was only politically possible because it was limited to *public* broadcasters. Will British lawmakers have the appetite to take on the Big Content and Big Tech giants who would lose out if creators had meaningful rights to negotiate fresh deals in other contexts?

## 2.7 CONCLUSION

Neither of the statutory reversion rights to have originated from Britain was designed in a way that would have allowed them to meaningfully benefit creators. The *Statute of Anne*'s author-protective intent was defeated by allowing publishers to extract the reversion right up front. The Imperial right was also designed to fail, by kicking in far too late (at a point most works had long ended their commercial lives) and by vesting in estates long after most of them had been wound up. Despite its deficiencies, the *Mbube* and *Redwood* cases still demonstrate the importance of reversion rights in correcting the injustices that can result from current contracting practice, and hint at the potential upside that could come from designing them in ways designed to further copyright's access and reward aims.

The use-it-or-lose-it model observed in some Commonwealth nations, in Africa and the Pacific presents a different, and intriguing, model which we examine more fully in Chapter 4 and our recommendations in Chapter 6. But the most effective intervention discussed in this chapter has undoubtedly been the UK's Terms of Trade reform that limited what creators can be obliged to give away. While not strictly a reversion right, it provides additional real-world evidence of the potential upside that could follow from introducing author-protective rights aimed at re-balancing bargaining power between creators and investors. Recent law reform developments in Canada, South Africa and the UK suggest that the *concept* of reversion is very much alive in lawmakers' minds as a way of addressing those imbalances.

# 3

# US Termination Rights

## INTRODUCTION

The British reversionary story is not the only one that shows how reversion's potential has been thwarted by poor design and systematic undermining by rightsholders. The United States has a long history of time-based reversion rights intended to benefit creators, first via a renewal right, and later via rights to unilaterally terminate copyright grants they had made decades before. In each case, however, these interventions failed to make any meaningful difference to the balance of power between creators and rightsholders, and did little to direct more money into creators' pockets.

This chapter traces that history of failure, and argues it should come as no surprise that the current US termination right is generating few benefits for authors: its design ensured its ineffectiveness from the very beginning.

## 3.1 US REVERSION RIGHTS HAVE BEEN CONSISTENTLY UNDERMINED

### 3.1.1 *1790: The Mirroring of the Two-Term* Statute of Anne *Model*

The US mimicked the *Statute of Anne* when it enacted its first Federal copyright law in 1790, granting 14 years of copyright and then 14 more to the author if they were still alive at the end of the first.[1] But unlike the *Statute of Anne*, which explicitly returned the rights to authors, the 1790 Act allowed the renewal term to go to authors or their executors, administrators or assigns.[2]

[1] *Copyright Act of 1790*, 1 Stat 24, § 1; Lionel Bently and Jane C Ginsburg, '"The Sole Right ... Shall Return to the Authors": Anglo-American Authors' Reversion Rights from the Statute of Anne to Contemporary U.S. Copyright' (2010) 25 *Berkeley Technology Law Journal* 1475, 1549.

[2] *Copyright Act of 1790* (n 1); Sidney J Brown, 'Renewal Rights in Copyright' (1942–3) 28(4) *Cornell Law Quarterly* 460, 461; Adam R Blankenheimer, 'Of Rights and Men: The Re-alienability of

It was unclear from the get-go whether the reference to 'assigns' meant that the author could transfer their rights for both terms in their initial contract, and Bently and Ginsburg argue that the more likely intention was that they could not.[3] Unsurprisingly, however, publishers routinely claimed to take the full duration of both terms upfront, before the value of the work was known.

Various draft bills were proposed to clarify this point in favour of authors, but never actually passed into law.[4]

### 3.1.2 1831: *The Two-Term System Remains, but Is Undermined by Rightsholder Contracting Practices*

The US retained the reversionary term in its 1831 law, after the British had abandoned its dual-term model. But despite the problem being well known, its revised law still failed to include any explicit prohibition on investors extracting rights over the reversionary term at the same time as the first.[5] Unsurprisingly, publishers took full advantage of that omission, and by the 1870s, publishing contracts 'systematically' provided for both terms to be extracted in full, with authors receiving no special payment for the second.[6] Although it was by no means clear that this was actually permitted under the law, the practical effect of this conduct was to deprive authors of the ability to re-license still valuable works once their copyrights were renewed.

In the lead-up to what became the 1909 US copyright law, it was proposed to extend copyright terms to the author's lifetime plus 50 years.[7] However, disputes broke out about what would happen to existing copyrights. There was consensus that they should also be extended – the dispute was over whether it should be authors or publishers that benefited from the windfall.

An early draft proposed limiting publishers' rights to the term they had actually contracted for, returning them to authors to enjoy the benefit of any additional years of protection after that.[8] But publishers objected fiercely, insisting instead that they get the benefit of the extension even though they had never bargained for (or paid for) those rights.[9]

Termination of Transfer Rights in Penguin Group v. Steinbeck' (2009) 24(1) *Berkeley Technology Law Journal* 321, 323.

3 Bently and Ginsburg (n 1) 1550.

4 A Bill for the Encouragement of Learning, and for the Promotion of the Useful Arts, HR 38, 11th Congress (1811); A Bill for the Encouragement of Learning, and for the Promotion of the Useful Arts, HR 75, 10th Congress (1808); A Bill for the Encouragement of Learning, and for the Promotion of Useful Arts, 7th Congress (1803), cited in Bently and Ginsburg (n 1) 1551.

5 Bently and Ginsburg (n 1) 1551.

6 Ibid 1554.

7 A Bill to Amend and Consolidate the Acts Respecting Copyright, HR 19853, 59th Congress (1906) cited in ibid 1555.

8 Ibid 1555–6.

9 Ibid 1556.

The Publishers Copyright League proposed that the new term of life plus 50 years incorporate a second renewal term that could be added to an initial fixed term and first renewal.[10] Sneakily though, they included language stating that this additional renewal term would only be enjoyed by the author or their heirs if the copyright had not been previously assigned.[11] Since publishers had been routinely extracting authors' rights in full for decades by this point, this would have meant an enormous windfall for publishers – all the while professing their 'willing[ness] that . . . [authors] should have the full benefit of this extension of those copyrights'.[12]

Bently and Ginsburg describe this proposal as a 'wolf in . . . sheep's clothing' that would have given publishers something they'd never before had – 'explicit statutory recognition' that authors could assign reversionary and renewal rights before they had even had a chance to vest.[13]

### 3.1.3 1909: *An Additional 14-Year Term, Undermined*

#### 3.1.3.1 The Poor Design of the 1909's Two-Term System

Ultimately, Congress abandoned the life plus 50 years proposal, and in 1909 simply extended the renewal term from 14 years to 28.[14] Congressional lawmakers seemed to understand how beneficial reversionary rights could be to authors – at least when they were able to hold on to them. There was powerful real-world evidence of this in the experience of Samuel Clemens (better known by his pen name, Mark Twain). He had sold *Innocents Abroad* very cheaply for the first term, but had somehow managed to keep hold of the renewal rights.[15] That was just as well, because it ended up being his best-selling work during his lifetime. If the rights had not reverted for the renewal term, nearly all of the profits would have ended up in other people's pockets.

Congress acknowledged this, and expressed its intention for authors to benefit from their statutory reversion terms.[16] And yet somehow, once again, they failed to make it explicit in the 1909 Act that publishers could not extract authors' renewal rights at the same time as the initial term. Publishers continued to take advantage of the uncertainty by insisting they could,[17] and, since few authors had the means or

10 Ibid.
11 Ibid.
12 Ibid 1557.
13 Ibid.
14 Ibid 1560.
15 Ibid 1559.
16 Ibid 1559–60; *Fred Fisher Music Co v M Witmark & Sons*, 318 US 643, 653–5 (1943).
17 In *Fred Fisher* (n 16) 658, the Court found that 'in the actual practices of authors and publishers' there continued to be widespread assignment of renewals following the enactment of the Copyright Act of 1909. See also Blankenheimer (n 2) 325.

power to challenge them, the question of whether advance transfers of rights were binding remained unresolved for another 30 years.

#### 3.1.3.2 The Supreme Court Undermines Creator Rights

This uncertainty was finally resolved in 1943, when the Supreme Court in *Fred Fisher Music Co v Witmark* found that publishers *could* take both terms from the author in the first instance.[18] The case involved three composers of the music and lyrics to the song 'When Irish Eyes Are Smiling', who assigned copyright to music publishers, M Witmark & Sons in 1912 for the *first* copyright term. But five years later, one of the song's lyricists, George Graff Jr, granted his rights in the *renewal* term to Witmark for 'When Irish Eyes' and 69 other songs for US$1,600, and a power of attorney for Witmark to complete the processes necessary to renew the copyright for its second term, as he was 'in need of immediate funds'.[19] When the 28-year term was up, Witmark registered the renewal and transferred the second term to itself.[20] But Graff had a change of heart and sought to register the renewal *himself*, following which he assigned the renewal interest to Fisher Music Co.[21]

The dispute between Fisher and Witmark eventually came before the Supreme Court mainly on this point of law: could copyright in the renewal term be assigned before the renewal right had accrued? The Supreme Court found that it could.[22] Although Congress had clearly indicated that authors were given two terms so they could negotiate the second term of exploitation from positions of greater bargaining power, the Supreme Court's decision ensured that rightsholders could prevent them from doing so.

Extraordinarily, Justice Frankfurter phrased his rubbing out of authors' rights in a way that suggested he was doing them a favour:[23] 'We are asked to recognize that authors are congenitally irresponsible, that frequently they are so sorely pressed for funds that they are willing to sell their work for a mere pittance, and therefore assignments made by them should not be upheld.'[24] But, his Honour continued,

> We cannot draw a principle of law from the familiar stories of garret poverty of some men of literary genius … We do not have such assured knowledge about authorship … or the psychology of gifted writers and composers, as to justify us

[18] *Fred Fisher* (n 16).

[19] Theodore R Kupferman, 'Renewal of Copyright – Section 23 of the Copyright Act of 1909' (1944) 44(5) *Columbia Law Review* 712, 720.

[20] Ibid.

[21] Ibid.

[22] Ibid 720–1.

[23] For a detailed overview of Supreme Court copyright jurisprudence in the twentieth century, see Marci A Hamilton, 'Copyright at the Supreme Court: A Jurisprudence of Deference' (2000) 47 *Journal of the Copyright Society of the U.S.A.* 317.

[24] *Fred Fisher* (n 16) 656.

as judges in importing into Congressional legislation a denial to authors of the freedom to dispose of their property possessed by others.[25]

His Honour's reasoning was that it may well be that authors 'have habits making for intermittent want, [but] they may have no less a spirit of independence which would resent treatment of them as wards under guardianship of the law.'[26]

The authors who had advocated so strongly for statutory clarification that their reversion rights couldn't be prematurely extracted may well have been taken aback by the nature of this solicitude. By the time of this decision publishers had a track record of systematically extracting broad rights from authors for at least 70 years, with none but the most powerful and successful authors typically having any choice about whether to give them up.[27]

Nonetheless, the *Fred Fisher* Court found that the thing authors would most resent (amidst their struggles to pay their bills and provide for their families) was whether the law took an overly paternalistic view of their copyright interests![28]

The *Fred Fisher* decision is perhaps unsurprising given the Supreme Court's early twentieth-century deference to freedom of contract.[29] But it also demonstrates the importance of precise drafting that accurately gives effect to the legislative intent: the law could not have been undermined if authors' rights had been properly protected in the first place.

The Supreme Court did subsequently provide one small consolation prize for destitute families of deceased authors – a ruling that, if the author assigned the right and then died, the 28-year renewal term would go to heirs free and clear: they would not be bound by the author's own earlier grant.[30] But investors promptly made sure to take this away too. They started requiring creators not only to give up their own rights, but to obtain their family members' agreement to give up their rights too.[31] Until that happened, they couldn't get paid. A 'considerable amount of trafficking' grew up around these rights.[32] This anecdote from music publishing veteran Jay Morgenstern shows just how seriously investors took this. As he tells the story, a music studio 'demanded all of the signatures and we were able to comply. [Then] the author died while his wife was expecting. Everybody at the studio went

[25] Ibid 657.

[26] Ibid 657.

[27] Bently and Ginsburg (n 1) 1554.

[28] For further detail on the implications of *Fred Fisher* (which is beyond the scope of this book), see, e.g., Kupferman (n 19) 719–21; Dorothy M Schrader, 'Vesting Date of the Renewal Copyright Interest' (1972) 19(4) *Bulletin of the Copyright Society of the U.S.A.* 277, 290–2.

[29] See *Lochner v New York*, 198 US 45 (1905); see further Hila Keren, 'Undermining Justice: The Two Rises of Freedom of Contract and the Fall of Equity' (2016) 2(1) *Canadian Journal of Comparative and Contemporary Law* 339, 342–3, 347–53.

[30] *Miller Music Corp v Charles N Daniels Inc*, 362 US 373 (1960); see also Bently and Ginsburg (n 1) 1563.

[31] Bently and Ginsburg (n 1) 1563.

[32] Ibid 1563 n 416, citing Report of the Register of Copyrights, 1199, 1253.

into cardiac arrest thinking that the new heir could renege on the license at reversionary time.'[33]

Renewal rights obviously had potential value – if they didn't, there would have been no reason for rightsholders to cling to them so tightly. Authors should have been able to share meaningfully in that by having the right to re-negotiate their deals during the renewal term, once everyone had a better idea of how much their work was worth. However, the design and interpretation of this regime ensured that it could be largely captured by investors instead. This undoubtedly harmed the public interest in access as well. As we've seen elsewhere, just because a publisher holds the rights doesn't mean they will actually exploit them. If authors had been free to negotiate fresh deals, as Congress intended, it would have increased the chance of the rights ending up in the hands of an investor who actively wished to do so.

### 3.1.4 1976: *The New Copyright Act's 'Inalienable' Termination Right*

The renewal structure's failures influenced Congress to create an entirely new reversion scheme as part of the 1976 *Copyright Act*, which remains the law today. But as we show below, this too was undermined by poor design and fierce rightsholder lobbying. The result is a case study in what *not* to do if you want a reversion right that will meaningfully benefit creators.

#### 3.1.4.1 A Radical Proposal: Automatic 20-Year Reversion Except in Cases of Continuing Royalties

In the lead-up to the revision of federal copyright law, the Copyright Register, Abraham Kaminstein, had been scathing about the renewal right's failures. He pointed out that its primary purpose had been to protect authors and their heirs against 'unprofitable or improvident disposition[s]', and that because the law had been interpreted to allow authors to transfer their renewal rights in advance, it had 'largely failed to accomplish its primary purpose.'[34]

In response to these failures, the Copyright Office advanced an initial proposal for rights to revert 20 years after transfer unless the contract provided continuing royalties for use.[35]

Publishers and other rightsholders lambasted the proposal, claiming that would not give them enough time to 'recoup their investment[s]' and would 'make [copyrights] … less valuable.'[36] And in any event, they insisted, 'authors, if they

33 Ibid citing email from Jay Morgenstern to Jane Ginsburg.

34 Register of Copyrights, 8th Cong, 1st Sess, 1961 report on the General Revision of the US Copyright Law 53, 92 (Comm Print 1961).

35 Copyright Law Revision Part 3 (US Government Printing Office, 1964) 277.

36 Ibid (summarised by Register).

ever were, are no longer in a weak bargaining position and need no special protection of the sort contemplated here'.[37] Authors weren't happy about it either, though their reasons were very different: they thought it would be too easy for publishers to evade the law by paying nominal royalties for the renewal period, and asked for stronger protections.[38]

#### 3.1.4.2 Automatic Reversion and a 'Bestseller' Clause

The Copyright Office took the authors' point, and suggested two new alternatives for consideration. In a proposal evocative of the 1737 British bill that would have limited transfers to 10 years, Alternative A would have seen rights revert automatically to authors 25 years after transfer.[39] Alternative B would have given authors the right to apply to a court to reclaim their rights if, after 20 years, the profits earned by investors were 'strikingly disproportionate' to the author's share.[40]

Alternative B was discarded quickly, with authors and investors both concerned about its potential costs and uncertainty.[41] But it was Alternative A on which investors really unleashed their ire. Many of their arguments echoed Justice Frankfurter in suggesting the proposed protection was insulting to authors. In transcripts of the negotiations to thrash out the law, content industry representatives variously described it as making authors out to be 'improvident', 'nincompoops' and 'fools'.[42]

It turned out, however, that authors didn't want copyright investors to protect them from the new law. In fact, they were 'ardently' in favour of reversion protections: to the point they would oppose any amendment of the copyright law in the event they weren't included. Irwin Karp, representing the Authors' League of America in those negotiations, explained that this vehement support was not because authors were improvident or foolish, but because the opposite was true. '[P]rudent, provident author[s]' want to limit their grants of rights, because of that information problem we've talked about before: they know their value can't be properly assessed at the time the initial bargain is made.[43] However, they rarely have the opportunity to do so. 'The reason you need a reversion', Karp explained, 'is because the imbalance in bargaining positions makes it impossible for the author to obtain the sort of bargain that he would like to obtain'.[44] In the publishing industry, for example, '[t]he basic terms of a book contract are the same wherever you go. You

37 Ibid (summarised by Register).
38 Ibid 277–8.
39 Ibid 16.
40 Ibid.
41 Ibid 278–80, 282–3, 288–9, 292.
42 Ibid 282, 285; Copyright Law Revision Part 4 (US Government Printing Office, 1964) 250, 275.
43 Copyright Law Revision Part 3 (n 35) 286.
44 Ibid.

can't, no matter how strongly you bargain as an author, limit the lease of rights to publish a book.'[45]

Copyright investors argued their businesses would be ruined if authors were limited to granting them just 25 years of rights. A film industry representative claimed that it might not be enough time to make a motion picture, 'for various complicated reasons'; book publishers claimed it would be 'devastating';[46] and the music industry claimed it would 'mean the death knell'.[47] But Karp, the authors' representative, persuasively demolished those claims. Under the then-current law, as he pointed out, investors lost their rights if the author died before the 28th year was up. No evidence had been presented of suffering by content companies as a result, so ergo, a term around that length must be ample.[48]

Rightsholders also solemnly exhorted the importance of freedom of contract. Horace Manges, speaking for the book industry, was particularly unsympathetic to those who came off second best in their deals. '[I]mprovident bargains are made by all classes of people, but the law does not give them another chance to change a disadvantageous contract.'[49]

But Karp had yet a powerful response to this argument too, pointing out that, at that exact moment, book publishers were attempting to interfere with retailers' freedom of contract by setting the prices at which books must be sold. In his acid observation, 'Each of us will object to certain interferences and support other interferences, depending on whether we are the owner of the ox who was gored or whether we want to gore somebody else's ox.'[50]

#### 3.1.4.3 The Eventual Compromise

Congress eventually passed the 1976 *Copyright Act* with two new termination rights – one applying to pre-1978 grants and the other to those that came after.[51] To terminate rights transfers, applicants must serve a notice on the grantee or their successor setting out the effective termination date, work title, author, and other key information such as details of the grant in question.[52] Those notices had to be issued not less than 2 years and not more than 10 years before the termination date,[53] and had to be validly served on the rightsholder as well as filed with the Copyright Office.[54]

45 Ibid 287.
46 Ibid 281.
47 Ibid 283.
48 Ibid 293.
49 Ibid 282.
50 Ibid 287.
51 17 USC §§ 203; 304(c), (d).
52 17 USC §§ 203(a)(4); 304(c)(4); Code of Federal Regulations § 201.10(b).
53 17 USC § 203(a)(4).
54 Ibid.

The base fee for recording a notice is US$125 (at the time of writing), and increases with the number of grants included in the notice.[55]

Lawmakers were explicit that they were necessary because of the power dynamics typical of creator-investor relationships: 'A provision of this sort is needed because of the unequal bargaining position of authors, resulting in part from the impossibility of determining a work's value until it has been exploited.'[56] As we show in Section 3.2, however, the operation of this creator-focused scheme has been anything but, with the law proving to be unclear, complex, susceptible to undermining by rights-holders, and generating little benefit for creators.

## 3.2 HOW THE CURRENT US TERMINATION SYSTEM (ACTUALLY) WORKS

Despite Congress's good intentions, the termination legislation they ultimately enacted gored the authors' ox deep. The provisions were a far cry from the Copyright Office's original author protective proposal. Rights cannot be reclaimed until 35 years after transfer. Terminations must be initiated by authors in accordance with complex technical rules. And numerous carveouts introduce substantial new uncertainties that have been exploited by investors to even further reduce the practical benefit of the new rights for their intended beneficiaries.

In this section, we explain how the scheme works in practice, with a focus on the main controversies:

(a) whether sound recordings are exempt from termination;
(b) the complexities of the termination procedure;
(c) whether rights are in fact 'inalienable'; and
(d) the way it disproportionately benefits the most commercially successful creators.[57]

[55] US Copyright Office, 'Calculating Fees for Recording Documents and Notices of Termination in the Copyright Office (Fees in effect as of March 20, 2020)', Circular 12A, 1–2 <https://www.copyright.gov/circs/circ12a.pdf>.

[56] Robert Brauneis and Roger E Schechter, Copyright: A Contemporary Approach 568 (*Thomson Reuters*, 2012) 755, cited in Dylan Gilbert, Meredith Rose and Alisa Valentin, 'Making Sense of the Termination Right: How the System Fails Artists and How to Fix It' (*Public Knowledge*, 2019) 11 <https://publicknowledge.org/wp-content/uploads/2021/11/Making-Sense-of-the-Termination-Right-1.pdf>.

[57] We do not claim to provide a comprehensive explanation of the termination system or systematically review the considerable literature on this system. Useful sources for further exploration of the myriad issues surrounding the termination system include: Kate Darling, 'Occupy Copyright: A Law & Economic Analysis of U.S. Author Termination Rights' (2015) 63 *Buffalo Law Review* 147; Richard Arnold and Jane C Ginsburg, 'Foreign Contracts and U.S. Copyright Termination Rights: What Law Applies?' (2020) 43 *Columbia Journal of Law & the Arts* 437; Jorge L Contreras and Andrew T Hernacki, 'Copyright Termination and Technical Standards' (2014) 43 *University of Baltimore Law Review* 221; Peter S Menell and David

Consistent with the history we've chronicled so far, there is a huge gap between this legislation's stated intention of protecting authors, and its actual real-world impact.

### 3.2.1 *Are Sound Recordings Exempt from Termination?*

One of the most controversial aspects of both 1976 Act termination rights concerns scope. Congress learned from the decades of uncertainty around prior reversion regimes, and finally made termination rights inalienable – their authors cannot contract them away.[58] However, there's a big exception. US law features the legal fiction that works 'for hire' are authored by the employer – even when that is a corporation, incapable of authoring anything.[59] Although termination rights are inalienable, the law provides that in cases involving works 'for hire' their actual creator never had authorship rights in the first place, meaning that there's nothing for them to terminate.[60]

#### 3.2.1.1 The Work-for-Hire Exception

The extent to which this carveout would affect creators was always going to depend on how works 'for hire' was defined. In the negotiations to craft the new *Copyright Act*, rightsholders succeeded in obtaining a broad definition that included not just all works created by employees in the scope of their employment, but also works within nine other defined classes – so long as the parties expressly agreed on that designation in writing (Table 3.1).[61]

As you can see, the additional carveouts focus largely on circumstances in which recognition of individual authorship would undermine the feasibility of making the work in the first place (such as documents prepared for the benefit of a corporate employer), or where the existence of multiple authors might make individual ownership unworkable (as can be the case for compilations and collective works).

Nimmer, 'Pooh-Poohing Copyright Law's "Inalienable" Termination Rights' (2010) 57 *Journal of the Copyright Society of the U.S.A.* 799; Andrew Paster, 'Rethinking Copyright Termination in a Global Market: How a Limitation in U.S. Copyright Law Could Be Resolved by France's Droit D'Auteur' (2017) 23 *Southwestern Journal of International Law* 375; Sean Stolper, 'Termination Rights: An In-Depth Look at Looming Issues under the Copyright Act of 1976' (2011–12) 13 *Texas Review of Entertainment and Sports Law* 33; Melville B Nimmer, 'Termination of Transfers under the Copyright Act of 1976' (1976–7) 125 *University of Pennsylvania Law Review* 947.

58 17 USC §§ 203(a)(5); 304(c)(5).

59 Copyright laws elsewhere in the world also grant first ownership of copyright in commissioned works to the commissioner, rather than the creator: see, e.g., *Copyright Act 1994* (NZ) s 21(3); *Copyright Act* (Hong Kong, Cap 528) s 15(1). Cf. Chapter 4 as to the lack of those carveouts in Europe.

60 Gilbert et al (n 56) 16.

61 17 USC § 101 (definition of 'work made for hire').

TABLE 3.1 *Works that can be excluded from termination under 17 USC §§ 203 and 304 as works-made-for-hire under 17 USC § 101*

| Type of exclusion | Description |
|---|---|
| In their entirety | Works prepared in the scope of employment |
| By express agreement, having been specially ordered or commissioned for use: | As a contribution to a collective work |
| | As part of a motion picture or other audiovisual work |
| | As a translation |
| | As a supplementary work[62] |
| | As a compilation |
| | As an instructional text[63] |
| | As a test |
| | As answer material for a test |
| | As an atlas |

When rightsholders lobbied for those carveouts from the termination right, they focused particularly on the potential problems termination would cause for the creation of encyclopedias and textbooks, which tend to have many different authors updating them regularly over time.[64] That is a valid point: after 35 years it would indeed be very difficult to untangle any individual's contributions, and allowing any one individual to terminate could risk a much larger investment.

In practice, however, these carveouts have not been limited to circumstances such as that. Rightsholders have taken advantage of drafting ambiguities to assert that they apply well beyond the scope they were obviously intended to cover. As foreshadowed above, this has most notably occurred in the context of sound recordings – the category of works most likely to have enduring value decades after they first hit the market. As we'll show, their attempts to broaden the reach of these carveouts has done much to subvert the law's intended benefits.

#### 3.2.1.2 Record Companies Try to Include Sound Recordings as Works-for-Hire: And Succeed (Temporarily)

In 1999, more than a decade before the first § 203 terminations could be initiated, a congressional staffer quietly inserted four words into the *Satellite Home Viewer*

62 Defined in 17 USC § 101 as:

> ... a work prepared for publication as a secondary adjunct to a work by another author for the purpose of introducing, concluding, illustrating, explaining, revising, commenting upon, or assisting in the use of the other work, such as forewords, afterwords, pictorial illustrations, maps, charts, tables, editorial notes, musical arrangements, answer material for tests, bibliographies, appendixes, and indexes....

63 Defined in 17 USC § 101 as: 'a literary, pictorial, or graphic work prepared for publication and with the purpose of use in systematic instructional activities'.

64 Copyright Law Revision Part 4: Further Discussion and Comments on Preliminary Draft for Revised US Copyright Law (US Government Printing Office, 1964) 250.

*Improvement Act* that had the effect of adding sound recordings to the *Copyright Act*'s definition of works for hire. The 11th-hour change occurred without any debates,[65] and artist representatives didn't find out about it until after it had been signed into law.[66] Uproar ensued. The resulting investigation discovered that the amendment had been inserted at the request of the Recording Industry Association of America (RIAA) – the industry lobby group representing the interests of the world's most powerful record labels – rather than any elected member of Congress.[67]

While Marybeth Peters, the then Register of Copyrights, denounced the 'middle of the night' amendment for having been made 'without any input from performers',[68] the RIAA played innocent, describing it as a mere 'technical' change.[69] US law permits technical amendments to statutes to bypass some of the usual lawmaking processes, but that is limited to fixing obvious mistakes like typos – not changing the substance of what has been deliberately decided by Congress.[70] But Hilary Rosen, the RIAA's then-president and CEO, falsely claimed that 'in everybody's view this was a technical issue', because 'record companies have long registered recordings with the Copyright Office as works-for-hire'.[71] As one legal writer retorted, 'Rosen's idea of "everybody" … must not include the artists, their attorneys, Intellectual Property professors and authors, top officials at the Copyright Office, or the courts for that matter, because all believe differently.'[72] As if there wasn't already enough stench around this surreptitious manoeuvre, the congressional staffer who had clandestinely slipped in the amendment, Mitch Glazier, was hired by the RIAA just a few months later.[73] He subsequently became, and is at the time of writing, its chair and CEO.[74]

[65] Ryan A Rafoth, 'Limitations of the 1999 Work-for-Hire Amendment: Court Should Not Consider Sound Recordings to Be Works-for-Hire When Artists' Termination Rights Begin Vesting in Year 2013' (2000) 53 *Vanderbilt Law Review* 1021, 1023.

[66] Mary LaFrance, 'Authorship and Termination Rights in Sound Recordings' (2002) 75 *Southern California Law Review* 375, 375–6.

[67] Ibid 375. See further David Nimmer and Peter S Menell, 'Sound Recordings, Works for Hire, and the Termination-of-Transfers Time Bomb' (2001) 49(2) *Journal of the Copyright Society of the USA* 387, 392; William Henslee and Elizabeth Henslee, 'You Don't Own Me: Why Work for Hire Should Not Be Applied to Sound Recordings' (2011) 10 *The John Marshall Review of Intellectual Property Law* 695, 702; Bill Holland, 'Acts' Reps Decry Copyright Clause', *Billboard* (online, 15 January 2000) 75; Rafoth (n 65) 1025.

[68] Holland (n 67); Rafoth (n 65) 1025.

[69] Holland (n 67).

[70] Rafoth (n 65) 1024.

[71] Holland (n 67) 75 (second quote summarised by Holland); Henslee and Henslee (n 67).

[72] Phillip W Hall Jr, 'Smells Like Slavery: Unconscionability in Recording Industry Contracts' (2002) 25(1) *Hastings Communications and Entertainment Law Journal* 189, 215.

[73] Peter J Strand, 'What a Short Strange Trip It's Been: Sound Recordings and the Work Made for Hire Doctrine' (2000) 18(3) *Entertainment and Sports Lawyer* 12, 12.

[74] RIAA, 'About RIAA' (Web Page, 2024) <https://www.riaa.com/about-riaa/board-executives/>.

We've told this story in detail because it demonstrates the lengths powerful rightsholders will go to avoid meaningful reversion rights – that is, those that might actually help level the playing field for creators. If they didn't have such potential, the music industry would have had no cause to go to such extremes to undermine them.

The RIAA's sneaky change didn't remain on the statute books for long. Recording artists were outraged when the theft came to light, and began a fierce and coordinated campaign to have it rolled back, finally succeeding after almost a year of gruelling and expensive efforts.[75]

In practice though, the artists' victory has been far less effective than they would have hoped. Although the labels' brazen attempt to steal musicians' reversion rights over sound recordings was ultimately defeated, they still consistently resist efforts to terminate sound recording transfers on the grounds that they fall within the carveouts. Label licensing agreements routinely designate sound recordings as works-for-hire.[76] Most commonly, they argue that's because they're part of an audiovisual work, because they're specifically ordered or commissioned for use as a contribution to a collective work, or because they're compilations.[77] The latter arguments ignore the fact that sound recordings typically have none of the features that justified compilations and collective works from being made excludable in the first place, and they're made even though labels argue albums are *not* compilations with equal fervour when that outcome would increase the sum payable to them by way of statutory damages for infringement![78] Some leading industry contract templates even designate artists as their employees exclusively for the purpose of the copyright ownership clause.[79] Recording artists are obviously not label employees (and certainly aren't treated as employees when it comes to minimum pay or worker protections), but if successful, such machinations would deny artists their right to terminate even sound recordings which are obviously outside the enumerated categories.

While some federal courts have explicitly recognised that sound recordings aren't one of the specified carveouts, there is a lack of specific higher court authority that could provide certainty to artists as to whether the labels' claims have merit.[80]

75 Strand (n 73).

76 E.g. Donald C Farber (ed), *Entertainment Industry Contracts: Negotiating and Drafting Guide* (LexisNexis, 2024) form 159-2, cl 4(a); 159-1, cl 9, 159-3, cl 4; David Nimmer, *Nimmer on Copyright* (LexisNexis, 2024) form 465-30.03A(2), cl 10.2.

77 See Hector Martinez, 'Cash from Chaos: Sound Recording Authorship, Section 203 Recapture Rights and a New Wave of Termination' (2014) 4(2) *Pace Intellectual Property, Sports & Entertainment Law Forum* 445, 468.

78 See 17 USC § 504(c); Kike Aluko, 'Terminating the Struggle over Termination Rights' (2019) 10 *Harvard Journal of Sports & Entertainment Law* 119, 127.

79 Farber (ed) (n 76) form 159-3, cl 4; see also Alexander Lindey, 'Lindey on Entertainment, Publishing and the Arts' (*Thomson Reuters*, 2024-1 ed) § 9:39, cl 5(c) ('employer for hire').

80 See further *Lulirama Ltd v Axcess Broadcast Services, Inc*, 128 F 3d 872, 878 (5th Cir, 1997); *Ballas v Tedesco*, 41 F Supp 2d 531, 541 (DNJ 1999); *Staggers v Real Authentic Sound*, 77 F Supp 2d 57, 64 (DDC 1999), all cited at Martinez (n 77) 469 n 48.

The dearth of litigation is unsurprising. Litigation is expensive, particularly in the US where even successful claimants usually have to bear their own costs.[81] Termination cases have sometimes been instituted by stars with deep pockets, including Sir Paul McCartney,[82] Boston country music star Dwight Yoakam,[83] or as class action lawsuits like those headed by singer John Waite and New York Dolls frontman David Johansen.[84] But labels typically ensured those cases are settled, usually with non-disclosure agreements, preventing not only judicial precedent but also the kind of knowledge transfer that might benefit artists more broadly.[85]

The upshot of all this is that, almost half a century after the 1976 law was enacted, many potential beneficiaries remain in limbo about whether they have any rights at all. The label arguments may well fail if and when they're finally tested in court, but until then the practical effect of the legislation is as if the RIAA's legislative heist had in fact succeeded: few artists can use their statutory termination rights to get a better deal for their sound recording copyrights.

This situation is especially aggravating given the changing economies around music distribution. As we explained in Chapter 1, in the 1970s royalty rates as low as 4 per cent were not uncommon, while deals inked today are likely to pay at least six times that amount.[86] If heritage artists were able to use their reversion rights the way Congress intended, they could renegotiate those contracts to let them share more fairly in the fruits of their labour. As matters currently stand, however, record labels simply add that windfall to their profits instead. Though it's artists' strong moral

81 See generally Peter Karsten and Oliver Bateman, 'Detecting Good Public Policy Rationales for the American Rule: A Response to the Ill-Conceived Calls for Loser Pays Rules' (2016) 66(3) *Duke Law Journal* 729; John Leubsdorf, 'Does the American Rule Promote Access to Justice: Was That Why It Was Adopted?' (2019) 67 *Duke Law Journal Online* 257.

82 Eriq Gardner, 'Paul McCartney Sues Sony to Regain Rights to Beatles Songs', *The Hollywood Reporter* (online, 18 January 2017) <https://www.hollywoodreporter.com/business/business-news/paul-mccartney-sues-regain-rights-beatles-songs-965684/>.

83 Eriq Gardner, 'Dwight Yoakam Sues Warner Music to Reclaim Rights to Recordings', *The Hollywood Reporter* (online, 9 February 2021) <https://www.hollywoodreporter.com/business/business-news/dwight-yoakam-sues-warner-music-to-reclaim-rights-to-recordings-4129591/>.

84 Bob Fredericks, 'David Johansen and Other Artists Sue Sony, UMG for Song Rights', *New York Post* (online, 6 February 2019) <https://nypost.com/2019/02/06/david-johansen-and-other-artists-sue-sony-umg-for-song-rights/>.

85 Ashley Cullins, 'Paul McCartney Reaches Settlement with Sony/ATV in Beatles Rights Dispute', *The Hollywood Reporter* (online, 29 June 2017) <https://www.hollywoodreporter.com/business/business-news/paul-mccartney-reaches-settlement-sony-atv-beatles-rights-dispute-1018100/>; Bill Donahue, 'Sony Music Settles Class Action Lawsuit Filed by Recording Artists over Termination Rights', *Billboard* (online, 28 February 2024) <https://www.billboard.com/business/legal/sony-music-settles-class-action-lawsuit-over-termination-rights-1235617233/>; Blake Brittain, 'Warner Music, Country Star Dwight Yoakam Settle Copyrights Dispute', *Reuters* (online, 15 February 2022) <https://www.reuters.com/legal/transactional/warner-music-country-star-dwight-yoakam-settle-copyrights-dispute-2022-02-14/>; see also Gilbert et al (n 56) 12 in relation to non-disclosure agreements; John Oullette, 'How Record Labels and Music Publishers Deal with Copyright Issues' (Conference Paper, International Summit of the Music & Entertainment Industry Educators Association, 16–17 May 2022) 74.

86 See Chapter 1, Section 1.1.4.3.

claims that justify beyond-incentive copyrights, the termination law's failure ensures those rewards fatten the wallets of executives and shareholders instead.

### 3.2.2 *Termination Rights Are Difficult to Exercise*

The termination law's second major failing arises from its complexity. As the proposed rights worked their way through the legislative process, the substantive and procedural processes for reclaiming rights became ever more complicated, sometimes ambiguous, and often impossible for laypeople to understand. Indeed, former Register of Copyrights Maria Pallante describes the termination provisions as 'almost incomprehensible on their face, particularly for the authors, widows, widowers, children and other heirs who need to navigate them'.[87] As composer Dr Elizabeth Vercoe explains, this is a real deterrent to use: 'the process is complex and few of the composers are sufficiently persistent to jump over the hurdles required to file for terminations.'[88] Copyright law academic Pamela Samuelson agrees, describing the process as 'so cumbersome and complicated that most authors will not realistically have a meaningful opportunity to terminate'.[89]

#### 3.2.2.1 Creators Can Easily Misinterpret Termination's Procedural Requirements

The legislation's detailed prescriptions ensure that those who aren't entirely deterred from exercising their rights have plenty of opportunity to get something wrong. Consider the example of artist Daniel DeCarlo, who worked for Archie Comics for over 40 years, during which time he created popular characters such as Josie and the Pussycats, Cheryl Blossom and Sabrina the Teenage Witch. Months after losing his job due to a breach of contract lawsuit he filed against Archie Comics,[90] he sought to terminate the transfers to some of his work, but the US District Court for the Southern District of New York declared his notices invalid[91] – DeCarlo had understood the termination clock began 35 years after initial *publication* of the

87 R Anthony Reese, 'Termination Formalities and Notice' (2016) 96 *Boston University Law Review* 895, 898, citing Maria A Pallante, 'The Next Great Copyright Act' (2013) 36 *Columbia Journal of Law & the Arts* 315, 316.

88 'Q&A with Dr. Elizabeth Vercoe on Terminating Transfers of Copyright', *Authors Alliance* (20 October 2020) <https://www.authorsalliance.org/2020/10/20/qa-with-dr-elizabeth-vercoe-on-terminating-transfers-of-copyright/>.

89 Reese (n 87) 899.

90 Robert J Hughes, 'Comics Artist Fired over Suit', *The Wall Street Journal* (online, 26 May 2000) <https://www.wsj.com/articles/SB958703392758999862>.

91 Robin Finn, 'The Battle for a Comic-Book Empire that Archie Built', *The New York Times* (online, 13 April 2012) <https://www.nytimes.com/2012/04/15/nyregion/the-battle-for-a-comic-empire-that-archie-built.html>.

works in 1967, but the Court confirmed it began from the dates of the *agreements* (1988 and 1996).[92]

DeCarlo is not the only one confused. Our study of copyright termination notice records unearthed at least 24 titles from nine § 203 notices with effective dates of termination *before* 1 January 2013. It's not clear if this was due to errors when those notices were recorded by the Copyright Office, or whether the creators themselves entered the wrong dates.[93] In any case, it should have been apparent that pre-2013 dates would be legally invalid, since that was the first year any § 203 termination could take effect.[94]

#### 3.2.2.2 Compliance Can Be Difficult Even When Interpreting Termination Procedures Correctly

Even where applicants interpret the requirements correctly, compliance can still be difficult. For example, since decades must pass before a termination notice can be issued, it can be difficult to determine precisely when it needs to be filed, or the date on which termination can have legal effect. There are any number of good reasons why, decades after a copyright agreement was executed, it might not be possible for its author to lay hands on it – and that can prevent them from being able to supply the key details needed to comply with the detailed substantive and procedural requirements of the notice process. The challenges are magnified when the transfers are evidenced over multiple documents or involve multiple parties.

Innocent errors won't automatically invalidate notices so long as they don't 'materially affect the adequacy of the information required to serve the purposes of [the termination provisions]'.[95] However, while courts have sometimes let minor defects slide,[96] the overall approach has been to require strict compliance with termination formalities.[97] Legal representation can help

92 *Archie Comic Publications, Inc v Daniel S. DeCarlo* SDNY No 00 CIV 5686 (LAK, 3 December 2001) 9–11 (Kaplan J). Two years later the District Court for the Southern District of New York confirmed these notices were 'null and void' because of this misunderstanding: *Archie Comic Publications, Inc v DeCarlo* 2003 US Dist LEXIS 4800 (SDNY, 31 March 2003) 56–7.

93 Joshua Yuvaraj et al, 'U.S. Copyright Termination Notices 1977–2020: Introducing New Datasets' (2022) 19(1) *Journal of Empirical Legal Studies* 250, 269.

94 Ibid.

95 *Code of Federal Regulations*, Part 201, § 201.10(e)(1), (2).

96 See, e.g., *Yoakam v Warner Music Group Corp*, 2021 US Dist LEXIS 164915, 11–19; *Johansen v Sony Music Entertainment, Inc*, 2020 US Dist LEXIS 56675 (SDNY, 31 March 2020) 14; *Mtume v Sony Music Entertainment*, 408 F Supp 3d, 471, 476–8 (requiring 'more factual development to determine if harmless error would apply to this case' (at 477) and therefore declining to dismiss the action); *Stillwater Ltd v Basilotta*, 2017 US Dist LEXIS 170176, 12.

97 See Guy A Rub, 'Stronger than Kryptonite? Inalienable Profit-Sharing Schemes in Copyright Law' (2013) 27(1) *Harvard Journal of Law & Technology* 49, 59 citing *Burroughs v Metro-Goldwyn-Mayer, Inc.*, 491 F Supp 1320, 1325–6 (SDNY, 1980); *Nance v Equinox Music*, No 09-cv-7808, 2010 WL 4340469, 3 (ND Ill, 22 October 2010). See also Debora Halbert, 'Letting

creators get that right,[98] but are very expensive – another disincentive to creators enforcing their rights.[99]

The termination system's complexity reduces its effectiveness as a mechanism to reward creators and promote widespread access to knowledge and culture. The best practice principles we set out in Chapter 6 prompt lawmakers to reflect on what is actually necessary to best achieve copyright's access and reward goals.

### 3.2.3 *An Inalienable Right: So far as That Goes*

The creators who campaigned for reform to the existing US termination law lost on many fronts, but secured one huge victory: Congress, after decades of dodging this question, finally made termination rights inalienable. The legislation expressly permits the termination of transfers 'notwithstanding any agreement to the contrary, including an agreement to make a will or any future grant'.[100] This is a huge improvement on the previous law, which allowed rightsholders to exercise their outsized bargaining power to snap up the benefit of the renewal term at the time the initial contract was entered into.[101]

But the efficacy of this new inalienability 'shield' in upholding the interests of authors and heirs has been undermined, as with other parts of the 1976 termination law, by its poor design. Keenly aware of the money and power at stake, rightsholders have developed ingenious arguments to test, and exploit, weaknesses in this shield. Controversies have thus arisen about precisely how inalienable termination rights are, of which we now examine the three most prominent:

(a) creators' testamentary freedom being curtailed;
(b) the risk of statutory heirs losing their US termination rights; and
(c) the risk of creators losing their US termination rights through the application of foreign law.

#### 3.2.3.1 Creators' Testamentary Freedom Being Curtailed

When Congress finally got serious about protecting authors against being obliged to give up their termination rights, it got *very* serious. While creators may leave their copyrights to any person they choose (and those testamentary transfers are not themselves terminable[102]), they can't bequeath the rights to terminate any previous

Anarchy Loose on the World: The Anarchist Cookbook and How Copyright Fails the Author' (2022) 55(2) *Akron Law Review* 283, 306.

98 Ann Bartow, 'Using the Lessons of Copyright's Excess to Analyze the Political Economy of Section 203 Termination Rights' (2020) 6(1) *Texas A&M Journal of Property Law* 23, 29.

99 Molly van Houweling, 'Authors versus Owners' (2016) 54(2) *Houston Law Review* 371, 383–4.

100 17 USC § 203(a)(5); 17 USC § 304(c)(3).

101 See Section 3.1.3.2.

102 17 USC §§ 203(a), 304.

transfers – those beneficiaries are designated via the statute.[103] This bifurcated system means that the owner of the copyright might not be the person who comes to own the termination rights.

That was the situation that emerged with the estate of Nobel Laureate John Steinbeck: he bequeathed the entirety of his copyright interests to his third wife, Elaine, but the *Copyright Act* split the associated termination interests between his wife and two children from a previous marriage.[104] When Elaine died, the termination rights were controlled exclusively by the two children, even though she had explicitly excluded them from her will.[105] A similar situation arose with Ray Charles' estate. He had left his copyrights to his charitable foundation, but since the statute gave the termination rights to his children, they were able to exercise them in a way that diverted the proceeds away from people with disabilities.[106]

It's obviously important to prevent creators from being pressured to bequeath their reversionary interests in ways that benefit the current licensees, but facts such as these are a reminder that it's also important to protect creators' wishes when it comes to the future stewardship of their works.[107] While a detailed consideration of the pros and cons of the current US approach is outside the scope of this book, we flag it to note that any policy discussion around the inalienability of reversion rights will need to grapple with the issue – a matter we return to in Chapter 6.[108]

### 3.2.3.2 Statutory Heirs Losing Their US Termination Rights

The statutory bifurcation between who an author (A) can leave their *copyrights* to (their estate, E), and who the *termination rights* will pass to automatically (the statutory successors, S) creates potential situations where E, in tandem with a grantee, can pre-emptively renegotiate a new deal for the rights and eliminate S's termination rights entirely in respect of that copyright. At first glance, this scenario appears to fly in the face of Congress's intention to protect the author and their *statutory* heirs by

[103] 17 USC §§ 203(a)(2), 304(c)(2).

[104] *Penguin Group (USA) Inc. v Steinbeck*, 537 F 3d 193 (2d Cir, 2008) 202–3.

[105] Ibid 197, see also 202–3.

[106] *Ray Charles Found. v Robinson*, 919 F Supp 2d 1054 (CD Cal, 2013) 1065–6; 'Complaint for (1) Declaratory and Injunctive Relief; (2) Breach of Contract; (3) Breach of the Implied Covenant of Good Faith and Fair Dealing', 4–5 <https://docs.justia.com/cases/federal/district-courts/california/cacdce/2:2012cv02725/528058/1>.

[107] We note protecting creators' testamentary freedom can be justified by recourse to natural rights theory, which also undergirds copyright's reward goal (although of course we acknowledge there are other jurisprudential justifications for testamentary freedom). See further Tonya M Evans, 'Statutory Heirs Apparent: Reclaiming Copyright in the Age of Author-Controlled, Author-Benefiting Transfers' (2016) 119(1) *West Virginia Law Review* 297, 314; Lee-ford Tritt, 'Liberating Estates Law from the Constraints of Copyright' (2006) 38(1) *Rutgers Law Journal* 109, 118–20; Eva E Subotnik, 'Copyright and the Living Dead? Succession Law and the Postmortem Term' (2015) 29(1) *Harvard Journal of Law and Technology* 77, 95–6.

[108] See Chapter 6, Section 6.1.6.1.

giving *those* heirs the right to terminate grants. The question that remains unanswered is whether these agreements can be ruled unenforceable as 'agreements to the contrary'. Courts have not settled the matter to date, leaving the potential for statutory heirs to be disinherited of these valuable termination rights.[109]

Steinbeck's two children found this out after they sought to terminate a 1938 grant Steinbeck made to The Viking Press, who eventually assigned the rights to publisher Penguin.[110] Penguin refused, arguing that a 1994 agreement with Steinbeck's widow Elaine (who inherited the copyright upon Steinbeck's passing) effectively 're-grant[ed] publishing rights to [those] ... works'.[111] The Second Circuit agreed. The 1994 agreement was clearly intended to *contractually* terminate the 1938 agreement, which meant there was nothing for Steinbeck's children to use the *statutory* termination right under § 304(d) of the Act on.[112] And the 1994 agreement was not an 'agreement to the contrary' under § 304(c)(5) of the Act.[113] Even if it *had* removed a termination right, that right would not have been exercisable *when* the 1994 agreement was executed (because § 304(d) related to works that benefited from the 20-year copyright term extension in 1998) – so any rights the 1994 agreement purported to bypass had not come into existence when it was executed.[114] The upshot of this decision was that creators/heirs had *one* chance to use the termination right, but that Elaine had effectively used up this chance through the 1994 agreement.[115]

The Ninth Circuit reached the same conclusion in a case involving the estate of Winnie the Pooh creator AA Milne.[116] Milne had initially granted US and Canadian rights to producer Stephen Slesinger in 1930, and Slesinger granted these rights to Disney in 1961.[117] By this point Milne was deceased, having bequeathed the interests in the Pooh works to a trust benefiting first his widow, then his son

[109] A detailed treatise on the agreement to the contrary problem and the competing arguments around this issue is beyond the scope of this book. For a more comprehensive analysis of these issues and the relevant case law see, e.g., Blankenheimer (n 2); Menell and Nimmer (n 57); Allison M Scott, 'Oh Bother: Milne, Steinbeck, and an Emerging Circuit Split over the Alienability of Copyright Termination Rights' (2007) 14(2) *Journal of Intellectual Property Law* 357; Peter S Menell and David Nimmer, 'Judicial Resistance to Copyright Law's Inalienable Right to Terminate Transfers' (2010) 33(2) *Columbia Journal of Law and the Arts* 227; Michael J Bales, 'The Grapes of Wrathful Heirs: Terminations of Transfers of Copyright and Agreements to the Contrary' (2010) 27(3) *Cardozo Arts & Entertainment Law Journal* 663; Roxanne E Christ, '*Milne v. Slesinger*: The Supreme Court Refuses to Review the Ninth Circuit's Limits on the Rights of Authors and Their Heirs to Reclaim Transferred Copyrights' (2007) 14(1) *UCLA Entertainment Law Review* 33; Michael A DeLisa, 'The Right of Termination in Copyright Law: The Second Circuit's Decision in *Penguin Group (USA) Inc. v Steinbeck* Bodes Well for Authors' (2009) 43(1) *Loyola of Los Angeles Law Review* 273.

[110] *Penguin Group* (n 104) 196.

[111] Ibid 199; Menell and Nimmer (n 109) 231.

[112] *Penguin Group* (n 104) 200–2.

[113] Ibid 202.

[114] Ibid 202–3.

[115] Ibid 204.

[116] *Milne v Stephen Slesinger, Inc*, 430 F 3d 1036 (9th Cir, 2005).

[117] Ibid 1039–40.

Christopher and granddaughter Clare.[118] Christopher favourably renegotiated these agreements in 1983 (the Pooh trust being estimated to have made a net gain in the hundreds of millions of dollars[119]) on the proviso that he would not exercise his § 304 termination rights under the original agreement.[120] Clare sought to terminate the 1930 agreement in 2002 (renegotiating the grant of the rights she expected to regain with Disney on the same day[121]), but would only have had the right to do so if the 1983 deal was an invalid 'agreement to the contrary'.[122] The Ninth Circuit held that it wasn't, since the 1983 agreement had effectively replaced the one from 1930.[123] In any event, it reasoned, there was no need for termination here because the 1983 agreement had achieved substantially the same goal, giving the authors/heirs a second opportunity to profit from the work.[124]

Both *Milne* and *Steinbeck* suggest a creator's estate can disinherit statutory heirs of the termination right (to the extent they are different) by executing a subsequent agreement that replaces the old grant and leaves nothing to terminate under the statute.[125] The subsequent agreement may well be lucrative for the copyright heirs (e.g. Milne's 1983 agreement) or lead to greater access to knowledge and culture. But as we showed in Chapter 1, such success is simply not guaranteed. In the meantime, enforcing such agreements enables rightsholders to deprive statutory beneficiaries (under the Act it is the creator's family) of their right to terminate, and all the intended benefits that could flow from being able to negotiate from a more informed bargaining position as to the value of the work.

There is some uncertainty as to whether the *Milne* and *Steinbeck* approaches will be followed.[126] Amidst this uncertainty, statutory termination heirs and testamentary beneficiaries (if different parties) should ensure they are as aligned as possible on the exploitation of the works and termination. Otherwise, these kinds of disputes are likely to keep arising until either Congress or the Supreme Court brings clarity to this area of the law.

[118] Ibid 1039.
[119] Ibid 1040–1.
[120] Ibid 1040.
[121] Ibid 1041.
[122] Ibid 1042.
[123] Ibid 1044.
[124] Ibid 1048; Menell and Nimmer (n 57) 809.
[125] See, e.g., Blankenheimer (n 2) 338; Menell and Nimmer (n 57) 819.
[126] Note however in *Classic Media, Inc v Mewborn*, 532 F 3d 978 (9th Cir, 2008) the Ninth Circuit found a subsequent agreement *was* an 'agreement to the contrary' and therefore that the purported termination of the grant in a previous agreement was valid. This was due to facts like the subsequent agreement not expressly revoking the prior agreement (as Milne's had) and there being no indication the terminating party had wanted to waive their termination right in the subsequent agreement. Despite this apparent split in the Ninth Circuit, scholars have generally approached *Steinbeck* and *Milne* as the main cases that 'open the door' to termination alienability again: see, e.g., Menell and Nimmer (n 109) 233–5; Menell and Nimmer (n 57) 815–17; Blankenheimer (n 2) 335–8. See further *Marvel Characters, Inc. v Simon* 310 F 32 280 (2d Cir, 2002).

### 3.2.3.3 Can US Termination Rights Become Alienable by the Operation of Foreign Law?

Rightsholders have also tried to undermine attempted terminations of US copyrights under the 1976 system by securing creator agreement to, and then relying on, choice-of-law/choice-of-forum clauses to have exploitation contracts adjudicated under foreign domestic law and secure rulings preventing the effect of those terminations, whether in foreign or US courts.[127] This strategy directly challenges termination's inalienability, especially given rights grants covering all or most of the world are prominent in leading industry templates (and most creators are likely to have difficulty negotiating substantive departures from these standard form agreements)[128] – rightsholders could simply insist that any disputes are governed by laws and fora without such 'inalienable' creator protections.

3.2.3.3.1 UNDERMINING US REVERSIONARY SYSTEMS USING FOREIGN LAW BEFORE 1976. A 1963 judgment of the High Court of England and Wales, *Campbell Connelly & Co Ltd v Noble*,[129] had already shown that the two-term renewal system under the 1909 Act was susceptible to this sort of undermining. There, a worldwide assignment of copyright, governed by English law, was held to assign not just the first term but the renewal term of US copyright as well.[130]

But was the 1976 Act, with its express provision for inalienability, better protected against such incursions under foreign law? The answer thus far remains uncertain. Another High Court decision from 2016 appeared to fling wide the door to wholesale undermining of the 1976 termination rights by the application of foreign law to

[127] For examples of these types of clauses in publishing contracts, see, e.g., Lynette Owen (ed), *Clark's Publishing Agreements* (Bloomsbury, 11th ed, 2022) 59 and Farber (ed) (n 76) form 41-1 Author-Publisher Hardcover Trade Book Contract with Commentary, cl 32; for recording contracts, see Nimmer (n 76) form 30.03A(2) Recording Agreement Exclusive Service/Long Form, cl 16.8, 16.9. See generally John F Coyle, 'A Short History of the Choice-of-Law Clause' (2020) 91(4) *University of Colorado Law Review* 1147; Maxwell J Wright, 'Enforcing Forum-Selection Clauses: An Examination of the Current Disarray of Federal Forum-Selection Clause Jurisprudence and a Proposal for Judicial Reform' (2011) 44(4) *Loyola of Los Angeles Law Review* 1625; John F Coyle, '"Contractually Valid" Forum Selection Clauses' (2022) 108(1) *Iowa Law Review* 127; John F Coyle and Robin J Effron, 'Forum Selection Clauses, Non-Signatories, and Personal Jurisdiction' (2021) 97(1) *Notre Dame Law Review* 187; Tanya J Monestier, 'When Forum Selection Clauses Meet Choice of Law Clauses' (2019) 69(2) *American University Law Review* 325; Chukwuma Samuel Adesina Okoli, 'The Significance of a Forum Selection Agreement as an Indicator of the Implied Choice of Law in International Contracts: A Global Comparative Perspective' (2023) 28 *Uniform Law Review* 197.

[128] See, e.g., Owen (ed) (n 127) 5; Nimmer (n 76) form 30.B(1) Exclusive Songwriting Agreement, cl 3.1; Nimmer (n 76) form 30.03A(2) Recording Agreement Exclusive Services/Long Form, cl 2(B); Donald Cameron et al, *Information Technology and Entertainment – Canadian Forms & Precedents* (LexisNexis, 2024) 5F11 Exclusive Songwriter and Co-publishing Agreement – Output during Term Version, cl 1(a); see Chapter 5, Section 5.3.1.

[129] [1963] 1 All ER 237 (Ch).

[130] *Campbell Connelly & Co Ltd v Noble* [1963] 1 All ER 237, 244.

contracts assigning US copyrights, although (as we explain in Section 3.2.3.3.2) this outcome is by no means certain.

3.2.3.3.2 UNDERMINING THE 1976 TERMINATION RIGHTS: BREACH OF CONTRACT IN A FOREIGN JURISDICTION. *Gloucester Place Music Ltd v Le Bon and Ors* is arguably the most prominent twenty-first-century example of rightsholders *neutralising* the US termination rights.[131] The case involved the spat between members of the world-famous pop band Duran Duran and music publisher Gloucester Place Music.[132] The band members tried to statutorily terminate the grants of US copyrights made as part of a 1980 worldwide copyright assignment to Gloucester (previously known as Tritec Music).[133] But Gloucester brought legal action in the High Court of England and Wales claiming the filing of the notices was a breach of contract.[134]

The contracts specified that English law applied, and since neither party disputed the choice of law question, the Court did not have the opportunity to determine it.[135] In these circumstances Justice Arnold decided, 'not without hesitation', that the band members exercising their termination rights *was* a breach of the relevant contracts under UK law.[136] The clause assigning worldwide rights was 'wide and general', and in context required the worldwide copyrights to stay with Gloucester for the whole copyright term.[137] Further, the band members had agreed they would not transfer the rights to any other person, which Justice Arnold interpreted to mean 'any person other than [Gloucester]'.[138] Any exercise of the US statutory termination rights would thus deprive Gloucester of the ownership promised by the contract.[139] Duran Duran was granted leave to appeal the decision in 2017, but the dispute was subsequently settled.[140]

3.2.3.3.3 UNDERMINING THE 1976 TERMINATION RIGHTS: A POTENTIAL CLOSURE OF THE LOOPHOLE. *Gloucester Place* illustrates the potential for rightsholders to bypass the clear congressional intent for termination to be inalienable by

[131] *Gloucester Place Music Ltd v Le Bon and Ors* [2016] EWHC 3091 (Ch).
[132] Ibid.
[133] Ibid [1]–[4].
[134] Ibid [1].
[135] Ibid [14].
[136] Ibid [44].
[137] Ibid.
[138] Ibid.
[139] Ibid.
[140] Chris Cooke, 'Duran Duran Given All Clear to Appeal Reversion Right Ruling', *Complete Music Update* (online, 7 February 2017) <https://archive.completemusicupdate.com/article/duran-duran-given-all-clear-to-appeal-reversion-right-ruling/>; Alex Woolgar, 'Duran Some Interesting Arguments with a View to Reclaim, but Le Bon et al Come Undone in an Ordinary World: No Rio-version of US Copyright' (2018) 40 *European Intellectual Property Review* 134, 138; Arnold and Ginsburg (n 57) 443.

simply enforcing a clause that prescribed the law *and* forum for any dispute. But the extent of this potential is not clear. In 2019 the US Second Circuit refused to uphold a similar claim by Bixio Music against renowned Italian composer Ennio Morricone,[141] even though the parties had agreed Italian law applied.[142] One of the Second Circuit's reasons was that the contract provided worldwide rights were granted 'for the maximum total duration permitted by the laws in force in each country in the world',[143] and for US rights this was 35 years 'plus such additional period as the assignor allows until the exercise of the option to terminate'.[144]

Arnold (who adjudicated *Gloucester Place*) and Ginsburg (who was an advocate in *Morricone*) subsequently published a joint paper arguing that *Morricone* suggests that the termination right limits the scope of US copyright in a way that restricts what can actually be assigned by contract: '[I]t suggests that a U.S. copyright should be conceptualized as being inherently contingent upon the author's exercise (or not) of her right of termination.'[145] In their view, this means any assignment of US copyright, even in a contract governed by English law, would not preclude the exercise of statutory termination rights.[146] We're yet to see whether this will be accepted by future foreign courts, but the outcome in *Morricone* and the public argument raised by these two distinguished experts makes it certain that choice of law won't simply be conceded the next time the issue comes up. In the meantime, creators are left sitting with the uncomfortable possibility that their termination rights are perhaps not as inalienable as Congress intended them to be.

#### 3.2.3.4 Alienability under the 1976 Termination System: Balance Askew

The controversies we examined in Section 2.3 show the 1976 system's approach to alienability is askew. On the one hand, it may be *too* restrictive on creators by forcing the bifurcation of their termination rights (which go to statutory heirs) and copyrights (which go to their estate). This could lead to situations where the statutory heirs reclaim copyright in ways the creators did not envision or desire. Whether this imposition on testamentary freedom is desirable is a discussion beyond the scope of this book, but the debate highlights the importance of crafting reversion systems with a clear vision of the obligations those inheriting reversion rights should have in relation to the exercise of those rights (which we integrate into our best practice analysis in Chapter 6).

141 *Ennio Morricone Music Inc v Bixio Music Group Ltd* 936 f 3d 69 (2d Cir, 2019). For more detail on the *Morricone* litigation, see, e.g., Arnold and Ginsburg (n 57) 441–3.

142 *Ennio Morricone* (n 141) 72.

143 Ibid 70 (emphasis removed).

144 Ibid 73.

145 Arnold and Ginsburg (n 57) 443.

146 Ibid 449.

On the other hand, the 1976 system has been shown to be vulnerable to rights-holder undermining through exploitation contracts. They have successfully disenfranchised statutory heirs by renegotiating rights grants with the estates, and in *Gloucester Place* they neutralised the termination right entirely by bringing a successful breach of contract action in the UK (albeit in a decision of a lower court, and where choice of law was not disputed). Generally speaking, reversion systems are instituted because contractual practices are undesirable; subverting creator/heir access to these systems maintains the undesirable status quo. Examples like these inform our recommendations in Chapter 6 for strict limits on contracting out, whether in domestic or foreign settings, when crafting domestic reversion mechanisms.

### 3.2.4 *The 1976 Termination System Privileges Famous, Successful Creators (and Is of Limited Utility to the Rest)*

#### 3.2.4.1 A 35-Year Termination Time Limit Works Mostly for Successful Creators

Even if the previous three issues were rectified with the termination system, the 35-year period for most post-1977 copyright grants means most works are unlikely to be worth terminating.[147] This is yet another example of a poorly designed system relative to its creator-protective goals (and more broadly copyright's access and reward goals). It is most likely to benefit the highly successful creators whose works *are* likely to retain value after 35 years. But those superstars are the artists (and works) that generally need termination the least. They have already been, and continue to be, handsomely rewarded from their creative labour,[148] and their works are more likely to be in demand (and therefore available to the public as knowledge and culture).[149] But for the vast majority of creators it is not likely to be worth filing to terminate after 35 years. Without termination intervening in the creative lifecycle, it's likely that knowledge and culture will continue to be locked away from the public once their initial commercial shelf-life is exhausted.

[147] See, e.g., Kevin J Hickey, 'Copyright Paternalism' (2017) 19(3) *Vanderbilt Journal of Entertainment & Technology Law* 415, 464; Darling (n 57) 196–7, 203; Yifat Nahmias, 'The Cost of Coercion: Is There a Place for "Hard" Interventions in Copyright Law?' (2020) 17(2) *Northwestern Journal of Technology and Intellectual Property* 155, 210.

[148] See, e.g., Billie Schwab Dunn, 'How "The Tortured Poets Department" Will Boost Taylor Swift's Net Worth', *Newsweek* (online, 19 April 2024) <https://www.newsweek.com/taylor-swift-tortured-poets-department-album-boost-net-worth-1891641>.

[149] See, e.g., Paul J Heald, 'Property Rights and the Efficient Exploitation of Copyrighted Works: An Empirical Analysis of Public Domain and Copyrighted Fiction Bestsellers' (2008) 92(4) *Minnesota Law Review* 1031, 1044.

#### 3.2.4.2 The Formal § 203 Termination Process Has Been Used Sparingly, and by Successful Creators

Our recent world-leading empirical study into copyright termination notices, referred to above, adds further weight to this argument.[150] The study (the full methodology, results and limitations of which are set out in our published paper) was a whole-of-universe study of all termination notice records on the online US Copyright Office Catalog. Of course, a termination notice being filed doesn't mean it occurs, because terminations can be challenged (as we showed above with sound recordings and works-made-for-hire).

Additionally, notices are not valid just because they are filed with the Copyright Office – errors could still invalidate them. The actual notices themselves are also not generally available for analysis online, meaning most researchers are reliant on the data uploaded to the Catalog (which contains flaws and inconsistencies).[151] And perhaps most importantly, the *filing* of a termination notice is only part of the termination system's *impact*. The other part is the *indirect* impact of the *prospect* of termination on rightsholder behaviour, for which we have located only anecdotal evidence.[152] Further research using other data sources and methods (e.g. interviews with creators and rightsholders) could usefully begin to fill these gaps in our knowledge as to termination's impact.

Despite their unavoidable limitations, the Catalog records still allow us to draw some preliminary conclusions: how little the termination system has been used and how it may skew towards famous creators.

Comparing our data against complementary Copyright Office registration data compiled by leading US copyright scholars Robert Brauneis and Dotan Oliar, we found that at most, the number of works subject to termination notices in our dataset was approximately 1.6 per cent of the number of copyright registrations in the years

[150] This was the first published whole-of-universe study into online records of termination notice data (noted whenever someone files a termination notice with the Copyright Office). Despite the considerable challenges of navigating an ageing, non-intuitive database, we extracted, cleaned, analysed and presented for public consumption two innovative new datasets of termination notice records from 1977 to mid-2020, covering both § 203 and § 304 notices. The datasets themselves carry enormous value for policymakers, law reform and industry stakeholders seeking to understand, apply and reform copyright reversion mechanisms in the US and beyond. See, e.g., Richard Osborne and Hyojung Sun, 'Rights Reversion and Contract Adjustment', [2.3.1] <https://www.gov.uk/government/publications/economics-of-streaming-contract-adjustment-and-rights-reversion/rights-reversion-and-contract-adjustment>; Brief of Public Knowledge, Lita Rosario-Richardson, Esq., Library Futures Institute, and Fight for the Future as *Amici Curiae* in Support of the Petition, *Markham Concepts et. al v Hasbro, Inc et al* (No 21-711), Supreme Court of the United States, 8, 9.

[151] Physical copies of notices may be available for searching at the Library of Congress by members of the public. For more information on searching the Copyright Office see, e.g., 'Searching the Copyright Office and Library of Congress Records', *Stanford Libraries* <https://fairuse.stanford.edu/overview/copyright-research/searching-records/>.

[152] See, e.g., Osborne and Sun (n 150) n 46.

that would have corresponded to those notices (1978–85).[153] We then looked at the top 10 list of creators by the number of works they had subject to termination notices, and found several prominent artists: funk legend George Clinton accounted for 2.49 per cent of *all* works, pop duo Hall and Oates made up 1.02 per cent and country songwriter Harlan Perry Howard accounted for 1.58 per cent.

These figures were even more telling for the relatively few literary works that were subject to termination (n = 840): that list was dominated by heavyweights from romance (Debbie Macomber, Nora Roberts, Linda Howard, Jayne Krentz), horror and science fiction (Stephen King) and children's fiction (Ann M Martin). *Sweet Valley High* author Francine Pascal was the most active author, with notices covering 305 of her titles – 36.3 per cent of all literary works with notices issued under § 203.

Our preliminary findings suggest a system where few creators see value in terminating their rights formally, while the top 10 lists feature industry stalwarts with 'bestseller' works – it's great for them to re-exploit their works, but not for most other creators. This is consistent with our argument that a 35-year term[154] is a poorly designed, excessively lengthy time period. It also suggests lawmakers may have too readily jettisoned the shorter 20- and 25-year models proposed in the copyright revision hearings in the face of rightsholder lobbying, despite strident advocacy for creators by Karp and his ilk.[155]

However, these findings inform our best practice analysis in Chapter 6 about crafting time limits that better help creators recapture and disseminate their works while they retain commercial (and cultural) value, particularly in light of the innovative new distribution models we outlined in Chapter 1.

## 3.3 CONCLUSION

In this chapter we laid out in stark detail just how ineffectively statutory reversion rights have been developed and operated in the US. Rightsholders fought hard to reduce the value of termination rights to authors, by blowing out the time before they can be exercised, insisting on onerous and expensive formalities,[156] and carving

[153] Yuvaraj et al (n 93) 268–9. Note at 269 that copyright registration is not required, but 'there are robust incentives to do so: it is a prerequisite to filing an infringement claim, and, done early enough, can entitle the rightsholder to statutory damages and attorney's fees').

[154] Although note this may be 40 years from the grant if the grant conveys a publication right: '… or, if the grant covers the right of publication of the work, the period begins at the end of thirty-five years from the date of publication of the work under the grant or at the end of forty years from the date of execution of the grant, whichever term ends earlier'. 17 USC §§ 203(a)(3).

[155] See Section 3.1.4.2.

[156] *Copyright Law Revision: Hearings on H.R. 4347, H.R. 5680, H.R. 6831, H.R. 6835 Before the Subcomm. on Courts, Civil Liberties, and the Administration of Justice of the House Judiciary Comm.*, 89th Cong, 1st Sess, 65 (1965) 994. The Copyright Committee of the Motion Picture Association of America insisted that 'the compromise provisions' which carved out works for hire, required the termination right to be executed upon formal notice in writing, and extended the time limit to 35 years before termination could be effected 'provide a minimal basis on which motion picture interests can learn to live with these provisions'.

out as many works as possible. Once enacted, they embarked on a systematic campaign to reduce the value of the rights still further by insisting on the broadest possible definitions of 'work for hire', settling lawsuits with NDAs to avoid precedents and prevent the kind of knowledge spread that could help artists successfully navigate the legislation's ambiguities, and attempting to subvert Congress's intention to make termination rights inalienable by entering into new deals with heirs.

Congress itself is also to blame here, repeatedly passing poorly designed laws: failing to specify key inclusions/exclusions, mandating complex formalities and enshrining a lengthy pre-termination waiting period that renders it near-irrelevant for non-superstar creators. And the role of the courts can't be overstated, as the Supreme Court and various circuits of the Court of Appeals handed down rulings that opened the door for rightsholders to undermine termination's intent through their contracting practices.

Nevertheless, the lessons we have learned from the sinking ship that is the US termination system will usefully inform our best-practice reversion principles in Chapter 6. And hope can be drawn from the fact the record industry attempted to steal back the termination rights of recording artists via their clandestine, dead-of-night manoeuvre, showing that they believe that meaningful reversion rights have real potential to shift money and power from labels to artists. While the US system is far from ideal, that should give hope to creators that there is a better way.

# 4

# Statutory Reversion Rights in Europe

## INTRODUCTION

As we've seen, reversion's potential to redress creator-rightsholder imbalances has been severely undermined in the Commonwealth and US by a combination of rightsholder lobbying, poor design and ambiguous drafting. In this chapter we now ask – have European nations done a better job?

Reversion rights have been a longstanding feature of continental copyright laws, where they've been implemented with a much richer and more diverse array of triggers than the simple time-based mechanisms favoured by common law nations. This notably includes a wide variety of 'use-it-or-lose-it' rights, which premise retention by rightsholders on works' continued availability. By freeing up unused rights for fresh investment, such mechanisms have obvious promise as a way of furthering both copyright's access and rewards goals.

The range and scale of European reversion rights over time combines with space and language constraints to prevent us attempting any comprehensive history. Instead, we more modestly seek to determine their relative efficacy by examining the laws of key European nations immediately before and after implementation of the 2019 EU Digital Single Market Directive ('DSM Directive'), together with the evidence we've been able to find out about their effects. Curiously, despite the broader range and availability of reversion rights on the continent, we find little evidence that they've had more practical benefit (for authors or the public) than the reversion rights of common law nations – though once again, we argue that this is attributable to deficiencies in their design and implementation rather than the concept itself.

## 4.1 EARLY ORIGINS OF REVERSION ON THE CONTINENT

Whilst a comprehensive history isn't feasible, we *can* share two key eighteenth-century developments that help explain the early origins of the flourishing that was to follow, whilst also confirming that European legislatures have not been immune from the kind of undermining by rightsholders that has so impacted reversion rights in Britain and the United States.

### 4.1.1 *The 1741 Danish Copyright Ordinance and Copyright's Access Goal*

Use-it-or-lose-it rights in continental Europe can be traced to its first copyright statute – the 1741 Danish Copyright Ordinance (the 'ordinance').[1]

The ordinance prohibited anyone from publishing, reprinting, importing reprints or selling any book or writing that had been lawfully acquired by someone else.[2] However, those exclusive rights came with a twist: a corresponding responsibility to keep that material available to the public. The law gave publishers between three months and a year to reprint titles that went out of print. If they failed to do so, their right would lapse, and anyone would be free to print the work.[3]

This law demonstrated a clear intent by lawmakers to promote not just the initial creation of works, but ongoing investments in their continued availability – in other words, a strong and explicit support of copyright's access aims.

This mechanism put unused rights into the public domain, rather than returning them to authors, but it's a clear ancestor of the use-based reversion rights that would begin to emerge in Europe soon after. The framers of the ordinance viewed failure to continue exploiting a work as abandonment of rights: 'other persons must be allowed to publish the same writing, since it is to be assumed that the rightful owner has relinquished his right to it because of the long delay.'[4] If the rightsholder was not going to use the rights, that should not necessarily mean that society loses access. Others should have an opportunity to invest in them instead.

In Chapter 2 we invited readers to consider how the 1737 English bill proposing limiting transfers to 10 years would have radically changed the power balance between authors and publishers.[5] It's equally worth considering how different access

[1] Ordinance that no person shall publish, reprint, import reprinted or sell any book or writing lawfully acquired by another (DA: 7. januar 1741. Forordning Anlangende at ingen maa oplægge, eftertrykke eller eftertrykt indføre, eller falholde nogen Bog eller Skrift, som en anden paa lovlig Maade sig haver forhvervet): Jesper Jakobsen, 'Commentary on the Danish Copyright Ordinance (1741)' in Lionel Bently and Martin Kretschmer (eds), *Primary Sources on Copyright* (1450–1900) (2023) <https://www.copyrighthistory.org/cam/tools/request/showRecord.php?id=commentary_sc_1741> referring to Robert Darnton, *Pirating & Publishing* (Oxford University Press, 2021) 7.

[2] Danish Copyright Ordinance, Copenhagen (1741), Lionel Bently and Martin Kretschmer (eds), *Primary Sources on Copyright (1450–1900)*, tr Mersiha Bruncevic, 3 <https://www.copyrighthistory.org/cam/tools/request/showRepresentation.php?id=representation_sc_1741&pagenumber=1_1&show=translation>.

[3] Ibid 4. Note Jakobsen's commentary indicates the reprinting periods are 'within one year, half a year or four years', but this text is not present in Bruncevic's translation. See further Jakobsen (n 1).

[4] Ibid.

[5] See Chapter 2, Section 2.1.

would look today had the copyright laws that followed the first European copyright statute followed suit in premising exclusivity privileges on continued availability – that is, if they had continued to tie ongoing rights to ongoing responsibilities.

### 4.1.2 *The 1794 Prussian Law and Copyright's Reward Goal*

Our second historical vignette concerns a reversion mechanism that was included in the penultimate draft of what eventually became the 1794 Prussian law (*Allgemeines Landrecht für die Preußischen Staaten*, or 'General National Law for the Prussian States'[6]). That draft incorporated rigorous protections for authors, most relevantly by limiting the publisher's rights to publication of a book's first edition. If they wished to publish a second, they would need to obtain the consent of the author or their heirs to do so, and authors would themselves be entitled to publish a second edition after all copies of the first were sold.[7]

Effectively then, the idea was to return the right to publish each subsequent edition to authors or their heirs, which they could then exploit at a time when all parties had a better idea of the work's commercial value.[8] This was particularly important at that time because, as we discussed in Chapter 2, authors were often paid by way of lump sum rather than having any ongoing right to royalties.[9]

At the 11th hour, however, intense opposition from prominent Berlin publisher Friedrich Nicolai led to sweeping changes that eliminated many of the draft's author-protective features.[10] Under the version that was enacted into law, publishers' rights were still limited to the work's first edition (though the definition was broadened to include 'any subsequent volumes and sequels'), and, more significantly, that limitation could be eliminated by contract.[11] That radically altered the proposed bargain by permitting publishers to negotiate up front for exclusive rights over all subsequent editions, and locking authors and their heirs into terms that had been agreed before anybody had a clear idea of the work's value. This shows once again how concerned publishers are to prevent meaningful reversion rights from being enacted, and demonstrates that Europe was not immune from the same kind of rightsholder undermining that so influenced author-protective laws in Britain and the US.

6 Friedmann Kawohl, 'The Berlin Publisher Friedrich Nicolai and the Reprinting Sections of the Prussian Statute Book of 1794' in Ronan Deazley, Martin Kretschmer and Lionel Bently (eds), *Privilege and Property: Essays on the History of Copyright* (OpenBook Publishers, 2010) 218.

7 Ibid.

8 The commentary is unclear on whether 'editions' here meant print runs or amended versions of the works.

9 See Chapter 2, Section 2.1.

10 For a detailed analysis of these changes, see Kawohl (n 6) 228–9.

11 Ibid 232.

## 4.2 TIME AND EXPLOITATION-BASED TRIGGERS IN EUROPE

Two main categories of reversion right emerged from these origins: those with time-based triggers (analogous to those we've already seen in common law nations) and 'use-it-or-lose-it' formulations (which, as introduced previously, allow authors to reclaim rights previously granted where rightsholders don't exploit them, or exploit them inadequately). Below, we briefly explore key varieties of each type as they existed in EU Member States in the lead-up to the DSM Directive. In doing so, we draw substantially on the work of Yuvaraj and Furgal carried out as part of the Author's Interest Project in 2019 and 2020, which we commend to readers interested in diving deeper.[12]

### 4.2.1 *Time-Based Triggers*

Time-based mechanisms might return rights to authors after a certain period, or limit the amount of time an author can license rights. Either way, the effect is the same: rights boomerang back to the progenitors of the work, creating possibilities for fresh investments in making them available to the public and for creators to share in their value.[13]

#### 4.2.1.1 Spanish Origins

The earliest time-based European mechanism we have identified was part of Spain's 1879 Act, and returned rights to authors' estates 25 years after death.[14] At that time Spanish copyrights lasted for 80 years after the author's death, much longer than

[12] Joshua Yuvaraj, 'Data for Legal Mapping Study into Copyright Reversion Laws Applicable to Book Publishing Contracts (up to March 2019)', *Bridges* (Monash University) <https://doi.org/10.26180/16416747.v3>; Joshua Yuvaraj, 'Back to the Start: Re-envisioning the Role of Copyright Reversion in Australia and Other Common Law Countries' (PhD Thesis, Monash University, 2021) ch 5; Ula Furgal, *Reversion Rights in the European Union Member States* (CREATe Working Paper 2020/11).

[13] We do not include in this analysis laws that make exclusive rights grants non-exclusive after a period of time, like the German law applicable to lump sum exploitation contracts after 10 years: Furgal (n 12) 98, Gesetz über Urheberrecht und verwandte Schutzrechte (Urheberrechtsgesetz) (1965) (Law on Copyright and Related Rights (Copyright Law) (1965) (Germany)) § 40. We also do not include provisions allowing creators to withdraw rights grants for 'moral rights considerations' (e.g. the work no longer matches the author's moral values), as these typically require creators to compensate investors for that withdrawal (and are conceptualised as moral rights, which are beyond the scope of this book to address). See further ibid 11. Last we do not cover provisions that restrict what rights can be assigned or licensed by contract, as such restrictions are not strictly reversion rights and merit separate examination.

[14] Ibid 10, Ley de 10 de enero de 1879 de propiedad intelectual (Law 22/1987 on Intellectual Property (Spain)) art 6.

surrounding nations,[15] and lawmakers were motivated by a desire to 'reconcile the legitimate interests of the author during his life and the consideration owed to his family'.[16]

The Spanish scheme was criticised for interfering with the law of succession and making negotiating copyright treaties with other countries more difficult,[17] but was nonetheless exported to parts of Africa and the Americas together as part of Spain's colonial rule.[18] And, although there's no documented link, its close resemblance to the Imperial law discussed in Chapter 2 (passed some 40 years later) suggests the Spanish law may have provided inspiration for that as well.[19]

#### 4.2.1.2 Time-Based Triggers as of 2020

In Europe, however, the Spanish formulation was an outlier. Time-based triggers were relatively rare in continental Europe, compared to the use-based triggers we discuss below.[20] Those countries that did adopt them tended to make them considerably shorter than the Spanish model, allowing authors to benefit in their lifetimes. Examples include:

[15] Brander Matthews, 'The Evolution of Copyright' (1890) 5(4) *Political Science Quarterly* 583, 593–4.

[16] José Bellido, Raquel Xalabarder and Ramón Casas Vallés, 'Commentary on Spanish Copyright Law (1879)' in Bently and Kretschmer (eds), *Primary Sources on Copyright (1450–1900)*.

[17] Ibid.

[18] James J Guinan, Jr, 'Duration of Copyright', Study No. 30, January 1957, Copyright Law Revision: Studies Prepared for the Subcommittee on Patents, Trademarks, and Copyrights of the Committee of the Judiciary, United States Senate, Eighty Sixth Congress, Second Session, Pursuant to S. Res. 240 (US Government Printing Office, 1961) 60 <https://www.copyright.gov/history/studies/study30.pdf>, referring to Colombia, Cuba and Panama. A version of this law appears to still be in effect in Equatorial Guinea: Ley de 10 de enero de 1879, de la Propiedad Intelectual [Law of January 10, 1879, on Intellectual Property] (Equatorial Guinea) (tr Google Translate) art 6, *WIPO Lex* <https://www.wipo.int/wipolex/en/legislation/details/10624>; Barbara Ringer, Study 31, Copyright Law Revision: Studies prepared for the Subcommittee on Patents, Trademarks, and Copyrights of the Committee on the Judiciary: United States Senate, 86th Congress, 2nd Session (US Govt Printing Office, 1961) 208. However, copyright protection appears to also be found in the Penal Code of the Republic of Equatorial Guinea (1963) and Annex VII of the Bangui Agreement Instituting an African Intellectual Property Organization (Act of December 14, 2015): European Commission, 'IP Country Fiche: Equatorial Guinea' 26–9 <https://intellectual-property-helpdesk.ec.europa.eu/system/files/2022-09/IP-Country-Fiche_Equatorial-Guinea_0.pdf>.

[19] Given the recency of the Spanish provision relative to the Imperial Act (32 years), its similarity (automatic reversion to the estate 25 years after the author's death), and the fact we don't clearly know what motivated the latter's introduction, it is certainly plausible British lawmakers were aware of, and were influenced by, this Spanish system. For more on the origins of the Imperial reversion right see Joshua Yuvaraj and Rebecca Giblin, 'Why Were Commonwealth Reversionary Rights Abolished (and What Can We Learn Where They Remain)?' (2019) 41(4) *European Intellectual Property Review* 232; Elena Cooper, 'Reverting to Reversion Rights? Reflections on the Copyright Act 1911' (2021) 43(5) *European Intellectual Property Review* 292.

[20] Furgal (n 12) 10.

1. Bulgaria, limiting copyright transfers to 10 years in length;[21]
2. Italy and Spain, limiting the duration of publishing contracts (to 20 and 15 years respectively);[22]
3. France, limiting rights granted by playwrights to five years;[23]
4. Spain, limiting assignments of rights in 'theatrical and musical performance' rights to five years.[24]
5. Portugal, mandating that grants of exclusive rights in works lapse if the work 'has not been used' after seven years.[25]

In addition, there is an EU-wide time-based reversion right that originated in the 2011 Term Extension Directive ('TED'), which we discuss in more detail next.

#### 4.2.1.3 Term Extension Directive

In 2011 the EU Parliament extended protection for recordings to 70 years from first lawful communication or publication, although rights in recordings that had not been lawfully communicated or published 50 years after fixation would still expire after that 50 years.[26] Our focus here is not on the debatable merits of that extension,[27] but on the

[21] Ibid 30–1, Закон за авторското право и сродните му права (1993) (Copyright and Related Rights Law (1993) (Bulgaria)) art 37(2).

[22] Ibid 133, Legge 22 aprile 1941, n. 633 Protezione del diritto d'autore e di altri diritti connessi al suo esercizio, Pubblicata nella Gazz. Uff. 16 luglio 1941, n. 166 (Law No 633 of 22 April 1941, Protection of copyright and other rights related to the exercise thereof, Published in Official Journal No 166 of 16 July 1941) (Italy)) art 122; 217–18, Ley de Propiedad Intelectual, regularizando, aclarando y armonizando las Disposiciones Legales Vigentes sobre la Materia (aprobado por el Real Decreto legislativo N° 1/1996 de 12 de abril de 1996, y modificado hasta el Real Decreto-ley N° 17/2020, de 5 de mayo de 2020) (Law on Intellectual Property, Regularizing, Clarifying and Harmonizing the Applicable Statutory Provisions (approved by Royal Legislative Decree No. 1/1996 of April 12, 1996, and amended up to Royal Decree-Law No. 17/2020 of May 5, 2020) (Spain))) art 69(4). Furgal notes that 'Nine [EU Member States] indicate a maximum term ... of at least some types of agreements or agreements concerning some types of works', but does not specify what these states are: ibid 11.

[23] Ibid 79–80, Code de la propriété intellectuelle 1992 (Intellectual Property Code 1992 (France)) art L132–18, 19.

[24] Ibid 218 (Spain) art 75.

[25] Ibid 167, Código do Direito de Autor e dos Direitos Conexos, Decreto-Lei n.° 63/85 – Diário da República n.° 61/1985, Série I de 1985-03-14 (Code of Copyright and Related Rights, Decree-Law n.° 63/85 – Diário da República n.° 61/1985, Series I of 1985-03-14 (Portugal)) art 43(5).

[26] Term Extension Directive, art 1(2)(a), (b).

[27] For further information on the arguments surrounding the TED, see, e.g., Agnieszka Vetulani-Cęgiel, 'EU Copyright Law, Lobby and Transparency of Policy-Making: The Cases of Sound Recordings, Term Extension and Orphan Works Provisions' (2015) 6 *Journal of Intellectual Property, Information Technology and E-Commerce Law* 146; <https://www.scribd.com/document/14561635/Open-Letter-EC>; Richard Osborne (19 May 2023): UK Music before and after Covid-19, *International Journal of Cultural Policy*; Susanna Monseau, '"Fit for Purpose": Why the European Union Should Not Extend the Term of Related Rights Protection in Europe' (2009) 19(3) *Fordham Intellectual Property, Media & Entertainment Law Journal* 629.

accompanying time-based 'use-it-or-lose-it' reversion right that instrument gave to performers. In sum, it allowed performers to terminate contracts and regain rights in recordings 50 years after lawful communication/publication, so long as those works were not available in sufficient quantity or sufficiently available for public access.[28] If they wish to exercise the right, performers must notify the producer, who then has a year to fulfil *both* sale and public availability criteria, or else the rights revert.[29]

The rationales for the TED's extension of sound recording copyrights are firmly rooted in creators' moral claims, with the Directive's recitals referring to the 'socially recognised importance of the creative contribution of performers' and the undesirability of still-living creators being unable to benefit financially from their work, or prevent 'objectionable' uses.[30] The accompanying termination right is consistent with this recognition of an ongoing connection between creator and output: if their recordings are no longer being made available or sold, it's the performer who has the greatest interest over what happens to them in their final 20 years of copyright.

Despite these laudable intentions, the evidence to date suggests that, in practice, the right has gone all but unused. We canvass that evidence and the probable reasons for the law's failure below.[31]

#### 4.2.1.4 Time-Based Triggers: Author Benefits during Their Lifetimes

The above analysis shows that, while relatively rare, time-based triggers were present in EU Member States as of 2020, and that they often came into effect much more quickly than the US (35 years) or the UK/Commonwealth (25 years after the author's death). As we explore further in Chapter 6, shorter time limits may encourage investors to actually use the rights they have been granted, while also allowing creators to renegotiate grants more frequently from a bargaining position informed by their work's actual value.

### 4.2.2 *Exploitation-Based Triggers*

European countries have additionally developed a wide range of reversionary mechanisms linking control of rights to their ongoing exploitation. In this section we identify key examples of use-it-or-lose-it rights that existed as of 2020 through the lens of the biggest controversies that surround them, namely:

1. What kind of circumstances gave rise to a right to revert?
2. To what extent (if any) can rightsholders bypass these rights via contract?

28 Term Extension Directive, art 1(2)(c).
29 Ibid art 1(2)(c).
30 Ibid recitals 4, 5.
31 See Section 4.3.1.1.

#### 4.2.2.1 What Circumstances Gave Rise to a Right to Revert as of 2020?

Use-it-or-lose-it rights may be general or specific to particular industries or situations.

4.2.2.1.1 GENERAL RIGHTS. The general model typically enables authors to reclaim rights over any kind of work in cases involving a lack of exploitation. The earliest historical example we could find was enacted in Austria in 1936, and entitled creators to reclaim their rights if they were not being used or if they were being used in a way that was prejudicial to the author's interests.[32]

Some countries, like Croatia, Romania, the Netherlands, Hungary, Germany, the Czech Republic, and Austria, had reversion thresholds that permit creators to reclaim rights that are being inadequately exploited.[33]

Others, however, only appeared to allow reversion in cases of *complete* non-use. For example, Poland allowed creators to revert rights if the rightsholder had failed to begin disseminating the work within the agreed time (or two years if there was no agreed time for dissemination).[34] And the Danish provision only allowed termination for non-exploitation three years after the author had discharged their obligations.[35]

We'll discuss the competing merits of inadequate versus no exploitation thresholds below, in relation to Article 22 of the DSM Directive.

4.2.2.1.2 INDUSTRY OR SITUATION SPECIFIC RIGHTS. Some European jurisdictions adopted approaches that tailor reversion rights to specific creative industries or situations.

[32] Loi fédérale concernant le droit d'auteur sur les oeuvres littéraires et artistiques et les droits connexes (loi sur le droit d'auteur de 1936, publiée au Journal officiel fédéral n° 111/1936 (BGBI. n° 111/1936)) (WIPO Lex, translated from French by WIPO Translate, 20 March 2024) s 29(1); Furgal (n 12) 8.

[33] Furgal (n 12) 36, Zakon o autorskom pravu i srodnim pravima (2003) (Copyright and Related Rights Act (2003) (Croatia)) art 45; 180–1, Legea nr. 8 din 14 martie 1996 privind dreptul de autor şi drepturile conexe Publicat în Monitorul Oficial nr. 489 din 14 iunie 2018 (Law no. 8 of 14 March 1996 on copyright and related rights (Romania)) art 48; 153–4, Wet van 23 september 1912, houdende nieuwe regeling van het auteursrecht (Auteurswet 1912) (Copyright Act 1912 (the Netherlands)) § 25e; 112–13, 1999. évi LXXVI. törvény a szerzői jogról (Act LXXVI of 1999 on copyright (Hungary)) § 51; 99–100 (Germany) s 41(1); 54, Zákon ze dne 3. února 2012 občanský zákoník (Sbírka zákonů č. 89/2012) (Act of 3 February 2012 Civil Code (Collection of Laws No. 89/2012) (Czech Republic) § 2378; 14–15, Bundesgesetz über das Urheberrecht an Werken der Literatur und der Kunst und über verwandte Schutzrechte (Urheberrechtsgesetz) (1936) (Federal Act on Copyright in Works of Literature and Art and Related Rights (Copyright Act) (1936) (Austria)) § 29; 199–200, Zakon o avtorski in sorodnih pravicah (ZASP) (1995) (Copyright and Related Rights Act (ZASP) (1995) (Slovenia)) art 83; 188–9, Zákon z 1. Júla 2015 Autorský zákon (Copyright Act of 1 July 2015 (Slovakia)) § 73 ('If the transferee does not use the exclusive license in the agreed manner or to the agreed extent . . .').

[34] Ibid 161, Ustawa z dnia 4 lutego 1994 r. o prawie autorskich i prawach pokrewnych (Opracowano na podstawie: t.j. Dz. U. z 2019 r. poz. 1231, z 2020 r. poz. 288.) (Copyright Act 1994 (Poland)) art 57(1).

[35] Ibid 62, Lov om ophavsret (1995) (Law on Copyright (1995) (Denmark)) § 54(1).

For example, in countries including Portugal, Croatia, Finland and Sweden, contracts for rights in literary and musical works to be used in films could be terminated after certain delays in completing or distributing the resulting work.[36] Meanwhile, Spain provided that exclusive contracts for 'theatrical and musical performance[s]' could only last five years,[37] and authors could terminate them sooner if the work was not performed for a year after its initial performance.[38]

Such industry-specific approaches show a sensitivity to the fact that copyright covers a wide range of cultural products, emerging from fields that each have their own (often very different) economic and industrial realities.

Some particularly interesting reversion rights have been enacted in relation to book publishing, which as we explained in Chapter 1 has a particularly strong reversionary tradition. For example, a 2014 French law entitles book authors to reclaim rights in a variety of circumstances, including for lack of exploitation, failure to provide accurate accounting statements, and where (at least four years after a book's initial publication) no royalties have been paid for at least two years.[39] Unlike nearly every other European reversion right, this French law explicitly distinguishes between physical and digital exploitations: if publishers are appropriately exploiting a book in one form but not the other, authors can reclaim their neglected rights while leaving the other arrangements intact.[40] Meanwhile, Spanish and Lithuanian laws provide that if authors have licensed their publisher the right to publish their books in multiple languages, they can reclaim rights over any unused languages after five years.[41]

The above examples are framed in ways that support creators wishing to take advantage of the new exploitation opportunities that flow from digital technologies and the internet. In other cases, however, rights have become outdated. For example, Furgal identifies Romania, Slovenia and Spain as among those that define 'out of print' by the number of copies remaining in stock – a formulation that made sense in the print context but simply does not translate to the digital context.[42] This demonstrates the importance of regularly reviewing statutory reversion rights to ensure they're well suited to evolving social, technological and economic realities – a recommendation we develop more fully in Chapter 6.

[36] Ibid 170–1 (Portugal) art 136; 40, Zakon o Autorskom Pravu (1991) (Copyright Act (1991) (Croatia)) art 121; 233, Lag (1960:729) om upphovsrätt till litterära och konstnärliga verk (Act on Copyright in Literary and Artistic Works (Swedish Statute Book, SFS, 1960:729, as last amended by SFS 2018:1099) (Sweden)) art 40; 73–4, 8.7.1961/404 Upphovsrättslag (8.7.1961 Copyright, Consolidated text 372/2020 (published 18 May 2020) (Finland)) § 40.

[37] Ibid 218 (Spain) art 75(1).

[38] Ibid 219 (Spain) art 81(1).

[39] Ibid 82–3 (France) arts L132–17-2, L132–17-3, L132–17-4.

[40] Ibid 7 (France) art L132–17-2.

[41] Ibid 215 (Spain) art 62(3); 143–4, Lietuvos Respublikos autorių teisių ir gretutinių teisių įstatymas 1999 m. gegužės 18 d. Nr. VIII-1185 (Copyright Act 1999 Republic of Lithuania Law on Copyright and Related Rights 18 May 1999 No VIII-1185 (Lithuania)) art 45(3).

[42] Ibid 7.

As we explained in Chapter 1, it makes sense for publishers to draft contracts that take sweeping rights so they're covered in the eventuality they decide to use them, even though it's vanishingly rare for all of those rights to actually be exploited. It's not their role to consider the collateral damage that might result from such broad terms locking up rights to wide swathes of a nation's literary heritage. In the examples set out above, lawmakers appear to have recognised both of those realities, and intervened in an attempt to reach a more appropriate balance. Of course, whether or not those attempts have been successful depends on how these laws actually work in practice. There's little evidence available about that, but we canvass what we could find below.

4.2.2.1.3 SITUATION-BASED TRIGGERS: GOING OUT OF BUSINESS. In addition to industry-specific triggers, some nations also grant authors entitlements to reclaim their rights in specific situations, most notably where the rightsholder has gone out of business.[43] In Austria, this entitlement applied for grants of reproduction and distribution rights in all types of works.[44] Belgium, France, Italy, Luxembourg and Spain all gave authors who had signed publishing contracts the right to reclaim their rights in such circumstances,[45] although there were variations like the Spanish law preventing reversion where the publisher had gone into liquidation but reproduction had already commenced.[46]

Meanwhile, the French Intellectual Property Code allowed creators of audiovisual works to 'request the termination' of an audiovisual production contract if the company was pronounced in liquidation or it had not been engaging in 'business activities' for over three months.[47] The Belgian Code of Economic Law had a similar trigger for audiovisual works: creators of audiovisual works could 'request the termination of [the] . . . contract' if the producer had not undertaken any activity for over a year, or when the audiovisual work had not been resold within a year of the producer's liquidation.[48] In Austria, an author could 'withdraw' from a contract if an exploiter had taken exclusive reproduction and distribution rights but that exploiter had since become subject to insolvency proceedings.[49] However, they

[43] Some countries also have triggers like when a publishing business changes hands: see, e.g., ibid 215–16 (Spain) art 68(1)(f). For space reasons we don't propose to outline all these different types of situation-based triggers, but as noted above we recommend the work of Yuvaraj, 'Data for Legal Mapping Study' (n 12) and Furgal (n 12) for those interested in further study.

[44] Furgal (n 12) 18 (Austria) § 32.

[45] See, e.g., ibid 25, Code de droit économique – 28 Février 2013 (Code of Economic Law – 28 February 2013 (Belgium)) art XI 200; 78 (France) art L132–15; 137 (Italy) art 135; 148, Loi du 18 avril 2001 sur les droits d'auteur, les droits voisins et les bases de données (Law of 18 April 2001 on Copyright, Neighbouring Rights and Databases (Luxembourg)) art 17; 215–17 (Spain) art 68(f).

[46] Ibid 217 (Spain) art 68(f).

[47] Ibid 80 (France) art L132–30.

[48] Ibid 23 (Belgium) art XI 185.

[49] Ibid 18 (Austria) § 32.

could only do so if 'the reproduction of the work ha[d] ... not yet begun' at the commencement of the insolvency proceedings.[50]

Such interventions appear primarily concerned with ensuring that the disappearance of cultural investors will not result in works being unnecessarily lost, to the detriment of both the original author and the broader public. As we will explain more fully in Chapter 5, it's important to provide legal or contractual mechanisms for authors to regain rights if rightsholders go out of business – otherwise, administrators may be legally required to hold on to them as business assets, even if they are no longer in a position to meaningfully exploit the works.[51]

### 4.2.2.2 Other Carveouts

As shown above, European reversion rights may be limited by industry or situation. However, both general and specific rights sometimes had other carveouts as well.

4.2.2.2.1 EXEMPTING REVERSION WHEN RIGHTSHOLDERS ARE NOT RESPONSIBLE FOR INADEQUATE EXPLOITATION/NON-EXPLOITATION. Some provisions bar creators from enforcing the general use-it-or-lose-it provision in situations where the rightsholder was not responsible for the inadequate exploitation/non-exploitation,[52] for example where the author was instead responsible,[53] or where it was caused by a third party, 'a fortuitous event or force majeure'.[54] Dutch law prevented reversions from being enforceable where 'the other party [the rightsholder] has such an overriding interest in maintaining the agreement that the creator's interest must deviate according to standards of reasonableness and fairness'.[55]

4.2.2.2.2 EXEMPTING SPECIFIC WORKS FROM REVERSION. Some reversion rights exclude certain types of work. In Finland and Sweden, for example, the 'reversion' of exclusive rights to perform a work in public to non-exclusive rights following three years of non-use did not apply to cinematographic works;[56] and the right to terminate publishing contracts for failure to begin or continue exploiting their works did not apply to newspaper and periodical contributions, or compilations.[57]

Italian law excluded collective works from authors' right to terminate publishing and performance contracts where the works had not been published within

[50] Ibid § 32(2).
[51] See Chapter 5, Section 5.1.3.
[52] Furgal (n 12) 36 (Croatia) art 45.
[53] Ibid 54 (Czech Republic) § 2378; 153–4 (the Netherlands) art 25e(1); 189 (Slovakia) § 73(1); 199 (Slovenia) art 83(1).
[54] Ibid 181 (Romania) art 48(2).
[55] Ibid 153 (the Netherlands) art 25e(1).
[56] Ibid 71 (Finland) § 30; 231 (Sweden) art 30.
[57] Ibid 72–3 (Finland) §§ 33 and 38; 232–3 (Sweden) arts 33 and 38.

two years.[58] Its 20-year time limit on publishing contracts did not apply to 'encyclopaedias, dictionaries ... sketches, drawings, vignettes, illustrations, photographs and the like, for industrial use ... works of cartography ... [and] dramatic-musical and symphonic works'.[59] Bulgaria and Poland both had carveouts for architectural works.[60]

Whether each carveout category of work listed above should indeed be exempted is beyond the scope of this book. However, the range and variety of these carveouts indicates the importance of carefully considering works for which reversion is *not* appropriate (a recommendation we return to in Chapter 6).

4.2.2.2.3 CONTRACTUAL CARVEOUTS FOR WORKS MADE IN THE COURSE OF EMPLOYMENT. Work-for-hire carveouts (which, as we showed in Chapter 3, can be weaponised to disenfranchise creators of statutory reversion rights) were also present in some domestic European copyright laws.[61] Unlike the US termination system, rights in works made in the course of employment *could*, in some countries, revert to the employees, but employers could negate this by contract.

For example, under Lithuanian law, rights in works created by employees in the course of employment reverted after five years (except in the case of computer programs), unless their contracts specified otherwise.[62] Poland permitted employees who made works in the course of employment to regain rights if the employer had not distributed the work within two years, again unless contractually specified.[63] And in Slovenia, rights in works made by employees in the course of employment (except computer programs, collective works and databases) were presumed to have been assigned for 10 years, following which the rights would revert to the employee for reassignment to the employer.[64]

In all these cases, the statutory provisions expressly allowed employers to derogate from reversion rights through their employment contracts. However, some European countries imposed stronger protections for employees in respect of works they created in the course of employment. In the Czech Republic and Slovakia, rights in works created in the course of employment would revert to authors if the

[58] Ibid 135–6 (Italy) art 127.
[59] Ibid 134 (Italy) art 122.
[60] Ibid 30–1 (Bulgaria) art 37(2); 162 (Poland) art 57(3).
[61] Furgal's dataset conceptualised works made for hire as works made in the course of employment. We have applied this framework, noting we were not able to locate provisions in Furgal's dataset directly dealing with commissioned works as included in the definition of 'works-made-for-hire' under 17 USC § 101.
[62] See, e.g., Furgal (n 12) 142 (Lithuania) art 9.
[63] Ibid 158–9 (Poland) art 12(1).
[64] Ibid 205–8 (Slovenia) arts 101(1) and 102. We note that the two translations of the relevant provision provided by Furgal diverge on whether the employer is entitled to a new assignment on payment of adequate remuneration, or whether the employer can simply 'request' another exclusive assignment.

employer died or went out of business and there was no legal successor.[65] The laws of corporate succession affecting publishers and other rightsholders in these jurisdictions is beyond the scope of our analysis. However, we highlight these provisions as examples where employees had at least limited reversion rights that it appears employers could *not* derogate from via contract. As we discuss in Chapter 6, the non-derogability of reversion mechanisms (except in limited circumstances) is an important protection for creators, even if, as we discuss in Chapter 6, the nature and features of employment relationships may justify statutory carveouts.

#### 4.2.2.3 To What Extent Can Rightsholders Bypass These Rights via Contract?

As we've seen throughout this book, the practical impact of reversion rights can be much affected by whether rightsholders are able to eliminate them via contract. For example, in what Hugenholtz describes as a 'weak point', the author-protective provisions of Germany's *Verlagsgesetz* (Publishing Act) of 1901 were overridable by contract until at least 2000.[66]

Rightsholders have also sometimes attempted to contract *around* the operation of reversion rights, so that even if they operated as designed (e.g. rights *did* return to creators), the rightsholders would ultimately still get them back. For instance, Guibault and Salamanca report that publishers in Spain have tried to contract *around* the statutory 15-year limit on publishing contracts by including automatic renewal provisions in their contracts.[67] They provide limited detail, but 'automatic renewal' suggests initial contracts would contain clauses mandating that contracts would renew for an additional 15 years once the initial period expires, then the contract would renew for a new 15-year period.[68] If effective, such stratagems would prevent authors from renegotiating publishing agreements at or around the 15-year

[65] Ibid 49–50, Zákon č. 121/2000 Sb. ze dne 7. dubna 2000 o právu autorském, o právech souvisejících s právem autorským a o změně některých zákonů (autorský zákon) (Act No. 121/2000 Sb. of 7 April 2000 on Copyright, on Rights Related to Copyright and on Amendments to Certain Acts (Copyright Act) (Czech Republic)) § 58(2); 191 (Slovakia) § 90(7).

[66] See P Bernt Hugenholtz, 'The Great Copyright Robbery: Rights Allocation in a Digital Environment', paper presented at *A Free Information Ecology in a Digital Environment, Conference*, NYU School of Law (31 March–2 April 2000) 6 <https://www.ivir.nl/publicaties/download/thegreatcopyrightrobbery.pdf>.

[67] European Commission, Directorate-General for Communications Networks, Content and Technology, Olivia Salamanca and Lucie Guibault, *Remuneration of authors of books and scientific journals, translators, journalists and visual artists for the use of their works* (2016) 115 <https://data.europa.eu/doi/10.2759/14126>.

[68] We note Guibault and Salamanca give the example of a clause 'allowing termination lacking communication by the parties with a 60-days' notice': ibid n 369. However, it is unclear how this operates as an 'automatic renewal', so we have included the description for completeness only.

mark, when they would have a greater idea of the work's value (and would be able to negotiate from a position of greater bargaining power).

Some European nations took strict stances against contracting out. The Netherlands and Slovenia, for instance, completely prevented creators from waiving their general use-it-or-lose-it rights,[69] while Romania and Slovakia prevented their general use-it-or-lose-it rights from being waived 'in advance'.[70]

Other nations barred or permitted contracting out in specific situations. For example, in Hungary creators could waive their general use-it-or-lose-it rights for up to five years after the contract was executed or the work was delivered to the rightsholder, whichever was later.[71] The Austrian copyright law similarly prevented creators from signing away their reversion rights except during the first three years of any transfer.[72] In Germany, the general use-it-or-lose-it right could be contracted away if this was done via a collective agreement.[73]

And in Denmark, the general use-it-or-lose-it provision could not be waived, 'unless it is [for] a mere change of the outlined time limits'.[74] As discussed above, the Danish use-it-or-lose-it provision allowed creators to terminate contracts for non-exploitation within three years.[75] Allowing these time limits to be varied could mean that rightsholders require creators to agree to longer notice periods than are reasonably required. Whether such contractual practices have taken place in relation to Danish works would require further investigation beyond the scope of this book. However, we note the *allowance* for such variation creates the potential for rightsholders to effectively neuter creators' ability to regain their rights, by making them wait for lengthy periods before those rights return to them.

#### 4.2.2.4 A Rich Range of Reversion Rights – but What Was Their Impact?

The above analysis shows that, as of 2020, EU members had already made a broad range of reversion mechanisms available to authors. These went well beyond the unsatisfactory time-based triggers adopted across Anglo-America – but have they been any more effective in practice? In the following section we canvass the evidence.

69 Furgal (n 12) 155 (the Netherlands) art 25h; 200 (Slovenia) art 83(5).

70 Ibid 181 (Romania) art 48(5); 188–9 (Slovakia) § 73(4). On the material available to us the meaning of 'in advance' is unclear. The efficacy of such provisions would be undermined if agreements not to exercise those rights made shortly after initial exploitation contracts were enforceable.

71 Ibid 112–13 (Hungary) § 51(4).

72 Ibid 8 (Austria) § 29(3).

73 Ibid 99–101 (Germany) § 41.

74 Ibid 62 (Denmark) § 54(2).

75 Ibid § 54(1).

## 4.3 HOW EFFECTIVE WERE THESE RIGHTS IN PRACTICE?

### 4.3.1 *Little Evidence of Efficacy – or Harm*

Despite the range of statutory reversion rights in force across the EU before the DSM Directive, including the kind of use-it-or-lose-it rights that we argue show real promise for promoting both of copyright's core aims, there's little evidence any of them have meaningfully assisted creators in practice[76] – and indeed some evidence that they failed to do so.

One explanation for the lack of positive evidence is that there have been few attempts to measure the effects of continental reversion rights. We were able to identify just five studies to have done so, despite searching all databases to which we have access and seeking input from local experts.[77]

It may be that access and language issues have prevented us from locating further evidence, despite our best efforts. It is also possible that some statutory reversion rights are having meaningful impacts for creators, but those benefits simply haven't been measured or reported. However, the results of a 2013 EU consultation on copyright rules suggest that outcome is less likely. A report synthesising more than 9,000 responses to the consultation disclosed widespread discontent about the terms of exploitation contracts, with creators and their professional representatives accepting that rights often needed to be transferred to get works produced and distributed, but complaining about unfair terms arising from imbalances of bargaining power.[78] The issues they identified included widespread use of 'buy-out' contracts (which don't permit creators any right to participate in the ongoing success of their works via royalties), lengthy licence terms with no

[76] See, e.g., Martin Kretschmer, 'Copyright and Contract Law: Regulating Creator Contracts: The State of the Art and a Research Agenda' (2010) 18(1) *Journal of Intellectual Property* 141, 163 on the Italian time limit on publishing contracts: 'It is unclear what effect [this provision] … has in practice.'

[77] United Kingdom Intellectual Property Office, *Copyright Term Extension for Sound Recordings: Post Implementation Review* (1 October 2018) <https://assets.publishing.service.gov.uk/media/5bd046faed915d78b48aaba4/Copyright_term_extension_for_sound_recordings.pdf>; Ana Ramalho and Aurelio Lopez-Tarruella, *Implementation of the Directive 2011/77/EU: Copyright Term of Protection* (April 2018) <https://www.europarl.europa.eu/RegData/etudes/STUD/2018/604957/IPOL_STU(2018)604957_EN.pdf>; IViR, *Summary and Conclusions* (1 September 2020) <https://www.ivir.nl/publicaties/download/Evaluatie-ACR-Eindrapport-Summary-and-conclusions.pdf>; European Commission, Directorate-General for Communications Networks, Content and Technology et al (n 67); and Europe Economics, Lucie Guibault, Olivia Salamanca and Stef van Gompel, *Remuneration of Authors and Performers for the Use of Their Works and the Fixations of Their Performances* (2015) <https://op.europa.eu/en/publication-detail/-/publication/c022cd3c-9a52-11e5-b3b7–01aa75ed71a1>.

[78] European Commission, 'Report on the responses to the Public Consultation on the Review of the EU Copyright Rules' (July 2014) 78–9.

possibility of renegotiation or termination, and inadequate transparency around how rights are actually being used.[79]

If there were any examples of successful reversionary interventions in the laws of EU Member States, we would have expected to see them reflected in this evidence. Instead, the submissions called for EU-wide interventions to help creative workers secure better terms, including limiting the rights that could be transferred, giving creators the right to renegotiate contracts, imposing time limits on contracts, and making reversion rights available, especially in cases involving a lack of exploitation.[80] This all suggests that, while creators believed in the potential of reversion to help address these problems, existing legislative interventions were failing to do the trick. We now draw from the evidence that *is* available to us to identify the main reasons why those existing interventions may have been ineffective.

#### 4.3.1.1 Ineffective Triggers

If reversion rights are to meaningfully benefit creators, they need triggers that enable them to do so. However, some existing rights permit reclamation only in circumstances where the copyrights are all but valueless. This appears to be the case for the TED's hybrid time-and-exploitation based right, which doesn't let performers get their rights back until 50 years after transfer – and then only in cases where they aren't being made appropriately available, and where that hasn't been rectified within a year of giving notice to the rightsholder.[81]

You might wonder who would bother exercising such a tightly constrained right. The answer, according to the two studies to have evaluated the impacts of this law, is *nobody*.[82] As of 2018, it appeared that the right had not been invoked by a single performer. As Ramalho and Lopez-Tarruella note in their EU Parliament-commissioned evaluation, it had been available for a relatively short time at the time of these reviews, which might help contextualise this result.[83] Nonetheless, their finding of zero uptake remains remarkable and damning.

[79] Ibid 79.

[80] Ibid. End users of copyrighted content also recommended EU intervention, including through 'use-it-or-lose-it' rights: ibid 78. End users mainly comprised 'individual citizens, internet users and consumer associations': 3. See also European Commission, Directorate-General for Communications Networks, Content and Technology et al (n 67); who surveyed authors, journalists and visual artists and found they did not complain about not being to reclaim their rights as much as they highlighted issues with transparency. While Guibault highlighted the apparent disjuncture with author organisation claims that such rights were important, she also acknowledged the study may not have been representative and that most of the responses from book authors on this point were from the UK: 191, 224–6. This may mean the findings are not as generalisable to creators across the rest of Europe.

[81] See Section 4.2.1.3.

[82] Ramalho and Lopez-Tarruella (n 77) 26; United Kingdom Intellectual Property Office (n 77) 4.

[83] Ramalho and Lopez-Tarruella (n 77) 26.

#### 4.3.1.2 Uncertainty

Uncertainty can also play a key role in undermining reversion rights. As we saw in Chapter 3, lack of clarity about when rights accrue and what is required to exercise them can substantially depress creator willingness to actually do so.[84]

Researchers evaluating the 2015 Dutch Copyright Act identified various uncertainties impacting its general use-it-or-lose-it right, which applies in cases where rightsholders fail to exploit works to a sufficient extent within a reasonable period.[85] In particular, they expressed concern about the lack of clarity around the interrelationship between this right and one entitling termination for breach under the general Dutch law of contract, as well as the meaning of 'sufficient exploitation'.[86]

Ramalho and Lopez-Tarruella criticised the TED right for uncertainty also. This stemmed largely from the Directive's inclusion of 'obscure and/or undefined terms', particularly 'sufficient quantity' as the threshold for determining whether the performer can validly initiate the reversion process.[87]

Only two countries defined this term in their domestic implementations, leaving considerable confusion elsewhere.[88] The resulting conflict in Portugal helpfully illustrates the problem. There, the performers' collective management organisation took the view that 'sufficient quantity' should mean 'sufficient quantity to be acquired in normal market conditions, that is with a balanced distribution in the territory at stake', and that it should require producers to not just make recordings available on one online platform but on 'a "significant part" of those that are active in the market'.[89] But the producers' collective management organisation disagreed, arguing that 'sufficient quantity' should reflect 'market demand' and *only* cover physical copies.[90]

These diverging views could lead to very different outcomes, especially given the fact that physical distribution of sound recordings has been largely replaced by streaming. Under the producers' view, performers would have no redress so long as they were satisfying the (likely minimal) demand for physical copies. It is unclear which of these views (or some third alternative) will eventually prevail in Portugal, or how long it will take for the issue to be resolved throughout the remaining Member States. In the meantime, however, that avoidable uncertainty reduces the TED right's potential value to creators even further.

84 See Chapter 3, Section 3.2.1.
85 Furgal (n 12) 153–4 (the Netherlands) art 25e.
86 IViR (n 77) 4–5.
87 Ramalho and Lopez-Tarruella (n 77) 25.
88 Ibid 24–5.
89 Ibid 24.
90 Ibid.

#### 4.3.1.3 Lack of Information

Reversion rights may also be undermined by creators being unable to access the data necessary to gauge whether the trigger is made out. This was the crux of yet another criticism Ramalho and Lopez-Tarruella made of the TED right: it doesn't require producers to provide performers with access to the information they'd likely need to determine whether they were entitled to initiate the termination procedure. They recommended that Member States require producers to provide all necessary information to facilitate performers' exercise of the rights, for free and within a reasonable period, but noted that none had yet done so.[91]

#### 4.3.1.4 Enforcement Challenges

Rights are only useful to the extent they can be enforced – and enforcement is particularly challenging in the context of reversion. This was made particularly clear in a 2016 investigation commissioned by the European Commission ('the EC study') to evaluate how author-protective interventions in 10 EU Member States (including some reversion rights) affected creator remuneration.[92] Its economic modelling found that the imposition of contractual obligations such as reversion rights *could* strengthen authors' bargaining power, but that difficulties creators faced in actually enforcing those rights substantially weakened their efficacy.[93]

Of particular relevance, the study found that most of the statutory termination measures in the EU Member States surveyed (as well as clauses requiring initial publication or permitting a revision in remuneration) needed to be enforced by judges.[94] As well as making exercise of the rights unfeasibly expensive, the study's authors found this could deter creators in another way: '… requiring action to be taken by authors against the publishers … puts them in a position that might jeopardise their relationship with the latter; this could lead to authors being less willing to enforce such protective measures.'[95]

Creators are understandably concerned about the risks of retaliation or other adverse consequences if they take action against their investment partners to enforce their rights.[96] Such risks are exacerbated by the fact that, as explained in Chapter 1,

[91] Ibid 7.
[92] European Commission, Directorate-General for Communications Networks, Content and Technology et al (n 67).
[93] Ibid 238.
[94] Ibid.
[95] Ibid.
[96] See, e.g., Katherine Day, *Publishing Contracts and the Post Negotiation Space: Lifting the Lid on Publishing's Black Box of Aspirations, Laws and Money* (Taylor & Francis, 2023). We discuss these concerns in more detail in Chapter 5.

culture industries typically feature both a relatively small number of buyers for creative work and an oversupply of creative labour.

The aforementioned study evaluating the effects of author-protective reforms in Dutch copyright law found that such concerns are likely to play 'a major role' in explaining why its fair remuneration provisions had been so little used.[97] '[M]ost authors, out of fear of loss of contracts or blacklisting, do not dare to invoke or enforce their right to fair remuneration against exploiters.'[98]

Such concerns are less relevant in the context of rights that don't apply until the creator is near the end of their career (like the US termination right) or dead (like the Imperial right), but are nevertheless important and often overlooked when considering the real-world practicability of rights that rely on creators asserting them while their arts careers are still active.

#### 4.3.1.5 Poor Design

Reversion rights can be undermined by poor design in other ways as well, including by failure to consider their interactions with other parts of copyright law (and the potentially unforeseen market impacts of such interactions).

For example, Ramalho and Lopez-Tarruella report that the TED use-it-or-lose-it right will likely never be used in the UK as a result of the way it was implemented.[99] The *Copyright, Designs and Patents Act 1988* provides that when performers trigger that provision, the copyright in that sound recording expires.[100] This would mean that the producer would no longer be responsible to pay equitable remuneration for use of the recording, and the performer would then need to seek such remuneration from '[the] person who plays the sound recording in public or communicates the sound recording to the public' (which they are entitled to even after the sound recording's copyright expires).[101] As Ramalho and Lopez-Tarruella note, performers might be disincentivised from exercising the TED's use-it-or-lose-it provision because it's uncertain how they would get that equitable remuneration from the person who plays the recording in public or communicates it to the public.[102]

The UK Intellectual Property Office's ('IPO') study into the TED's implementation in the UK also highlighted potential issues with the use-it-or-lose-it provision when there are multiple performers. The IPO noted that under the UK's implementation of that provision, *all* the performers would lose out on access to

[97] IViR (n 77) 4.
[98] Ibid.
[99] Ramalho and Lopez-Tarruella (n 77) 26, *Copyright, Designs and Patents Act 1988* (UK) s 191HA(4).
[100] Ibid.
[101] Ibid s 182D(1).
[102] Ibid 26.

continuing royalties if one performer invoked the use-it-or-lose-it right.[103] Ramalho and Lopez-Tarruella found other EU Member States had implemented the provision so as to require some type of agreement between the joint performers, or a majority of them, to invoke the right.[104] But the lack of such procedures in the UK highlights how domestic lawmakers can fail to design reversion laws to operate well given the realities of how works are created and distributed.

#### 4.3.1.6 Rights Unsuited to the Digital Context

The lack of meaningful impact attributable to Europe's reversion rights in the lead-up to the Directive may be a consequence of their being out of date.

In her 2020 analysis, Furgal identified France as the only country to have dealt explicitly with digital exploitation, explicitly entitling authors to end publishing agreements for lack of exploitation in digital *or* physical form.[105] While various other countries gave authors statutory 'out of print' rights, their usefulness was often limited by outdated formulations based on the realities of traditional print publishing.[106] Allowing authors to reclaim rights when their book is 'out of print' or has 'less than 100 copies remaining in stock' makes little sense in the context of publishing industries increasingly reliant on digital distribution and print on demand.

In some cases, the transition to digital technologies has drastically changed the practical meaning of reversion rights from what lawmakers originally intended. Consider the general use-it-or-lose-it rights that are based on a complete lack of exploitation, for example. In the analogue era, making a work available to the public ongoing necessitated substantial investments in production and distribution. In those circumstances, *any* level of exploitation suggested that the investor was still demonstrating a meaningful commitment to the work.[107] In the digital era, however, most works can be kept available for remarkably little outlay, and so the mere fact a rightsholder is still technically making a work available to the public doesn't necessarily indicate an equivalent level of commitment to what it did in the past.

The significance of this shift was explicitly recognised in the evaluation of the Dutch use-it-or-lose-it right. Despite having a broader threshold than some of the laws we canvassed above (based on lack of sufficient exploitation, rather than no exploitation), the report criticised it for failing to take into account the changed realities that come with digital distribution: 'As a result of digitisation, a work can be

[103] United Kingdom Intellectual Property Office (n 77) 4.

[104] Ramalho and Lopez-Tarruella (n 77) 23–4.

[105] Furgal (n 12) 7 (France) art L132–17-2.

[106] Ibid.

[107] Joshua Yuvaraj and Rebecca Giblin, 'Are Contracts Enough? An Empirical Study of Author Rights in Australian Publishing Agreements' (2020) 44(1) *Melbourne University Law Review* 380, 389–90.

made available online indefinitely, almost at no cost.'[108] As Professor JG Visser has noted elsewhere, 'there will thus hardly ever be any question of [non-use]' under this provision.[109]

Concerned that authors might be prevented from reclaiming rights in circumstances where rightsholders are technically but not meaningfully exploiting them, the report's authors recommended that both availability and promotion of works be taken into account when determining the sufficiency of any exploitation.[110]

#### 4.3.1.7 Contracting Out

Finally, the ability of rightsholders to contract out of some European reversion rights may further explain their apparent lack of benefit for creators.[111] None of the studies we surveyed directly addressed this issue, but it's worth bearing in mind given the ongoing significance of this issue in the context of Commonwealth and US reversion rights, as well as the disproportionate bargaining power rightsholders often enjoy relative to creators. As we'll see, contracting out and many of the other problems identified above also affected the design and implementation of Article 22 of the DSM Directive, undermining the great promise of that instrument to harmonise, for the first time, baseline protections for creators across the Union.

## 4.4 ARTICLE 22: A MISSED OPPORTUNITY

### 4.4.1 *The Lead-Up to the Directive*

As we've seen, European creators expressed a strong desire for better reversion rights in the 2013 consultation even though the ones already on the books were largely letting them down – and they set their eyes on the EU to achieve reform.

There are two key reasons why EU intervention may have seemed a more attractive bet than domestic law reform.

First, creators from strongly laissez-faire traditions (such as the UK, which was then an EU member state, Ireland, Malta and Cyprus) may have believed that EU intervention was the only feasible way of achieving the kinds of author protections that had been largely absent in their own domestic copyright laws.[112]

[108] IViR (n 77) 5; see also 45–52 of the full study, downloadable via <https://repository.wodc.nl/handle/20.500.12832/2460>.The Dutch law was passed in 2015, but the sufficient exploitation use-it-or-lose-it right was already present in the 2012 Bill before the EU copyright consultation: Thomas Dysart, 'Author-Protective Rules and Alternative Licences: A Review of the Dutch Copyright Contract Act' (2015) 37(9) *European Intellectual Property Review* 601, 602.

[109] Dirk JG Visser, 'Dutch Copyright Contract Law' in Simon Geiregat and Hendrik Vanhees (eds), *Copyright Contracts Tomorrow* (LeA Uitgevers, 2023) 31–3.

[110] IViR (n 77) 5.

[111] See Section 4.2.2.3.

[112] Furgal (n 12) 7.

Second, creator groups may have been aware of Big Content's track record of derailing creator-favouring laws at the national level. One example was a proposed 2010 Dutch law that would have banned copyright assignments (permitting licences only) and allowed authors to terminate most licences after five years.[113] After furious responses claiming it would be the end of the Dutch publishing industry[114] and would 'lead to the destruction of knowledge and capital',[115] those provisions were dropped.[116] Creators seeking rights within the EU would still need to contend with fierce rightsholder lobbying, but if they succeeded in obtaining a strong reversion right, it would have to be implemented throughout all Member States with little opportunity for powerful rightsholders to derail it. That may have made the EU a better focus for creator efforts than individual legislatures.

Rightsholder responses to the 2013 consultation asserted that further regulation was not needed, that author and performer remuneration was adequate and the most important thing when considering fair remuneration is the author's freedom of contract.[117] However, the European Commission accepted the evidence of creators instead, and acknowledged the need for legislative intervention by way of what would become the 2019 Digital Single Market Directive.[118]

Its initial proposal was for a package of three author-protective provisions: a transparency obligation for rightsholders (e.g. to report on royalties to authors and performers), a 'bestseller' clause allowing renegotiation of disproportionate remuneration arrangements, and a voluntary alternative dispute resolution system accessible to creators.[119]

Creators responded by lobbying hard for reversion rights to be included as well,[120] further demonstrating their belief in reversion's potential to ameliorate problems

[113] Bart Lenselink, 'Copyright Contract Law' in Bernt Hugenholtz, Antoon Quaedvlieg and Dirk Visser (eds), *A Century of Dutch Copyright Law: Auteurswet 1912–2012* (deLex, 2012) 193.

[114] Submission by NUV Groep algemene uitgevers, 30 September 2010, 2 <https://www.internetconsultatie.nl/auteurscontractenrecht/reactie/f78ce01e-b5d8-420f-9070-1cbefaab3650> (translated by DeepL).

[115] Submission by Grope uitgevers voor vak en wetenschap, 28 September 2010 <https://www.internetconsultatie.nl/auteurscontractenrecht/reactie/ad94d033-8210-4e32-90b3-0808da35ac2c> (translated by DeepL).

[116] The time limit was abandoned in 2012 when the Dutch Government put forward its copyright amendment bill: Amendments to the Copyright Act and the related rights in the context of enhancing the position of authors and performing artists in contracts for copyright and neighbouring rights (Copyright Contract Act) Bill, Second House of Representatives, 2011–2012, 33 308, no. 2 (June 20, 2012), referred to in Dysart (n 108) 602 n 13).

[117] European Commission (n 78) 80.

[118] Impact Assessment (16 September 2016) 207–8 <https://www.eumonitor.eu/9353000/1/j4nvgs5kjg27kof_j9vvik7m1c3gyxp/vk7k8gzqvpwy/f=/12254_16_add_1.pdf>.

[119] Proposal for a Directive of the European Parliament and of the Council on copyright in the Digital Single Market, 14 September 2016, arts 14–16.

[120] See, e.g., Society of Authors, 'The Society of Authors' Response to the Intellectual Property Office's Calls for Views on the European Commission's Draft Legislation to Modernise the European Copyright Framework' (6 December 2016) 11 (archived on the Wayback Machine as of 27 March 2019) <https://web.archive.org/web/20190327101504/https://www.societyofauthors

with their contracts. That eventually caused the European Parliament to propose a general 'use-it-or-lose-it' provision that would allow authors and performers across the Union to revoke copyright grants where there was an 'absence of exploitation'. Under that initial draft, authors could revoke rights grants when there was 'an absence of exploitation' or where rightsholders had failed to comply with a separate transparency right, aimed at giving creators better visibility of how their works were being used, and their payments calculated.[121] Contracting out of the reversion right was excluded except 'if concluded by means of an agreement which is based on a collective bargaining agreement'.[122]

The DSM Directive was intended to 'achieve a well-functioning and fair marketplace for copyright' across the EU,[123] making this a once-in-a-generation opportunity to achieve a healthier balance between the interests of rightsholders (to have a reasonable opportunity to exploit rights and benefit from their investments), creators (to be able to reclaim and benefit from unused rights) and the public (to have better access to cultural heritage via rights being freed to facilitate new exploitations). Unfortunately, for the reasons we unpack below, the eventual Article 22 signally failed to provide the best practice solution creators were crying out for.

### 4.4.2 *The Eventual Article 22*

The enacted version differed markedly from Parliament's first proposal. We briefly canvass what that version looked like, before returning to trace its journey to enactment and then domestic implementation throughout the Union.

.org/SOA/MediaLibrary/SOAWebsite/Submissions/20161205-Submission-to-IPO-on-DSM-directive-dec-2016.pdf>, cited in Ula Furgal, 'Interpreting EU Reversion Rights: Why "Use-It-or-Lose-It" Should Be the Guiding Principle' (2021) 43 *European Intellectual Property Review* 283, 285; BASCA, 'British and EU Music Creators United in Calling for an EU-Wide Rights Reversion Mechanism' (19 October 2017) <https://web.archive.org/web/20180612142607/https://basca.org.uk/2017/10/19/music-creators-call-eu-wide-rights-reversion-mechanism/>; European Composer & Songwriter Alliance, 'A Fair Rights Reversion Mechanism: A Necessity for Europe's Creators' <https://composeralliance.org/media/53-briefingpapereurightsreversionmechanism.pdf>; see also Ed Johnson-Williams, 'Submission to the IPO Call for Views: Modernising the European Copyright Framework' (6 December 2016).

[121] Amendment 84 (new art 16a) (Draft Legislative Resolution).

[122] Amendment 84 (new art 16a(4)).

[123] *Directive (EU) 2019/790 of the European Parliament and of the Council of 17 April 2019 on copyright and related rights in the Digital Single Market and amending Directives 96/9/EC and 2001/29/EC* [2019] OJ L 130 ('EU DSM Directive') recital 3. The Directive was part of a wider copyright reform 'package', and the intention behind it was to modernise EU copyright protection in the face of '[r]apid technological developments', particularly in the context of the digital marketplace for copyrighted works. See Séverine Dusollier, 'The 2019 Directive on Copyright in the Digital Single Market: Some Progress, a Few Bad Choices, and an Overall Failed Ambition' (2020) 57 *Common Market Law Review* 979, 979–80; EU DSM Directive, recital 3.

Article 22, as enacted, required Member States to ensure authors or performers could wholly or partly revoke grants or exclusive licences of rights where there was a 'lack of exploitation'.[124] This revocation could only happen: (a) a reasonable time after the transfer, or the licence had concluded; and (b) once the author or performer had given notice as to when that exploitation needed to take place by.[125] The provision excluded reversion where 'the lack of exploitation [was] ... predominantly due to circumstances that the author or the performer can reasonably be expected to remedy'.[126] Article 22 could also not be enforced by creators of computer programs.[127]

Article 22 allowed Member States significant leeway to craft the reversion right according to their specific contexts. These included the relevant factors for different types of works and creative industries, the matter of how reversion would operate for coauthored works, whether authors should be prevented from exercising the right after a period justified by the industry or type of work, and whether authors were able to choose to only end the *exclusivity* of the grant/licence, rather than revoke it entirely.[128] While some of this discretion was appropriate, the breadth of it gave powerful rightsholders greater scope to intervene in domestic implementations than creators may have hoped for.

Article 22 was accompanied by several other author-protective provisions: a requirement that Member States impose obligations on rightsholders to provide creators with rights to 'appropriate and proportionate remuneration' (Article 18); regular information about how their works were being used and how their share of income was calculated (Article 19); additional remuneration if the success of their works makes their initial remuneration arrangements disproportionate (Article 20); and a voluntary alternative dispute resolution ('ADR') mechanism to resolve disputes related to the transparency and contract adjustment provisions (Article 21). Member States needed to 'ensure that any contractual provision that prevents compliance with Articles 19, 20 and 21 shall be unenforceable in relation to authors and performers' (Article 23). As we demonstrate below, this meant Member States could technically allow investors to contract out of the application of Article 22 and its intended benefits for creators, even though those states *could* (but were not required to) limit contracting out provisions to those 'based on a collective bargaining agreement'.[129]

The DSM Directive became law on 17 May 2019,[130] requiring Member States to implement the Directive's requirements into their domestic laws by

[124] EU DSM Directive, art 22(1); recital 80.
[125] Ibid art 22(3); recital 80.
[126] Ibid art 22(4); recital 80.
[127] Ibid art 23(2).
[128] Ibid art 22(2); recital 80.
[129] Ibid art 22(5).
[130] *Official Journal of the European Union* L 130 (Vol 62) 92.

June 2021.[131] Poland was the last Member State to implement the Directive in September 2024, despite previously challenging it.[132]

### 4.4.3 *How the Sausage Was Made*

Before getting into the specific deficiencies of this provision, it's worth providing a little more context about Article 22's passage into law, and the changes that were made along the way.

As noted above, the Parliament included reversion in its amended draft legislation after the Commission had failed to do so in its initial proposal.[133] The first draft had two triggers: authors could revoke rights grants when there was 'an absence of exploitation' or where rightsholders had failed to comply with the new transparency requirement.[134] Additionally, it excluded contracting out except where collectively bargained.[135]

Parliament passed that draft in September 2018,[136] but the reversion provision met substantial opposition during the subsequent trilogue negotiations between the Parliament, Commission and Council.[137] There were six rounds of negotiation, and as late as the fifth, still no agreement on whether to even *include* the reversion

[131] Legislative Train, JURI (Press Release, February 2024) <https://www.europarl.europa.eu/legislative-train/carriage/jd-directive-on-copyright-in-the-digital-single-market/report?sid = 7801>.

[132] Pawel Lipski, 'Poland: The DSM Directive finally implemented', Bird & Bird (19 September 2024) <https://www.twobirds.com/en/insights/2024/poland/the-dsm-directive-finally-implemented>; Paul Keller, 'TDM: Poland Challenges the Rule of EU Copyright Law', *Kluwer Copyright Blog* (Blog Post, 20 February 2024) <https://copyrightblog.kluweriplaw.com/2024/02/20/tdm-poland-challenges-the-rule-of-eu-copyright-law/>.

[133] See Section 4.4.1.

[134] Amendment 84 (new art 16a) (Draft Legislative Resolution). The Industry, Research and Energy Committee recommended more triggers, like a lack of reporting, non-payment and even inadequate promotion: Opinion of the Committee on Industry, Research and Energy for the Committee on Legal Affairs on the proposal for a directive of the European Parliament and of the Council on copyright in the Digital Single Market (1 August 2017), Amendment 58 (new art 15a), report referred to in Furgal (n 120) 285. However, these proposals were not adopted. The rationale for this draft is similar to recital 80 of the current DSM Directive, except that Parliament intended reversion to take place only after parties had used the ADR mechanism: Amendment 50 (new recital 43a). However, this was not implemented in the Directive's final text.

[135] Amendment 84 (new art 16a(4)).

[136] Amendments adopted by the European Parliament on 12 September 2018 on the proposal for a directive of the European Parliament and of the Council on copyright in the Digital Single Market (COM(2016)0593 – C8–0383/2016 – 2016/0280(COD)) Amendment 50: Proposal for a directive, recital 43a (new); Amendment 84: Proposal for a directive, Article 16 a (new) <https://www.europarl.europa.eu/doceo/document/TA-8-2018-0337_EN.html>.

[137] Kosta Hountalas, 'Proposed Changes to EU Copyright Law – Implications for Rights Holders in the News and Media Industries' (2018) 37(4) *Communications Law Bulletin* 21, 21.

right in the Directive.[138] After the fifth round, however, with most of the Directive's other content broadly agreed, a compromise text was finally agreed.[139]

That final version weakened the Parliament's original proposal in two critical ways.

First, it deleted the second trigger for reversion – the one that would have allowed creators to reclaim their rights in circumstances where rightsholders had failed to comply with their obligations under the accompanying transparency obligation. The impetus for this appears to have originated with the EU Presidency, which was adamant that it would *not* accept that trigger (albeit for reasons not apparent in the primary documents available to us).[140]

We've previously flagged that author-protective provisions are only helpful to the extent they can be enforced. Had creators been given the right to terminate their contracts where rightsholders failed to provide them with the data to which they were entitled by law, it would likely have made it much easier to get them to actually do so. Unfortunately, the deletion of the second trigger meant this potential was never realised.

Second, the compromise text flipped the contracting out restriction. Whereas previous contracting out was banned except when the result of collective bargains (reflecting the German contracting-out model for its own use-it-or-lose-it provision, discussed above[141]), Member States were now *permitted* (but not required to) impose such restrictions.[142] Effectively, that permitted rightsholders to contract out of domestic implementations of Article 22 unless Member States individually restricted them from doing so.[143] Once again, this left individual Member States vulnerable to lobbying from powerful corporations during their domestic implementations.

In addition, the law as passed changed the (now sole) reversion trigger from 'absence of exploitation' to 'lack of exploitation'.[144] However, it's not clear that this change made any substantive difference.

[138] Council of the European Union, *Proposal for a Directive of the European Parliament and of the Council on Copyright in the Digital Single Market – Update of negotiating mandate* (Note from Presidency to Permanent Representatives Committee, 2016/0280 (COD), 17 January 2019) 5 <https://www.politico.eu/wp-content/uploads/2019/01/Revised-mandate-Coreper.pdf>; see also Trilogue 4-Column document (version 5.1, 7 December 2018) 106–9 <https://www.europarl.europa.eu/RegData/publications/trilogue/2016/0280/NEGO_CT(2016)0280(2018-12-07)_XL.pdf>. The EU Council refused to include reversion at all, in contrast with the Parliament's proposal: Council of the European Union (n 138) 162–4, 276–80.

[139] Council of the European Union, 'EU Copyright Rules Adjusted to the Digital Age' (Web Page, 13 February 2019) art 22 <https://www.consilium.europa.eu/en/press/press-releases/2019/02/13/eu-copyright-rules-adjusted-to-the-digital-age/>.

[140] Council of the European Union (n 138) 5.

[141] See Section 4.2.2.3.

[142] Council of the European Union (n 138) 280.

[143] See Section 4.4.5.

[144] EU DSM Directive, art 22(1); Council of the European Union (n 138) 276.

Below, we critically evaluate the 'lack of exploitation' standard and rules around contracting out, including the further problems that emerged during Article 22's domestic implementations.[145]

### 4.4.4 *'Lack of Exploitation'*

One of the most significant problems with Article 22 arises from its 'lack of exploitation' trigger. As explained above, some countries with general use-it-or-lose-it rights before the DSM Directive had based them on no exploitation, while others had more creator-protective standards that allowed rights to be reclaimed where exploitation was inadequate.[146]

'Lack of exploitation' could have either meaning on its face, and neither view is unanimously adopted in the scholarship or by industry stakeholders.[147] Acknowledging the text's ambiguity, we proceed with a plain reading of the phrase in the context of the Directive's recitals, which suggest Article 22 is intended to be limited to situations where rights are 'not exploited at all'.[148] The equivalent phrases in the Directive's other published languages are consistent with 'no exploitation' as well.[149]

Problematically, this high threshold doesn't go as far as it might to further copyright's access and reward goals. As we've noted at various times throughout this book, digital technologies make it very easy and often virtually costless to make most works available online.[150] In this paradigm, mere availability of a work does not say the same thing about the rightsholder's commitment to it as it did in the analogue age. Under a 'no exploitation' standard, reversion can be avoided where

[145] Our discussion is not intended to be an in-depth review of art 22, but an examination of the areas we consider to be of most pressing concern with art 22 and its implementations. We acknowledge, however, a broader range of issues has been and will continue to be discussed in relation to art 22. For broader critiques of art 22 and the Directive generally, see, e.g., Dusollier (n 123); Ted Shapiro and Sunniva Hansson, 'The DSM Copyright Directive: EU Copyright Will Indeed Never Be the Same' (2019) 41(7) *European Intellectual Property Review* 404; Eleonora Rosati, *Copyright in the Digital Single Market: Article-by-Article Commentary on the Provisions of Directive 2019/790* (Oxford University Press, 2021) 2023; European Copyright Society, 'Comment of the European Copyright Society Addressing Selected Aspects of the Implementation of Articles 18 to 22 of the Directive (EU) 2019/90 on Copyright in the Digital Single Market' (2020) 2 *JIPITEC* 132. We also note our analysis of the law is based on the national legislation following implementation of the DSM Directive, which to the best of our knowledge is current at the time of writing (2024).

[146] See Section 4.2.2.1.1.

[147] Joshua Yuvaraj, 'Implementing copyright revocation in Ireland and Malta: lessons for lawmakers' (2023) 18(7) *Journal of Intellectual Property Law & Practice* 528, 532–3.

[148] EU DSM Directive, recital 80.

[149] EU Commentary, para 74, n 43. See also Séverine Dusollier and Léo Pascault, 'Contractual Protection of Authors and Performers in France after the CDSM Directive' in Simon Geiregat and Hendrik Vanhees (eds), *Copyright Contracts Tomorrow* (LeA Uitgevers, 2023) 83.

[150] See further Furgal (n 120) 290.

rightsholders have made it available for sale online, even if they're doing nothing to actively invest in making the work available in new formats, or promoting it to new audiences.[151]

While a standard based on no exploitation is better than no revocation right at all, we query whether it's desirable to allow rights to remain locked up on the basis of such minimal commitment – especially when others may be willing and able to do a better job.

A trigger based on exploitation being 'inadequate' in the circumstances would have been more consistent with promoting copyright's access and reward goals. We agree with the recommendation of von Gompel et al in their evaluation of the Dutch use-it-or-lose-it right that, in determining whether the exploitation threshold has been reached, consideration ought to be given not only to whether the work is available, but the extent to which it is being appropriately and actively promoted.[152] In determining whether exploitation is in fact appropriate in all the circumstances, relevant circumstances might include the author or an alternative investor being keen to re-launch the work to the public, or make it available in new formats.

As we will argue in Chapter 6, any such standard would need to be supported by regularly updated industry-specific guidelines to help creators identify whether their work would qualify – and give rightsholders certainty about what they needed to do to retain them.[153] Done well, such a standard could do a much better job of promoting public access to knowledge and culture, and helping creators achieve recognition and financial rewards for their work.

The 'no exploitation' standard also raises a controversy over whether an author can reclaim some of their rights in cases where some but not all are being exploited. For example, imagine a situation where a publisher is exploiting its print rights over a book, but not its audio or ebook rights. Can an author revert just the unused rights?

Commentary of the European Copyright Society published to assist the implementation process suggests that Member States would need to explicitly make it clear that reversion is available in relation to each right in order to achieve such an end, suggesting that simple enactment of Article 22's text would not be sufficient.[154] And the French implementation, for example, seems to rule this out explicitly. Its implementation provides that, 'when author has transferred, on an exclusive basis, all or part of her rights, she may, *in the absence of all exploitation of their work*,

[151] Dusollier and Pascault (n 149) 83.

[152] IViR (n 77) 5.

[153] See Chapter 6. On how sector-specific agreements could impose an inadequate exploitation threshold to strengthen a legislative 'no exploitation' reversion system, see, e.g., Pierre Sirinelli and Alexandra Bensamoun, 'The Transposition of Articles 18 to 23 of Directive 2019/790 of April 17, 2019, by Order No. 2021-580 of May 12, 2021, into the Common Law Regime for Copyright Contracts' (2021) 270(10) *Revue internationale du droit d'auteur* 137, 225–6. See further Dusollier and Pascault (n 149) 83–4.

[154] ECS Commentary 2020, 22, n 43. For a more detailed overview of the literature on lack of exploitation, see, e.g., Yuvaraj (n 147) 528.

automatically revoke all or part of this transfer'.[155] By contrast, as we saw above, France's existing use-it-or-lose-it provisions for books not only use broader 'inadequate exploitation' triggers, but allow authors to reclaim part of their rights (e.g. digital or print) if only one of them meets the threshold.[156]

Given the breadth of rights cultural investors tend to take in their dealings with creators, the fact that in winner-takes-all markets few works are likely to be fully exploited, and the ease with which minimal exploitation (such as making it available online) can be achieved, it's difficult to discern a normative case for so strictly limiting the reversion right's scope.

As the Directive only prescribes minimum standards,[157] EU Member States could have provided protections more in line with copyright's access and reward goals by implementing versions that included a broader trigger – for example by enabling authors to reclaim rights in case of inadequate exploitation, as well as no exploitation at all.[158] However, only a minority of countries took the opportunity to do so. Eight countries already had a pre-DSM Directive general use-it-or-lose-it right with a trigger that included inadequate exploitation: Slovenia, Romania, Germany, the Czech Republic, Croatia, Austria, the Netherlands and Slovakia.[159] Six of these countries maintained that standard through implementation, ensuring authors had a broader right than the minimum mandated via Article 22.[160] But the remaining two

155 Art L. 131-5-2-I CPI (emphasis added), in Dusollier and Pascault (n 149) 83. Cf. Brad Spitz, 'CDSM: French Transposition on the Remuneration of Performers', *Kluwer Copyright Blog* (Blog Post, 21 April 2023) <https://copyrightblog.kluweriplaw.com/2023/04/21/cdsm-french-transposition-on-the-remuneration-of-performers/> (interpreting the equivalent revocation right for performers as using 'lack of exploitation of his or her performance' as a threshold).

156 Dusollier and Pascault (n 149) 83.

157 See EUR-Lex, 'National Transposition' (Web Page) <https://eur-lex.europa.eu/collection/n-law/mne.html>.

158 See European Commission, 'Better Regulation in Europe: An OECD Assessment of Regulatory Capacity in the Original Member States of the EU: Project Glossary', definition of 'Gold Plating' <https://www.oecd.org/gov/regulatorypolicy/44952782.pdf>, referred to in OECD, 'Regulatory Impact Assessment across the European Union' in *Better Regulation Practices across the European Union* (2019) <https://www.oecd-ilibrary.org/sites/9b745623-en/index.html?itemId=/content/component/9b745623-en>. (However, it is important to ensure measures additional to the minimum requirements of a Directive do not cause additional burdens or harms. For more information, see generally Eduardo Magrani, Nevin Alija and Felipe Andrade, '"Gold-Plating" in the Transposition of EU Law' (2021) 8 *E-Pública* 45.)

159 Furgal (n 12) 8.

160 Bundesgesetz über das Urheberrecht an Werken der Literatur und der Kunst und über verwandte Schutzrechte (Urheberrechtsgesetz 1936, zuletzt geändert durch das Bundesgesetz BGBI. I Nr. 244/2021) ['Federal Law on Copyright in Literary and Artistic Works and Related Rights (Copyright Law 1936, as amended up to Federal Law published in the Federal Law Gazette I No. 244/2021 (BGBI.I No. 244/2021))', *Das Rechtsinformationssystem des Bundes* [The Legal Information System of the Republic of Austria] (Web Page) <ris.bka.gv.at/GeltendeFassung.wxe?Abfrage=Bundesnormen&Gesetzesnummer=10001848>] (Austria) (tr Microsoft Edge) § 29(1); Gesetz über Urheberrecht und verwandte Schutzrechte (Urheberrechtsgesetz, das zuletzt durch des Gesetzes vom 23. Juni 2021 geändert worden ist) ['Act on Copyright and Related Rights (Copyright Act, as amended up to Act of June 23, 2021)',

states, the Czech Republic and Romania, actually wound that protection back, reducing their standard to allow reversion for non-exploitation *only*.[161]

Most of the other Member States implemented the minimum 'no exploitation' standard, however (n = 18). Malta alone appeared to implement Article 22 by directly adopting its (rather ambiguous) 'lack of exploitation' language.[162]

It's unclear the extent to which countries decided to pass the minimum standard was influenced by rightsholder lobbying, as there was not always transparency around the implementation process. In Ireland, for example, which adopted an

*WIPO Lex* (Web Page) <wipo.int/wipolex/en/text/586964>] (Germany) s 41(1); 1999. évi LXXVI. törvény a szerzői jogról (Hatályos: 2024.02.17.-tól) ['Act No. LXXVI of 1999 on Copyright (consolidated text of February 17, 2024)', *Nemzeti Jogszabálytár* [National Legislation Database] (Web Page) <njt.hu/jogszabaly/1999-76-00-00>] (Hungary) (tr Microsoft Edge) § 51(1); Auteurswet 1912, tekst geldend op: 01-10-2022 ['Copyright Act 1912, as amended up to October 1, 2022', *Overheid.nl* (Web Page) <wetten.overheid.nl/BWBR0001886/2022-10-01/#HoofdstukI_Paragraaf6_Artikel16>] (the Netherlands) (tr Microsoft Edge) art 25e (1); Autorský zákon č. 185/2015 Z. z. (v znení č. 125/2016 Z. z., 215/2018 Z. z., 306/2018 Z. z., 71/2022 Z. z., 455/2022 Z. z.) ['Copyright Act No. 185/2015 Coll. (as amended by No. 125/2016, 215/2018, 36/2018, 71/2022, 455/2022)', *Zákony pre ľudí* [Laws for the People] (Web Page) <zakonypreludi.sk/zz/2015-185>] (Slovakia) (tr Microsoft Edge) § 73(1); Zakon o avtorski in sorodnih pravicah (Uradni list RS, št. 21/95 z dne 14.04.1995, kot je bil spremenjen 26.10.2022) ['Copyright and Related Rights Act (Official Gazette of the Republic of Slovenia, No. 21/95 of April 14, 1995, as amended up to October 26, 2022)', *WIPO Lex* (Web Page) <wipo.int/wipolex/en/text/587464>] (Slovenia) art 83(1).

161 Zákon občanský zákoník č. 89/2012 Sb. ze dne 3. února 2012 ['Civil Code Act No. 89/2012 Coll. of February 3, 2012', as amended up to Act No. 31/2024 Coll. of March 31, 2024, *Zakony pro lidi* [Laws for the People] (Web Page) <zakonyprolidi.cz/cs/2012-89/zneni-20240101>] (Czech Republic) (tr Microsoft Edge) art 2378; Legea nr. 8 din 14 artie 1996 privind dreptul de autor şi drepturile conexe ['Law No. 8 of March 14, 1996 on Copyright and Related rights' amended up to May 1, 2022, *Legislative Portal* (Web Page) <legislatie.just.ro/Public/DetaliiDocument/259087>] (Romania) (tr Microsoft Edge) art 48^1(1). See further Furgal (n 12) 20. See, e.g., Gregor Schmid et al, 'Transposing the DSM Copyright Directive in Germany, the Czech Republic and Slovakia', *Taylor Wessing* (Web Page, 27 May 2021) <https://www.taylorwessing.com/en/interface/2021/copyright-update/transposing-the-dsm-copyright-directive-in-germany-the-czech-republic-and-slovakia>; Josef Donát, 'The Future of Czech Copyright Law in Light of DSM Directive (Part II)', *Rowan Legal* (Web Page, 17 December 2021) <https://rowan.legal/en/114060/>. Czech parliamentary documents acknowledge this change in exploitation trigger (Czech Parliament, Draft Act amending Act No. 121/2000 Coll., on Copyright, on Rights Related to Copyright and on Amendments to Certain Acts (Copyright Act), as amended, and Act No. 89/2012 Coll., Civil Code, as amended (Explanatory Memorandum, Version for comments, 6 November 2020). Comments from Czech Government departments indicated they wanted to make their reversion provision consistent with the 'no exploitation' approach, which the Office of the Government of the Czech Republic – Compatibility Department considered was more consistent with art 22 in non-English languages (Czech Parliament, Draft Act Amending Act No. 121/2000 Coll., on Copyright, on Rights Related to Copyright and on Amendments to Certain Acts (Copyright Act), as amended, and Act No. 89/2012 Coll., Civil Code, as amended (Settlement of Comments, Version for Government Meeting, 22 April 2021)). Beyond this, we could not find indications as to why the Czech Government went with a narrower definition.

162 Copyright and related rights in the DSM Regulations, 2021 (Malta) reg 21(4)(b); Yuvaraj (n 147) 531–2.

explicit 'no exploitation' standard, the government's consultation did not ask for comment on the standard to be adopted, and did not make responding submissions available to the public.[163]

### 4.4.5 *Contracting Out*

#### 4.4.5.1 Contracting Out of Article 22 Is Now Allowed

We've seen throughout this book that when reversion rights can be avoided by contractual terms to the contrary, rightsholders routinely respond by using their superior bargaining power to require creators to sign away their reversion rights at the time they enter into the initial contract.[164] If we're concerned with ensuring that copyright law promotes ongoing access to works and recognition and rewards for creators, it's undesirable to allow rightsholders to so cheaply and easily eliminate protections designed to achieve this.[165]

EU lawmakers recognised and provided for the risk of contracting out by requiring Member States to ensure contracts can't bypass or neuter various other of the DSM's author-protective provisions, but not Article 22.[166] By doing so, they have suggested that it is indeed possible to do so.[167] Member States *can* limit contracting out of Article 22 to situations where the relevant provisions were 'based on a collective bargaining agreement'.[168] But again, this is permitted rather than

[163] See Yuvaraj (n 147) 533–4.
[164] See Chapters 2, 3 and 5.
[165] Section 4.5 deals with *direct* contracting out, for example by specifying that the implemented reversion provisions don't apply. Rightsholders could also adopt the approach that succeeded in *Gloucester Place v Le Bon*, discussed in Chapter 3 – specify the applicable law to be that of a jurisdiction where there are no reversion rights: see, e.g., Jane C Ginsburg, 'The Author as Revenue Sharer: Lecture in Memory of William R. Cornish' (2023) 18(11) *Journal of Intellectual Property Law & Practice* 787, 791–2. However, this is a problem with reversion rights generally rather than art 22, so we will instead address it in detail in our best practice analysis in Chapter 6.
[166] EU DSM Directive, art 23(1). Article 18 is also made non-mandatory, but a discussion of that provision is beyond the scope of this book.
[167] Yuvaraj (n 147) 530; European Copyright Society (n 145) [37]. Other commentators generally indicate parties can contract out of art 22: Ted Shapiro, 'Remuneration Provisions in the DSM Copyright Directive and the Audiovisual Industry in the EU: The Elusive Quest for Fairness' (2020) 42(12) *European Intellectual Property Review* 778, 784–5; Dusollier (n 123) 1026; Jane C Ginsburg, 'Authors' Remuneration: Reforms to Wish For' in Gustavo Ghidini (ed), *Reforming Intellectual Property* (Edward Elgar, 2022), 128; João Pedro Quintais, 'The New Copyright in the Digital Single Market Directive: A Critical Look' (2020) 42(1) *European Intellectual Property Review* 28, 40. The accompanying recitals say the same thing: arts 19–21 should be mandatory and parties should not be able to contract out of them, but they say nothing about art 22.
[168] EU DSM Directive, art 22(5).

mandatory, and thus further suggests that if they don't so regulate, exploiters will still be able to contract out of revocation unhindered.[169]

The enacted text effectively flipped the European Parliament's original reversion proposal, which prohibited rightsholders from contracting out *except* as part of a collective bargain.[170] The closed-door nature of (and lack of transparency around) the trilogue negotiations[171] makes it difficult to prove any causal connection between rightsholder lobbying[172] and the shift away from the right being mandatory, but there is no doubt that the change benefited big businesses over creators.

Failure to make Article 22 expressly mandatory, when most of the DSM's other author-protective provisions *are* mandatory, has been criticised for either 'lack[ing] ... coherence' or indicating a desire to prioritise rightsholder interests over those of creators,[173] neither of which are consistent with the Directive's creator-protective rationales.[174] It also made individual Member States vulnerable to lobbying from Big Content during the course of their domestic implementations: if they chose to actively depart from the DSM's text to make reversion rights inviolable, they would not have any cover from the EU in doing so.

#### 4.4.5.2 Some Courageous Implementations

Despite this, most (n = 19) of the EU Member States have implemented stricter approaches to contracting out than mandated by Article 22. Of these 19 states, only five (Croatia, the Netherlands, Slovenia, Spain and Slovakia), went further than required by the Directive, banning contracting out of the Article 22 equivalent in their domestic law completely.[175] The remaining 14 states permitted contracting out only in certain circumstances:

[169] Yuvaraj (n 147) 530.

[170] See Section 4.4.1.

[171] See further Päivi Leino-Sandberg, 'Transparency and Trilogues: Real Legislative Work for Grown-Ups?' (2023) 14 *European Journal of Risk Regulation* 271, 271, 278, 286, 290.

[172] As Leino-Sandberg notes, the '[European] Parliament has no rules that would even attempt to make external influence in legislative work efficiently visible with a view to enabling political accountability.' Ibid 283.

[173] Stéphanie Carre, Stéphanie Le Cam and Franck Macrez, 'Buyout Contracts Imposed by Platforms in the Cultural and Creative Sector', Study requested by the JURI Committee of the European Parliament, PE 754.184 (November 2023) 38 <https://www.europarl.europa.eu/RegData/etudes/STUD/2023/754184/IPOL_STU(2023)754184_EN.pdf>.

[174] See further EU DSM Directive, recitals 74 and 75.

[175] Zakon o autorskom pravu (NN 111/2021) ['Copyright and Related Rights Act (OG No. 111/2021)', *WIPO Lex* (Web Page) <wipo.int/wipolex/en/text/584899>] (Croatia) art 70(6); Auteurswet 1912, tekst geldend op: 01-10-2022 ['Copyright Act 1912, as amended up to October 1, 2022', *Overheid.nl* (Web Page) <wetten.overheid.nl/BWBR0001886/2022-10-01/#HoofdstukI_Paragraaf6_Artikel16>] (the Netherlands) (tr Microsoft Edge) art 25h; Autorský zákon č. 185/2015 Z. z. (v znení č. 125/2016 Z. z., 215/2018 Z. z., 306/2018 Z. z., 71/

1. Eleven limited contracting out to collective bargaining situations (as permitted by the Directive);[176]

2022 Z. z., 455/2022 Z. z.) ['Copyright Act No. 185/2015 Coll. (as amended by No. 125/2016, 215/2018, 36/2018, 71/2022, 455/2022)', *Zákony pre ľudí* [Laws for the People] (Web Page) <zakonypreludi.sk/zz/2015-185>] (Slovakia) (tr Microsoft Edge) § 73(4); Zakon o avtorski in sorodnih pravicah (Uradni list RS, št. 21/95 z dne 14.04.1995, kot je bil spremenjen 26.10.2022) ['Copyright and Related Rights Act (Official Gazette of the Republic of Slovenia, No. 21/95 of April 14, 1995, as amended up to October 26, 2022)', *WIPO Lex* (Web Page) <wipo.int/wipolex/en/text/587464>] (Slovenia) art 83 (5); Real Decreto Legislativo 1/1996, de 12 de abril, por el que se aprueba el texto refundido de la Ley de Propiedad Intelectual, regularizando, aclarando y armonizando las disposiciones legales vigentes sobre la materia ['Royal Legislative Decree 1/1996, of April 12, 1996, approving the revised text of the Law on Intellectual Property, regularizing, clarifying and harmonizing the legal provisions in force on the matter', *Agencia Estatal Boletín Oficial del Estado* [State Agency Official State Gazette] (Web Page) <boe.es/buscar/act.php?id = BOE-A-1996-8930>] (Spain) (tr Microsoft Edge) art 48bis(4). Note, however, that in Slovakia authors cannot waive the right in advance, which *could* open the door for rightsholders to bypass the statutory right.

176 Code de droit économique (mis à jour le 19 février 2024) ['Code of Economic Law (updated on February 19, 2024)', *ejustice* (Web Page) <ejustice.just.fgov.be/eli/loi/2013/02/28/2013A11134/justel#LNK0426>] (Belgium) (tr DeepL) art XI.167/4(5); Ο περί του Δικαιώματος Πνευματικής Ιδιοκτησίας και Συγγενικών Δικαιωμάτων Νόμος του 1976 (59/1976) ['The Copyright and Related Rights Act of 1976 (59/1976)', as amended up to Law No 155(I)/2022), *CyLaw* (Web Page) <cylaw.org/nomoi/enop/non-ind/1976_1_59/full.html>] (Cyprus) (tr Microsoft Edge) s 43(3(e)); Bekendtgørelse af lov om ophavsret (LBK nr 1093 af 20/08/2023) ['Promulgation of the Copyright Act (LBK no. 1093 of 20/08/2023)', *Retsinformation* (Web Page) <retsinformation.dk/eli/lta/2023/1093#idfad91e59-c2a8–41a8–94ab-ed28e6bd3b9a>] (Denmark) (tr Microsoft Edge) § 54(2); Upphovsrättslag 8.7.1961/404 (ändrad genom lag 21.12.2023/1216) ['Copyright Act (Act No. 404/1961 of July 8, 1961, as amended up to Act No. 1216/2023 of December 21, 2023)', *Finlex* <finlex.fi/sv/laki/ajantasa/1961/19610404>] (Finland) (tr Microsoft Edge) s 30b; Gesetz über Urheberrecht und verwandte Schutzrechte (Urheberrechtsgesetz, das zuletzt durch des Gesetzes vom 23. Juni 2021 geändert worden ist) ['Act on Copyright and Related Rights (Copyright Act, as amended up to Act of June 23, 2021)', *WIPO Lex* (Web Page) <wipo.int/wipolex/en/text/586964>] (Germany) s 41(4); Νόμος 2121/1993, Πνευματική Ιδιοκτησία, Συγγενικά Δικαιώματα και Πολιτιστικά Θέματα (επικαιροποιημένος μέχρι και τον ν. 5046/2023) ['Law No. 2121/1993 on Copyright, Related Rights and Cultural Matters (as amended up to Law No. 5046/2023)', *Οργανισμός Πνευματικής Ιδιοκτησίας* [Hellenic Copyright Organisation] (Web Page) <opi.gr/en/library/law-2121-1993>] (Greece) (tr Microsoft Edge) art 15B(6); Legge 22 aprile 1941, n. 633 sulla protezione del diritto d'autore e di altri diritti connessi al suo esercizio (Ultimo aggiornamento all'atto pubblicato il 30/12/2023) ['Law No. 633 of April 22, 1941, for the Protection of Copyright and Neighbouring Rights (last update to the act published on December 30, 2023)', *Normattiva* (Web Page) <normattiva.it/uri-res/N2Ls?urn:nir:stato:legge:1941-04-22;633!vig = >] (Italy) (tr Microsoft Edge) art 110-septies(5); Autortiesību likums (Ar grozījumiem: 05.04.2023) ['Copyright Law (as amended up to April 5, 2023)', *Latvijas Republikas tiesību akti* [Legislation of the Republic of Latvia] (Web Page) <likumi.lv/ta/id/5138-autortiesibu-likums>] (Latvia) (tr Microsoft Edge) art 45.3(7); 'Copyright and Related Rights in the Digital Single Market Regulations', *Malta Legislation* (Web Page) <legislation.mt/eli/sl/415.8/eng> (Malta) s 21(4)(c); Legea nr. 8 din 14 artie 1996 privind dreptul de autor şi drepturile conexe ['Law No. 8 of March 14, 1996 on Copyright and Related rights' amended up to May 1, 2022, *Legislative Portal* (Web Page) <legislatie.just.ro/Public/DetaliiDocument/259087>] (Romania) (tr Microsoft Edge) art 48^1 (8); Lag (1960:729) om upphovsrätt till litterära och konstnärliga verk ['Act (1960:729) on Copyright in Literary and Artistic Works', amended up to SFS 2022:1712, *Sveriges Riksdag*

2. Two (Austria and Hungary) retained their pre-DSM Directive restrictions on contracting out of their use-it-or-lose-it rights, preventing creators from waiving their statutory reversion rights beyond three and five years respectively;[177]
3. One (Estonia) permitted contracting out if it was to the author's benefit, but not their detriment.[178]

However, the eight remaining Member States enacted rights which were silent as to whether it was possible to contract out,[179] which (for the reasons explained above, and the fact that other author-protective provisions in the copyright laws of these countries *are* mandatory[180]) strongly suggests that it is. Given the ease with which such terms can be inserted into contracts and the disproportionate bargaining power

[Swedish Parliament] (Web Page) <riksdagen.se/sv/dokument-och-lagar/dokument/svensk-forfattningssamling/lag-1960729-om-upphovsratt-till-litterara-och_sfs-1960-729/>] (Sweden) (tr Microsoft Edge) s 29d(3).

[177] Bundesgesetz über das Urheberrecht an Werken der Literatur und der Kunst und über verwandte Schutzrechte (Urheberrechtsgesetz 1936, zuletzt geändert durch das Bundesgesetz BGBI. I Nr. 244/2021) ['Federal Law on Copyright in Literary and Artistic Works and Related Rights (Copyright Law 1936, as amended up to Federal Law published in the Federal Law Gazette I No. 244/2021 (BGBI. I No. 244/2021))', *Das Rechtsinformationssystem des Bundes* [The Legal Information System of the Republic of Austria] (Web Page) <ris.bka.gv.at/GeltendeFassung.wxe?Abfrage = Bundesnormen&Gesetzesnummer = 10001848>] (Austria) (tr Microsoft Edge) § 29(3); 1999. évi LXXVI. törvény a szerzői jogról (Hatályos: 2024.02.17.-tól) ['Act No. LXXVI of 1999 on Copyright (consolidated text of February 17, 2024)', *Nemzeti Jogszabálytár* [National Legislation Database] (Web Page) <njt.hu/jogszabaly/1999-76-00-00>] (Hungary) (tr Microsoft Edge) § 51(4).

[178] Autoriõiguse seadus vastu võetud 11.11.1992 ['Copyright Act adopted 11.11.1992', in force from January 1, 2023, *Riigi Teataja* [State Gazette] (Web Page) <riigiteataja.ee/en/eli/527122022006/consolide>] (Estonia) § 49/4 (2).

[179] Bulgaria, Ireland, France, the Czech Republic, Luxembourg. Lithuania, Portugal, Poland.

[180] ЗАКОН ЗА АВТОРСКОТО ПРАВО И СРОДНИТЕ МУ ПРАВА изм. и доп. ДВ. бр.100 от 1 Декември 2023г ['Law on Copyright and Related Rights amended and supplemented by SG 100 of December 1, 2023', *lex.bg* (Web Page) <lex.bg/mobile/ldoc/2133094401>] (Bulgaria) (tr Microsoft Edge) arts 38(6) and 39a(7); 'European Union (Copyright and Related Rights in the Digital Single Market) Regulations 2021 (S.I. No. 567/2021)', *WIPO Lex* (Web Page) <wipo.int/wipolex/en/text/586484> (Ireland) reg 31; Code de la propriété intellectuelle (version consolidée au 1 janvier 2024) ['Intellectual Property Code (consolidated version as of January 1, 2024)', *Légifrance* <legifrance.gouv.fr/codes/texte_lc/LEGITEXT000006069414?init = true&page = 1&query = Code+de+la+propri%C3%A9t%C3%A9+intellectuelle+&searchField = ALL&tab_selection = code>] (France) (tr Microsoft Edge) art L131–5-3 (stating that provisions are of 'public order', which means they cannot be contracted out of: see further Holfran Avocates, 'Contracting in France, What to Pay Attention To?' (Web Page, 10 November 2023) <https://holfran.com/en/contracting-in-france-what-to-pay-attention-to/>; Zákon občanský zákoník č. 89/2012 Sb. ze dne 3. února 2012 ['Civil Code Act No. 89/2012 Coll. of February 3, 2012', as amended up to Act No. 31/2024 Coll. of March 31, 2024, *Zakony pro lidi* [Laws for the People] (Web Page) <zakonyprolidi.cz/cs/2012-89/zneni-20240101>] (Czech Republic) (tr Microsoft Edge) ss 2374(2) and 2374a(4); Loi du 18 avril 2001 sur les droits d'auteur, les droits voisins et les bases de données (version consolidée applicable au 09/04/2022) ['Law of 18 April 2001 on copyright, related rights and databases (consolidated version applicable on April 9, 2022)', *Journal Officiel du Grand-Duché de Luxembourg* [Official Journal of the Grand Duchy of Luxembourg] (Web Page) <legilux.

culture investors typically have over creators, we expect that this will translate to this right being of even less benefit to creators in those nations.

## 4.5 A WASTED OPPORTUNITY

Continental Europe has a tradition of protecting authors' rights much more actively than common law nations, and that's reflected in the panoply of reversion rights that existed in the lead-up to the DSM Directive, as well as the author-protective provisions that instrument included.

However, few of the reversion rights we were able to identify have been implemented in a way likely to meaningfully change outcomes for creators, and Article 22 is perhaps the biggest disappointment of them all. The DSM Directive was a once-in-a-generation opportunity to remedy this by achieving meaningful, technologically appropriate rights, but it signally failed to do so. While the opacity of the process makes it difficult to understand exactly what determined the final framing, the inappropriately high exploitation threshold, elimination of reversion as a consequence for rightsholder failures to comply with their transparency obligations and approach to contracting out resulted in a right that we suspect will do little to secure a fairer share of rewards to creators, or promote better public access to valuable knowledge and culture. Article 22's use-it-or-lose-it right is better than nothing, but it's far from what could have been.

public.lu/eli/etat/leg/loi/2001/04/18/n2/consolide/20220409> (Luxembourg) (tr Microsoft Edge) art 13d; Lietuvos Respublikos autorių teisių ir gretutinių teisių įstatymas 1999 m. gegužės 18 d. Nr. VIII-1185 Vilnius ['Republic of Lithuania Law No. VIII-1185 on Copyright and Related Rights of May 18, 1999', consolidated version from January 1, 2024 to April 30, 2024, *Lietuvos Respublikos Seimo kanceliarija* [Chancellery of the Seimas of the Republic of Lithuania] (Web Page) <e-seimas.lrs.lt/portal/legalAct/lt/TAD/TAIS.81676/asr>] (Lithuania) (tr Microsoft Edge) arts 40.1(5), 40.2(3); Código do Direito de Autor e dos Direitos Conexos (aprovado pelo Decreto-Lei n.º 63/85 de 14 de março de 1985, e alterado até ao Decreto-Lei n.º 47/2023 de 19 de junho de 2023) ['Code of Copyright and Related Rights (approved by Decree-Law No. 47/2023 of March 14, 1985, and amended up to Decree-Law No. 47/2023 of June 19, 2023', *Procuradoria-Geral Distrital de Lisboa* [Lisbon District Attorney's Office] (Web Page) <pgdlisboa.pt/leis/lei_mostra_articulado.php?nid = 484&tabela = leis&so_miolo = >] (Portugal) (tr Microsoft Edge) art 44f(1).

# 5

# Contractual Reversion Rights

## INTRODUCTION

While we argue that reversion rights have real potential to re-draw copyright's broken bargain, none of the statutory interventions we canvassed across Chapters 2 to 4 has succeeded in doing so. Do those failures mean we should leave creator rights to be determined via private contracts rather than public regulation?

Cultural investors have long and consistently argued in favour of exactly that, lauding contracts as the best way of regulating the legal rights and responsibilities between themselves and the creators they work with.[1] You may recall that creator submissions to the 2013 EU reform consultation consistently criticised contracts for

[1] See, e.g., *Memorandum Statement by the Copyright Committee of the Motion Picture Association of America* before the Committee on the Judiciary House of Representatives Subcommittee No. 3, 89th Congress, 1st session 990 <https://babel.hathitrust.org/cgi/pt?id=pst.000014112416&seq=342&q1=freedom>; *Copyright Law Revision Part* 3 (US Government Printing Office, 1964), Philip B Wattenberg on behalf of Music Publishers' Association of the US, 285<https://babel.hathitrust.org/cgi/pt?id=pst.000014112416&seq=5&q1=wattenberg>; Thomas J Robinson, Motion Picture Association of America, 288; *Music Publishers Association, Submission to the European Commission Public Consultation on the Review of the EU Copyright Rules* 39; International Publishers Association, Submission to New Zealand Ministry of Business, Innovation and Employment, *Review of the Copyright Act 1994* [11] <https://www.mbie.govt.nz/dmsdocument/6707-international-publishers-association-review-of-copyright-act-1994-issues-paper-submission-pdf>; Publishers Association of New Zealand, Submission to New Zealand Ministry of Business, Innovation and Employment, *Review of the Copyright Act 1994* [11] <https://www.mbie.govt.nz/dmsdocument/6753-publishers-association-of-new-zealand-review-of-copyright-act-1994-issues-paper-submission-pdf>; National Council of Provinces Trade & Industry, Economic Development, Small Business, Tourism, Employment & Labour Committee, Parliament of the Republic of South Africa, *Copyright Amendment Bill & Performers Protection Amendment Bill: Public Hearings*, 21 February 2023 (Philippa Rafferty, Group Executive Legal and Business Affairs of eMedia Investments); National Council of Provinces Trade & Industry, Economic Development, Small Business, Tourism, Employment & Labour Committee, Parliament of the Republic of South Africa, *Copyright Amendment Bill & Performers Protection Amendment Bill: Public Hearings*, 7 March 2023 (Danny Dohmen, Immediate Past President of Licencing Executives Society of South Africa).

failing to safeguard their interests, providing evidence of the ways in which their unequal bargaining power led to unfair terms, a lack of transparency, and lack of scope to negotiate better deals.[2] Rightsholder responses to that review painted a very different picture, insisting that authors and performers were being 'appropriately remunerated thanks to existing law and practice in all sectors of the creative industries' and calling for creator rights to 'be regulated by the market'.[3] The most important issue, in the view of the publishers, producers and broadcasters who responded, was 'ensuring that there is contractual freedom, freedom of negotiation and the right for an author to choose his/her representative'.[4]

When statutory reversion rights come on the agenda, rightsholders resist with rhetoric that warns against 'statutory intrusion upon the sanctity of contract',[5] and argues that they would 'arbitrarily restrict… freedom to trade'.[6] They sometimes even argue that statutory interventions are unnecessary because such rights can already be incorporated via contracts. In Canada for example, in response to Bryan Adams' call for a new entitlement to revert rights 25 years after transfer, the Executive Director of the Professional Music Publishers Association told a parliamentary committee that if Adams wanted such a limit he should have simply negotiated it into his contract. 'There's nothing in the law that stops what we're discussing being effective in a contract. You could say that after 35 years the copyright would go back to the composer. That's already possible to do if we wish to do it.'[7] That's undeniable, so far as it goes, but disingenuously ignores the fact that they do *not* wish to do it, and that very few composers have the bargaining power to force them to do so.

We've previously shown that the highly unequal bargaining power between cultural investors and creative workers means that, in practice, contractual 'freedom' is usually illusory.[8] But do contracts nonetheless result in reversion rights that appropriately balance and promote copyright's access and rewards aims? We aim to answer that question in this chapter, primarily by drawing upon the results of two empirical studies. The first analyses half a century of publishing contracts sourced from the archive of the Australian Society of Authors to determine how they allocate rights, the way in which they provide for reversion and how those practices have evolved over time. The second investigates what happens when authors actually attempt to enforce their contractual rights.

2 European Commission, 'Report on the Responses to the Public Consultation on the Review of the EU Copyright Rules' (July 2014) 78–9.

3 Ibid 80.

4 Ibid.

5 *Motion Pictures Association of America, Comment to the Copyright Office Library of Congress in the Matter of Modernizing Recordation of Notices of Termination*, 4 <https://www.motionpictures.org/wp-content/uploads/2023/04/MPA-Comments-on-Termination-Recordation.pdf>.

6 National Council of Provinces Trade & Industry, 7 March 2023 (n 1).

7 INDU, *Evidence*, 1st Session, 42nd Parliament 19 September 2018, statement by Jérôme Payette (executive director of the Professional Music Publishers Association) 7.

8 See e.g. Chapter 1, Section 1.3.1.

As the following pages will show, we find that contractual practice results in similar failures to the statutory model, including outdated, missing and poorly designed rights, and a balance that favours the interests of rightsholders over those of creators or the public. We also find that author attempts to enforce contractual rights can result in an additional panoply of problems, including challenges determining whether a particular work is eligible to revert, getting publishers to respond to reversion requests, and even finding the relevant contracts in the first place. While some of these problems can be addressed, we conclude the chapter by identifying a number of structural features that make the deficiencies of contracts much harder to rectify than those of statutes, and argue that the best path towards reversion reforms that could meaningfully improve copyright's ability to achieve its aims involves some form of public intervention.

## 5.1 INTRODUCING REVERSION RIGHTS IN PUBLISHING CONTRACTS

### 5.1.1 *Out-of-Print Clauses*

As we've previously observed, book publishing is the creative industry with the longest and strongest history of contractual reversion, almost exclusively in the form of use-it-or-lose-it rights.[9] These practices recognise the importance of not just publishing books in the first place, but keeping them available ongoing. As leading British publisher Stanley Unwin observed in 1947, permitting authors to reclaim rights where publishers cannot or will not reprint their books is 'eminently just'.[10]

Such 'out-of-print' clauses are publishing's best-known reversion right. Traditionally, they entitled authors to reclaim rights granted under publishing contracts (usually excepting those that have previously been sub-licensed) once the book has gone 'out of print'. Sometimes such clauses operate automatically: for example, by reverting rights after the book has been out of print for more than six months.[11] More commonly however, reversion occurs after the author gives notice that the book is no longer available for purchase, and the publisher fails to re-print.[12]

Out-of-print clauses are intended to motivate publishers to keep books available, which clearly benefits the public (by promoting access) and authors (by ensuring

[9] See e.g. Chapter 1, Introduction.

[10] Stanley Unwin, *The Truth About Publishing* (Unwin Brothers, 5th ed, 1947) 97; see also Stanley Unwin, *The Truth About Publishing* (Lyons & Burford, 1995, reprinting the 1960 edition of the book published by George Allen & Unwin) 93.

[11] *The Publishers Weekly* (1906) No 1776, 667; *Harper & Bros v M A Donohue & Co* (1905) 144 F 491, [493].

[12] E.g., Alexander Lindey and Michael Landau, *Lindey on Entertainment, Publishing and the Arts* (Thomson Reuters, 3rd ed, 2024) s 5:109, cf. Lynette Owen (ed), *Clark's Publishing Agreements* (Bloomsbury Professional, 10th ed, 2017) 57.

they still have a chance to earn royalties).[13] When unused rights revert, the pool of potential beneficiaries also includes publishers whose fresh investments in previously neglected works pay off – as when Text Publishing republished the out-of-print *Women in Black* in an edition that went on to sell over 100,000 copies, be developed into a stage production and feature length film, and be translated for new audiences in Germany, Italy, France and Israel.[14]

#### 5.1.1.1 When Will a Title Be 'Out of Print'?

'Out of print' has had different meanings over time, and across different parts of the publishing industry.[15] Accordingly, authors' organisations have long insisted that contracts should provide clear, objective standards for determining a book's print status. In 1968, for example, the Society of Authors' (UK) model contract defined a book as being out of print if the publisher had 'fifty (50) copies or less in stock'.[16] By 1991, it was recommending that rights should revert if a book was out of print *or* average sales had fallen below 250 copies, and the publishers had declined to reprint.[17] US and Australian author organisations similarly recommended objective standards by around the same time.[18]

Rather than adopting objective criteria for determining print status, however, some publishing guides simply replaced outdated 'out of print' language with alternative formulations, like 'off the market', 'out of print in all editions', or

[13] The Authors Guild, 'A Publishing Contract Should Not Be Forever', 28 July 2015 <https://perma.cc/T3U6-FUKV>; Australian Society of Authors, *Australian Book Contracts* (Keesing Press, 4th ed, 2009) 24.

[14] Text Publishing, *The Women in Black* <https://perma.cc/GM63-3BYJ>; Text Publishing, *Ladies in Black* <https://perma.cc/7XUF-CFWL>; Andrea Hanke, 'Editorial: Rising Stars', *Think Australian*, Books+Publishing, 15 November 2018 <https://perma.cc/KW25-6483>; email dated 18 November 2019 from Anne Beilby (Rights and Contracts Director, The Text Publishing Company).

[15] E.g., JM Cavendish, *A Handbook of Copyright in British Publishing Practice* (Cassell 1974, 1st ed) 155: 'A book is said to be out of print ('o/p') when not enough copies are available from stock to satisfy reasonable public demand'; Jonathan Kirsch, *Kirsch's Handbook of Publishing Law* (Acrobat Books, 1995) 224: 'A book is "out of print," according to book industry practice, when it is no longer generally available to consumers through ordinary channels of trade in the book industry.'

[16] Andrew O Shapiro, 'The Standard Author Contract: A Survey of Current Draftsmanship' (1968) 18 *Copyright Law Symposium* 135, 165, referring to Society of Authors contract, cl 13(a).

[17] Denis De Freitas, 'Copyright Contracts: A Study of the Terms of Contracts for the Use of Works Protected by Copyright under the Legal System in Common Law Countries' (1991) 11 *Copyright* 222, 241.

[18] The US Authors Guild recommended that authors should be allowed to terminate publishing contracts if books were out of print *and* annual royalties did not meet a particular threshold after ten calendar years: see ibid 250. The Australian Society of Authors' 1994 model contract specified that 'a book shall be deemed to be out-of-print where the Publisher's stocks are less than fifty (50) or where less than twelve (12) copies are shown as having been sold in any six (6) months accounting period.' Australian Society of Authors, *Australian Book Contracts* (Keesing Press, 2nd ed, 1994) 36.

'not available in any edition'.[19] Such formulations require books to be entirely unavailable, including in digital form or via print-on-demand ('POD'), before authors could reclaim their rights.

In today's era of natively digital manuscripts, keeping a title available digitally or via POD requires virtually no investment – certainly far less than a fresh print run would require. But under these 'technical availability' standards, such minimal contributions can be enough to enable publishers to hold on to the rights forever, even if the book is no longer selling and no royalties are being paid.[20]

Writers have long expressed concern that these changed realities could radically alter their traditional bargain with publishers. In 1994, the US National Writers Union argued that out-of-print clauses needed to be 're-thought in the electronic era, when small quantities or even single copies of a work can be reproduced easily and cheaply'. The Union argued that 'the real criterion for whether a publisher can retain rights is whether the work is still being actively marketed', although instead of suggesting objective sales or stock-based thresholds it recommended that the publisher be required 'to notify the author when it has decided that it no longer makes sense to make even minimal efforts to promote the work'.[21]

In the succeeding decades, author associations around the English-speaking world have consistently warned their members about the dangers of out-of-print clauses being based on 'technical availability' standards that could be satisfied by eBooks or POD, as early as 2000 (Authors Guild, US),[22] 2001 (Australian Society of Authors),[23] and 2006 (Society of Authors, UK).[24] As the Society of Authors further explained in 2008:

> Publishers will be tempted to argue that a book is "available" – the term now often used in preference to "in print" – if it can be supplied as POD or as an eBook. It becomes all the more important for authors to ensure that they have the option of reverting rights if sales – preferably in units, but possibly in revenue – fall below figures agreed in the publishing contract.[25]

Authors have long raised this issue with the Australian Society of Authors, which noted in 2021 that 'being caught by the "never-out-of-print ebook/POD

19 Lynette Owen (ed), *Clark's Publishing Agreements: A Book of Precedents* (Bloomsbury Professional, 10th ed, 2017) 54; see also Roy Kaufman, *Publishing Forms and Contracts* (Oxford University Press, 2008) 19.

20 The Authors Guild (n 13).

21 US National Writers Union, *Statement of Principles on Contracts between Writers and Electronic Book Publishers* <https://perma.cc/66WZ-WGZZ>.

22 The Authors Guild, *Bulletin*, Spring 2000, 5.

23 Australian Society of Authors, *Australian Book Contracts* (Keesing Press, 3rd ed, 2001) 31.

24 Society of Authors, *The Author*, Winter 2000, 129.

25 Society of Authors, *The Author*, Autumn 2008, 94.

loophole" ... thwart[s] their ability to end publishing agreements and explore other options.'[26]

While there are some variations in the criteria different author associations recommend authors to use, especially the appropriateness of unit sales versus dollar amounts,[27] the message of each organisation has long been consistent: that objective criteria are needed to make it possible for authors to reclaim rights where publishers are no longer meaningfully investing in their books' success.

Despite these consistent calls, industry practice guides have been slow to adopt objective criteria to define out-of-print clauses. As late as 2010, *Clark's Publishing Agreements* ('*Clark's*'), a leading UK guide to publishing contracts,[28] still recommended that contracts give authors the right to reclaim their rights if their book was 'out of print in all editions' and the publisher had not at least commenced a new edition within nine months of having received a written request from the author to do so.[29] It did, however, acknowledge that the 'main trend' since its 2007 edition was the move to definitions based on objective criteria, and described the question of when a book is 'out of print' as 'one of the significant by-products of the move into the digital/electronic era'.[30]

It was not until 2013 that *Clark's* finally recommended permitting the author to reclaim their rights in a work if the work failed to meet a minimum sales threshold based either on quantity of copies sold or royalty value.[31] The 2017 edition noted that setting appropriate levels was an 'inexact science', but recognised that 'authors should be entitled to get their rights back if the publisher is not properly supporting

[26] Australian Society of Authors, 'APA Updates Code of Conduct following ASA Campaign' (Web Page, 3 November 2021) <https://www.asauthors.org.au/news/apa-updates-code-of-conduct-following-asa-campaign/>.

[27] The Australian Society of Authors is comfortable with sales measures (Australian Society of Authors, *Contracts* <https://perma.cc/PS4F-36ZY>), but the Society of Authors (UK) recommends that authors only agree to contracts that give them a right to recover their rights when the work is available only in digital/POD editions, or where 'sales have dwindled below an agreed level' (leaving it open whether that's calculated with reference to revenue or copies sold) (Society of Authors, *Before You Sign: Getting Your Rights Back* <https://perma.cc/PN8L-24W6>). By contrast, the Author's Guild (US) is wary of using unit sales as a benchmark: 'Publishers might ... be able to game the clause by offering one-cent e-books the way they've gamed existing clauses by using e-books and print-on-demand.' It prefers yearly income thresholds (e.g. US$250–$500), below which authors can terminate the contract and exploit their books via other means: The Authors Guild (n 13).

[28] *Clark's* has been described as an 'integral reference work for the publishing industry' (Huw Alexander, 'Clark's Publishing Agreements: A Book of Precedents (8th edn)' (2011) 22(1) *LOGOS: The Journal of the World Book Community* 68, 70) and Martin Woodhead, 'Clark's Publishing Agreements: A Book of Precedents, 9th edn' (2014) 27(4) *Learned Publishing* 315, 317.

[29] Lynette Owen (ed), *Clark's Publishing Agreements: A Book of Precedents* (Bloomsbury Professional, 8th ed, 2010) 55.

[30] Ibid 54.

[31] Lynette Owen (ed), *Clark's Publishing Agreements: A Book of Precedents* (Bloomsbury Professional, 9th ed, 2013) 55.

the book'.[32] That emphasis on 'proper support' confirms the continuing validity of the traditional 'out of print' bargain: publishers must exhibit some minimally meaningful commitment to ensure they hold onto the rights. The 2017 edition of *Clark's* stated that termination clauses based on minimum sales or minimum income 'have become the norm',[33] but even now some publishing guides do not reflect that.[34]

As of 2019, the leading author advocacy associations in the US, UK and Australia all reported that, whilst objective criteria have finally now been adopted by all or almost all major trade publishers, they were still seeing new contracts with 'out of print' defined by technical availability standards rather than objective criteria (particularly from academic publishers and small trade presses).[35]

### 5.1.2 *Other 'Use It or Lose It' Rights*

'Out of print' rights are the main form of 'use-it-or-lose-it' reversion right in publishing contracts, but others do exist. For example, contracts might take rights in multiple territories or languages, but then provide for their return if the publisher fails to exploit them within a certain period.[36]

The Society of Authors has observed that 'many publishers will agree' to such mechanisms on request.[37] However, not all authors know to negotiate for 'use-it-or-lose-it' rights to be included in their contracts, and many simply agree to whatever terms they were originally offered, particularly early in their writing careers.[38]

[32] Owen (ed) (n 19) 56.

[33] Ibid 34.

[34] E.g., Mark A Fischer, E Gabriel Perle and John Taylor Williams, *Perle, Williams & Fischer on Publishing Law* (Wolters Kluwer, 4th ed, 2019, last updated May 2019) ('*Perle*') 2–71; *Lindey* ss 5:14, cl 16, 5:109, 5:110; 5:117, 5:118; 5:163; *Entertainment Industry Contracts* (Matthew Bender, 2019) Form 41-1, cl 15(b), 15.

[35] Joshua Yuvaraj and Rebecca Giblin, 'Are Contracts Enough? An Empirical Study of Author Rights in Australian Publishing Agreements' (2020) 44(1) *Melbourne University Law Review* 380, 391, n 50.

[36] For instance, a template contract from 'Big 5' publisher Random House in *Lindey* allows the author to revoke the publisher's rights to license the work in the British Commonwealth (except Canada), South Africa and the Republic of Ireland if those rights have not been exercised within 18 months of the work first being published in the United States (*Lindey* (3rd ed) s 5:114, cl 1(b)). A further right of revocation is included for the 'right to license in all foreign languages and all countries' if no license or option is granted three years after the book is first published in the United States (*Lindey* (3rd ed) s 5:114, cl 1(c)). See also *Perle* (4th ed, 2019) 2–43; *Entertainment Industry Contracts: Negotiating and Drafting Guide* (10th ed, 1995) 41-17.

[37] The Society of Authors, 'Before You Sign | Getting Your Rights Back' (Web Page, 16 February 2018) <https://societyofauthors.org/News/Blogs/Before-you-Sign/February-2018/Before-You-Sign-Getting-Your-Rights-Back#:~:text=Many%20publishers%20will%20agree%20to,an%20agreed%20time%2C%20those%20rights>.

[38] Martin Kretschmer, 'Copyright and Contracts: A Brief Introduction' (2006) 3(1) *Student's Guides to the US Government Series* [3]; Lucie Guibault, 'Relationship between Copyright

If use-it-or-lose-it' clauses can be included on request, but not by default, that risks disproportionately disadvantaging emerging and less-well-resourced authors.

### 5.1.3 *Liquidation Rights*

Some publishing contracts also contain clauses allowing authors to reclaim rights in situations like publisher bankruptcy or liquidation, similarly to some of the European copyright laws surveyed in Chapter 4.[39] Whether they are enforceable depends on the jurisdiction and drafting. For example, in Australia the *Corporations Act 2001* (Cth) prevents termination of a contract if one party enters administration (as opposed to liquidation).[40] The Act also requires liquidators to maintain corporate assets, like publishing rights and earnings due to authors, for creditors.[41] Absent a contractual allowance, they may not be *able* to return rights to authors, even if they wished to do so.[42] For this reason it's important that contracts specify what happens when a publisher goes out of business, and leading publishing guides recommend allowing the author to terminate in such circumstances.[43]

## 5.2 HOW EFFECTIVE ARE REVERSION RIGHTS IN PUBLISHING CONTRACTS?

In 2020, we published a study that drew upon the Australian Society of Authors' archive of author contracts, comprising over 50 years of documents provided by members for the purpose of obtaining advice about their terms. There have been few previous attempts to investigate contractual practice around reversion,[44] probably because contracts (being spread across so many parties) are notoriously difficult to study, and we were keen to get a better understanding of how they allocated rights and responsibilities between the parties.

The archive's time span allowed us to not only investigate the ways in which publishers dealt with reversion rights in their contracts, but how those practices evolved in response to the major technological, cultural and economic shifts that

and Contract Law' in Estelle Derclaye (ed), *Research Handbook on the Future of EU Copyright* (Edward Elgar, 2009) 519; David Caute, 'A Survey of Publisher's Contracts' (1980) 99 (2569) *New Statesman; London* 892, 892.

39 See Chapter 4, Section 4.2.2.1.3.

40 See, e.g., *Corporations Act 2001* (Cth) s 451E(1); *Rathner, in the matter of Citius Property Ltd (Administrator Appointed)* [2023] FCA 26, [60] (finding the s 451E stay does not prohibit exercise of a contractual termination right arising on the other party entering liquidation).

41 *Corporations Act 2001* (Cth) s 420A(1).

42 See further Charles Clark, 'Contracts between Authors and Publishers' (1992) XXVI(4) *Copyright Bulletin* 17, 24.

43 See, e.g., Lynette Owen (ed), *Clark's Publishing Agreements* (Bloomsbury, 11th ed, 2022) 60–1, 102–3.

44 We review the existing literature at Yuvaraj and Giblin (n 35) 393–5.

occurred within that period, most notably publishing's transition from analogue to digital.

Our investigation addressed three key questions:[45]

1. What rights have authors assigned or licensed to publishers via publishing contracts?
2. What provisions have those contracts made to return rights to authors?
3. How have those practices evolved over time?

### 5.2.1 *Methodology*

Our full methodology is set out in the published paper,[46] but in brief: we selected a purposive sample of 145 contracts ('sample') that authors provided to the Australian Society of Authors for advice between 1960 and 2014.[47] The contracts related to a range of publishers across the period 1960–2014, with between one and six contracts per year (an average of 2.8). We excluded contracts with confidentiality clauses.[48] We coded the contracts to generate quantitative data using relevant variables (the duration of the grant, the presence and nature of reversion rights, etc.).

The findings of our study are not necessarily generalisable to Australian publishing contracts. The Australian Society of Authors had destroyed a portion of the archive in 2016 due to space constraints, and the contracts it does have relate only to the self-selecting category of authors who sought advice from them in the first place. However, our findings are consistent with publishing practice literature and experiences reported by leading author organisations.[49] These findings also have broad relevance through the English-language world because of the structural similarities between publishers, publishing's global nature,[50] and the general absence of statutory reversion rights for authors in these countries.[51] They also have broader normative implications for discussions about reversion law reform in relation to other

45 Ibid 395.

46 A detailed explanation of our method, including data collection, coding, reliability testing and limitations, can be found at ibid 395–402.

47 Contracts were examined under conditions of confidentiality and our findings do not necessarily reflect the Australian Society of Authors' views.

48 See further Yngvar Kjus, 'Twists and Turns in the 360 Deal: Spinning the Risks and Rewards of Artist-Label Relations in the Streaming Era' (2022) 25(2) *European Journal of Cultural Studies* 463, 467.

49 See Katherine Day, *Publishing Contracts and the Post Negotiation Space: Lifting the Lid on Publishing's Black Box of Aspirations, Laws and Money* (Taylor & Francis, 2023) 103; Yuvaraj and Giblin (n 35) 397.

50 See, e.g., Helge Rønning and Tore Slaatta, 'Marketers, Publishers, Editors: Trends in International Publishing' (2011) 33(7) *Media, Culture & Society* 1109, 1110; see further Giulia Trentacosti and Nick Pilcher, 'Dealing with the Competition of English-language Export Editions: Voices from the Dutch Trade Book Market' (2021) 37 *Publishing Research Quarterly* 278, 280–1 on the dominance of Anglo-American publishing.

51 See generally Chapters 2 and 3.

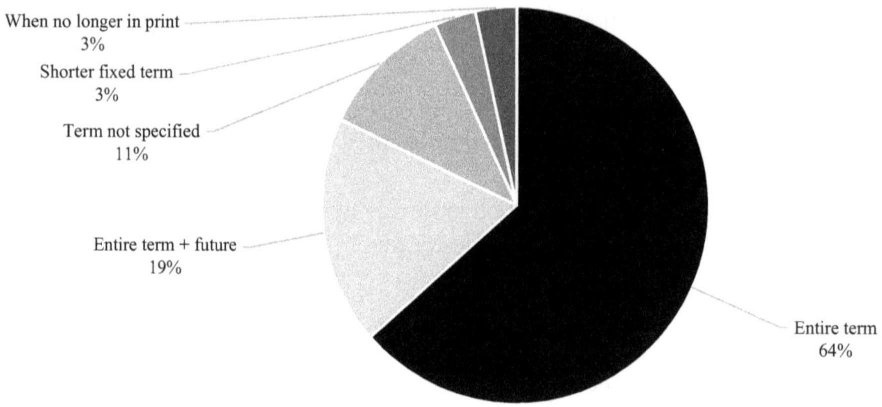


FIGURE 5.1 Length of publishing contracts.

industries (music publishing, recording, etc.), because the features of creative markets that lead to the adoption of reversion clauses in publishing contracts are often present in those fields as well.[52]

### 5.2.2 *Results*

#### 5.2.2.1 Publishers Took Extremely Broad Rights

5.2.2.1.1 MOST LICENCES WERE FOR THE ENTIRE TERM OF COPYRIGHT. Most contracts in the sample took rights for the entire term of copyright (Figure 5.1), which is consistent with the advice to publishers in leading industry guides.[53] Nineteen per cent even took rights for any and all *additional* terms of copyright that may be granted by lawmakers at some future time.[54] Just 6 per cent of contracts either specified a shorter fixed term, or limited the term until the work went out of print. The remaining 11 per cent did not specify a term, and under Australian law a reasonable term would be implied.[55]

52 See generally Section 5.3.

53 For sample clauses, see, e.g., Owen (ed) (n 43) 7, 10; Alexander Lindey, *Lindey on Entertainment, Publishing and the Arts* (Thomson Reuters, 2024-1 ed) § 5:14, cl 1; David Nimmer, *Nimmer on Copyright* (LexisNexis, 2024) form 26-1 cl 1; Donald C Farber (ed), *Entertainment Industry Contracts: Negotiating and Drafting Guide* (LexisNexis, 2024) form 41-1 cl 1.

54 See, e.g., Lindey (n 53) § 5:14, cl 1. Jones and Benson recommend that this allowance is made if publishers take rights for the entire term: Hugh Jones and Christopher Benson, *Publishing Law* (Routledge, 3rd ed, 2006) 77.

55 Andrew Robertson and Jeannie Paterson, *Principles of Contract Law* (Lawbook, 6th ed, 2020) 499 [23.75].

5.2.2.1.2 RIGHTS TAKEN WERE BROAD, AS WELL AS LONG. Most contracts took exclusive rights over printing and publishing (79 per cent). A further 17 per cent purported to take the entire copyright, which is common practice in relation to educational and academic texts but less so for trade books.[56]

Some contracts exhibited confusion as to precisely what was being taken. For example, a 1964 contract gave the publisher the copyright *and* an exclusive licence for printing, publishing and selling the book, even though the latter would not be necessary if the publisher owned the copyright. A 2002 contract said copyright belonged to the publisher but later listed the author's name after the copyright symbol, with an identical listing for the publisher: who did the parties to that contract believe actually owned the copyright? And a 2012 contract granted the publisher an irrevocable, perpetual exclusive licence – which it also made terminable on 10 days' notice. A licence cannot of course be simultaneously irrevocable and terminable. Inconsistencies like this suggested some publishers lacked the expertise or resources to draft appropriate contracts, and sometimes failed to even understand what they were taking.

Contracts were similarly expansive in the language and territory rights they gave publishers.[57] Eighty-three per cent granted worldwide printing, publishing and licensing rights without the author's further approval.

Nearly half (n = 72) explicitly took rights in all languages. A further 7 per cent allowed publishers to print and publish books in all languages so long as the author approved the sale of translation rights. Just 13 per cent specified that the publisher took English-language rights only.

We identified ambiguities in the context of language rights too. Two contracts were so unclear we could not determine the languages for which publishers had been granted printing, publishing and/or licensing rights. A further 29 per cent (n = 42) did not specify the languages in which the publisher could print, publish and/or license the book. However, 60 per cent (n = 25) of those then gave the publisher translation rights without requiring the author's approval.

In sum, the publishers captured by the sample took extremely broad rights:

1. 79 per cent took exclusive rights, including copyright assignments, for at least the entire copyright term;
2. 66 per cent expressly took term-long exclusive rights worldwide; and
3. 44 per cent expressly took term-long exclusive rights, worldwide, in all languages.

[56] See, e.g., Hugh Jones, *Publishing Law* (Routledge, 2016) 96; Lynette Owen, *Selling Rights* (Routledge, 5th ed, 2006) 29, 31; Lynette Owen, *Selling Rights* (Routledge, 6th ed, 2010) 39, 41; Owen (ed) (n 43) 82–3.

[57] We anticipate this proportion would have been lower had agented author contracts been available for study, because agents often prefer to sell world and language rights themselves (and will therefore withhold them from publishers if possible).

It's understandable that publishers wish to take broad rights upfront – they want to ensure their commercial interests are protected in the event one book turns out to be a runaway bestseller. However, such practices make it all the more important to provide clear and appropriate mechanisms for returning rights where (as is nearly always the case) they aren't all used. As we demonstrate in the following section, however, the sampled contracts showed much less consideration for the return of rights than for their initial extraction.

#### 5.2.2.2 Most Contracts Had Out-of-Print Rights, but These Were Slow to Evolve

Most contracts in the sample had out-of-print rights (n = 126, 87 per cent). Six of the 19 contracts without such rights were for educational and academic texts, for which it can be appropriate *not* to have such a clause because those texts are designed to be regularly revised, and can be originated by publishers rather than authors and are designed to be regularly updated.[58] But over half the contracts without out-of-print clauses involved trade non-fiction books, providing evidence that out-of-print clauses are less universal than the publishing industry sometimes represents them as being.[59]

5.2.2.2.1 MOST OUT-OF-PRINT FORMULATIONS WERE UNFIT FOR PURPOSE. Just 7 per cent of sampled contracts with out-of-print clauses (n = 9) accorded with best practice by using objective criteria to determine print status. One 2014 example defined 'out of print' as where there had been gross royalties of under AUD $100 across print and ebook sales during the previous 12 months. Such triggers gave authors clarity about the circumstances in which they could exercise their reversion rights. Welcomely, this example explicitly encompasses digital sales – something we saw in Chapter 4 is not always the case in European statutory formulations that provide objective criteria to define print status.[60]

The earliest contract we found referencing objective criteria was dated 1987, and five of the nine contracts that did so were dated 2009 or earlier. That suggests that at least some publishers were aware of the importance of evolving their definitions of 'out of print' during the shift to the digital era.

However, the overwhelming majority of contracts with out-of-print clauses (88 per cent) instead relied on technical availability standards (Figure 5.2). These included 'out of print and not available in any edition' (n = 54), 'out of print in all editions' (n = 21), 'out of print' (n = 18), and 'out of print or off the market' (n = 10). Other variants also appeared, and in fact became more common in the later years of the

58 See, e.g., Owen (ed) (n 43) 98; Nimmer (n 53) form 465-26-2, cl 11.
59 Rebecca Giblin, 'Does Australia Really Need Author Rights? A Response to Industry Pushback' (2019) 235 *Overland* <https://perma.cc/M55E-YYNG>.
60 See Chapter 4, Section 4.2.2.1.2.

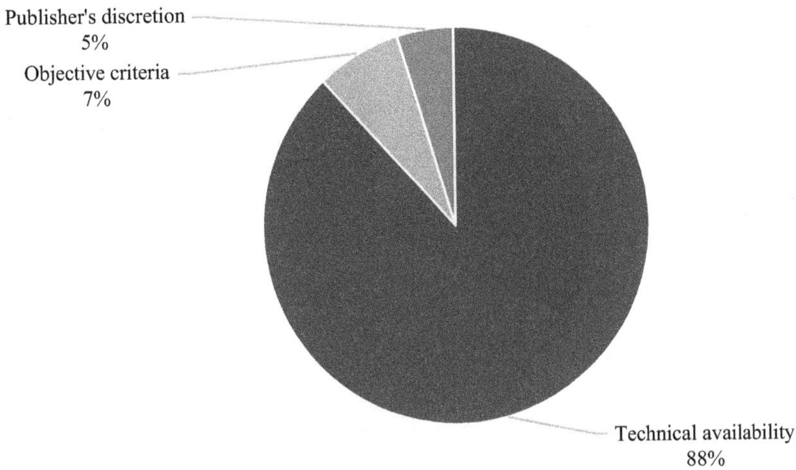


FIGURE 5.2 Standards determining whether a book is out of print.

sample.[61] We were unable to determine whether these various formulations had different meanings – would 'out of print' include books that were only available in digital editions? Would there be a different result for 'out of print or off the market'? That lack of clarity is likely to make it more challenging for authors to confidently ascertain the scope of their rights.

As explained above, formulations based on technical availability have long been inconsistent with industry best practice. That they were so prevalent in our sample despite the concerted, decades-long efforts of author advocates to reform them shows that it can take an inordinately long time for changes to industry reality to flow through to contractual practice.

The final six contracts with out-of-print clauses gave publishers the power to determine when a title was out of print, by, for example, declaring that demand or changed conditions don't justify further publication. Such formulations are also undesirable for lack of clarity, and for their reliance on intervention from publishers at a time when they're likely to have very little remaining interest in a particular title.

5.2.2.2.2 AUTHORS HAD TO WAIT A LONG TIME TO RECLAIM THEIR RIGHTS. Where a book did meet the out-of-print criteria, just four contracts provided for rights to revert immediately to authors upon notification to their publisher. It was much more common for authors to be obliged to give their publisher notice to reprint, and permitted to exercise their reversion right only after that notice expired (93 per cent, n = 117).

The notice framework is intended to balance the needs of publishers to profit from their investments with the interests of authors in reclaiming rights that are no longer

[61] Yuvaraj and Giblin (n 35) 408, n 107.

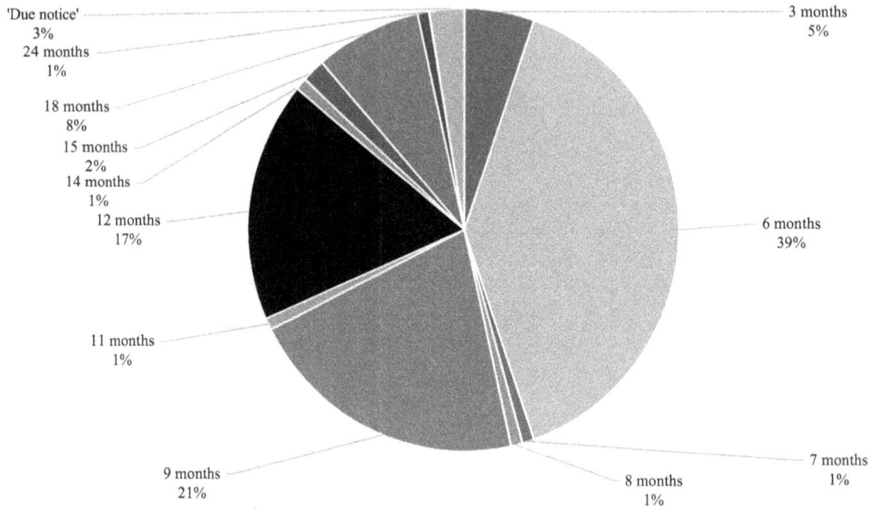


FIGURE 5.3 Periods of notice for publishers to reprint in contracts with out-of-print clauses.[62]

being meaningfully exploited. But the longer the notice period, the bigger the hurdle for authors wanting to capitalise on new exploitation opportunities. As shown in Figure 5.3, the explicit notice periods contained in the sample contracts varied between two months and two years. Some contracts didn't specify a time at all, but required authors to give 'due notice', adding an additional layer of uncertainty to the process.

Interestingly, we observed a general upward trend in the notice period to reprint (Figure 5.4), even though *Clark's* exhibited a *downward* trend in recommended notice periods across its various editions over time.[63] The *Clark's* reduction is consistent with technological advancements making it cheaper and faster to print books, including the kind of small print runs that were economically infeasible in prior eras. Logically this should have translated to publishers requiring less notice to reprint, not more. While the findings are not necessarily generalisable, they are consistent with the overall picture of publishers extracting broader rights from authors than what they actually need.

Sometimes contracts required authors to wait out multiple waiting periods before exercising their out-of-print rights. Sixteen per cent of contracts with out-of-print clauses imposed a waiting period after publication before the author could give notice to reprint. Five per cent imposed a waiting period after the work went out of print before the author could give notice to reprint. Notably, one 2011 contract

[62] We excluded three contracts from 1977, 1987 and 2014 because we could not confidently determine the notice periods. Also, 19 contracts indicated the period was to 'commence' the republication process. In these instances, we added six months to the contractual notice period, assuming it to be a reasonable time for the publisher to finalise reprinting.

[63] Yuvaraj and Giblin (n 35) 116–18.

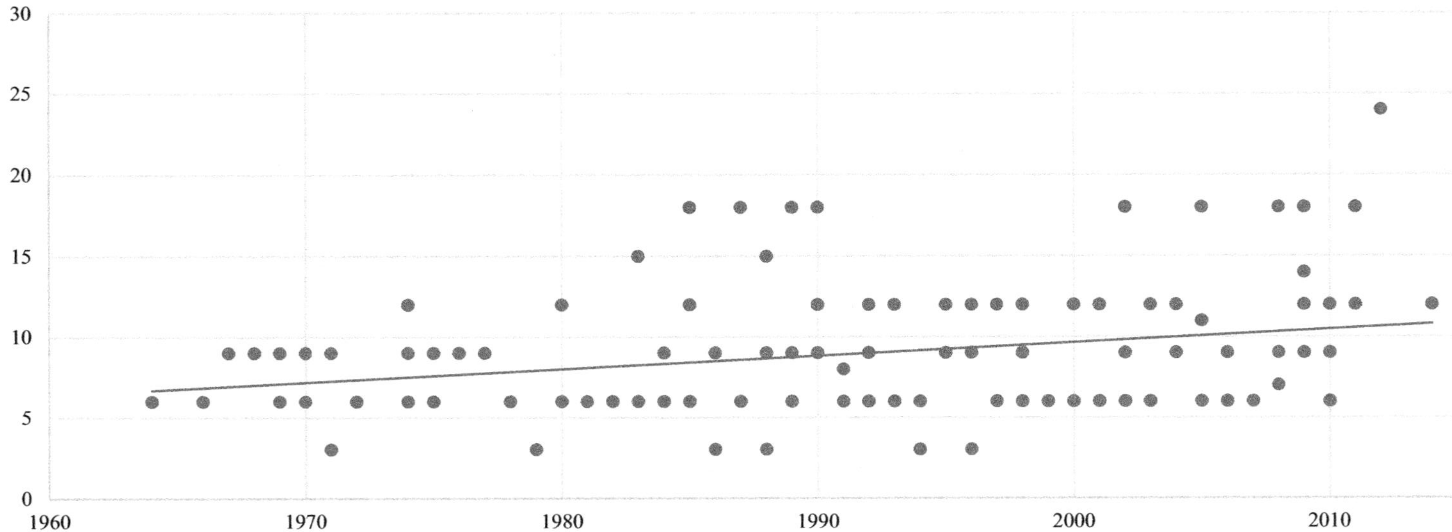


FIGURE 5.4 Notice to reprint (months over time) in contracts with out-of-print clauses.
The Y-axis charts the notice to reprint in months, while the X-axis lists the years of the contracts in the sample.

required *all three*: the author had to wait 12 months after initial publication, plus 12 months after the book went out of print to issue the notice to reprint, then wait a further 12 months after that to actually get their rights back in the event the book wasn't returned to market.

Long notice periods make it harder for authors to ascertain their rights, and make it more time consuming and expensive to exercise them. Even if they have an opportunity to partner with another investor to exploit unused rights, being obliged to wait years to actually reclaim them may mean the opportunity disappears by the time they are able to do so.

5.2.2.2.3 SOME CONTRACTS REQUIRED AUTHORS TO PAY TO RECLAIM THEIR RIGHTS. In the early days of publishing, authors were sometimes required to pay to reclaim rights to out-of-print titles.[64] By the 1970s, however, such requirements were seen as being of purely historic interest, with reductions in the cost of book publishing long having eliminated the need to impose them.[65]

Against that backdrop, we were startled to find six contracts in our sample, dated between 1964 and 1998, that still required the author to repay the unearned portion of their advance and/or contribute to the cost of plant used to print the book. This provides additional evidence that it can take decades for changed industry realities to be fully reflected in contractual practice.

### 5.2.2.3 Not All Contracts Provided for Return of Rights in the Event of Liquidation

Seventy per cent of the sampled contracts provided for authors to reclaim their rights if publishers went out of business, which suggests this issue is of considerable importance to authors. However, the remaining 30 per cent were silent on this issue, raising questions about what would happen to those titles in the event their publisher went under.

### 5.2.2.4 Almost No Contracts Provided Mechanisms to Return Unused Language and Territory Rights

As we saw above, the contracts in our sample took broad exclusive rights over a wide swathe of territories and languages, nearly always for the entire term of copyright.

64 Lionel Bently and Jane C Ginsburg, '"The Sole Right . . . Shall Return to the Authors": Anglo-American Authors' Reversion Rights from the Statute of Anne to Contemporary U.S. Copyright' (2010) 25(3) *Berkeley Technology Law Journal* 1475, 1512–13.

65 Stanley Unwin, *The Truth About Publishing*, rev Philip Unwin (George Allen & Unwin, 8th ed, 1976) 68. The most current edition of *Clark's Publishing Agreements* at the time of writing also expressly indicates repaying an unearned advance is not required for reversion under the out-of-print clause: Owen (ed) (n 43) 63.

Such practices would be less problematic if the contracts adequately provided for their return to authors in the event they went unused, and author associations routinely recommend that contracts incorporate mechanisms to do so.[66] Such rights operate in parallel to 'out of print' rights. For example, a book may still be in print in the UK, but not available in Australia, or in a Spanish language edition, or anywhere in digital form. Best practice would let the publisher hold on to the UK print rights, but permit the author to reclaim rights to unused territories, languages and formats after the publisher has had a reasonable opportunity to exploit them. However, just eight contracts in our sample (6 per cent) made any provision to return unexploited language or territory rights to authors.

### 5.2.3 *Publishing Contracts Are a Poor Repository of Reversion Rights*

The above results show that, when it comes to reversion rights, publishing contracts result in similar problems to those we identified in the context of Europe's statutory equivalents, including inconsistent coverage and outdated formulations. Strikingly, sometimes the problems were identical – such as reversion rights predicated on a book going 'out of print' – a standard that is either radically changed in meaning since the advent of the digital era, or lost meaning altogether, depending on how it's interpreted.[67]

We were particularly concerned by the extent to which the contracts in our sample were missing out-of-print clauses altogether (13 per cent), had out-of-print clauses based on problematic technical availability standards (88 per cent), failed to provide for reversion of unused languages and territories (94 per cent), and failed to provide for reversion in the event of publisher liquidation (30 per cent).

We were also concerned by the ambiguities and inconsistencies we identified in relation to these clauses. Within documents, we sometimes observed different fonts and inconsistent use of terminology, suggesting that these problems may sometimes have emerged from publishers cutting and pasting from different versions over time. While these inconsistencies may have resulted from good faith attempts to reflect changing practices, the results suggest not all publishers have the expertise or resources to draft contracts well.

The Australian Society of Authors successfully used *Are Contracts Enough?* as 'a catalyst' to lobby the Australian Publishing Association ('APA') to change its Code of Conduct,[68] which as a result now advises members to specify clear, objective criteria

66 The Society of Authors, 'CREATOR – Fair Contract Terms' (Web Page) <https://www.societyofauthors.org/Where-We-Stand/C-R-E-A-T-O-R-Campaign-for-Fair-Contracts>; International Authors Forum, 'Authors: Ten Principles for Fair Contracts' (Web Page) <https://www.internationalauthors.org/wp-content/uploads/2019/01/Authors-Ten-Principles.pdf>.

67 See Chapter 4, Section 4.3.1.6.

68 Australian Society of Authors (n 26).

for determining print status in their out-of-print clauses.[69] While this development is certainly welcome, its effects are limited. Not all Australian publishers are members, and not all members will follow the advice. Further, it does nothing to improve the situation for authors bound by existing deficient contracts (which as we've seen may last for a hundred years or more). And, finally, it addresses only one of the myriad deficiencies we have identified above. While it now addresses out-of-print rights for example, the APA's Code of Conduct remains silent about how to appropriately provide for the return of other unused rights.

### 5.2.4 *Enforcing Contractual Rights Is Problematic Too*

One limitation of our archival study was that it only looked at the text of the documents – not how they were applied in practice. That's potentially significant, because publishing industry practice sometimes sees publishers return rights to authors even in circumstances where the contract does not strictly require them to do so.[70] To more fully evaluate the degree to which a contract-based approach is problematic, it's necessary to understand what happens when authors actually seek to enforce their rights.

The Untapped experiment, introduced in Chapter 1, fills that gap.[71] Project member Airlie Lawson, a literary sociologist with some 20 years' experience in Australian and international publishing, worked closely with participating authors, agents and heirs ('participants') to secure the rights necessary to republish a collection of culturally important lost books under the Untapped imprint, first digitally, and later in print.

Rights to 115 titles had already been reverted at the time participants were approached about the project, demonstrating a strong degree of ongoing interest in rights that their publishers had found to be commercially exhausted.[72] The project team also assisted participants with navigating the reversion process for a further 46 titles, recording any challenges or obstacles they faced. The team then interviewed 23 participants (e.g. authors or heirs) to obtain a deeper understanding of their experiences actually exercising their reversion rights.

Preliminary results from this research are striking. They suggest participants faced a wide range of obstacles in the course of exercising their contractual reversion

69 Australian Publishers Association, 'Constitution and Code of Conduct' (Web Page) <https://publishers.asn.au/Web/Web/About-Us/Governance/Constitution-Code-of-Conduct.aspx>.

70 Interview with author association staff member A, 7 November 2018.

71 These findings are drawn from Paul Crosby, Tessa Barrington, Airlie Lawson and Rebecca Giblin, 'Untapped Potential: Results from the Australian Literary Heritage Project' (October 2024) <https://law.unimelb.edu.au/__data/assets/pdf_file/0007/5096446/Untapped-Research-Report_v4.pdf>. As indicated at p. 14 of the report, we intend to publish and make available a more detailed analysis of the project's findings via SSRN.

72 Crosby et al (n 72), 14.

rights. Their combined experiences generate important insights into the appropriateness of relying on contracts to secure rights reversion.

In some cases, participants struggled to identify their rights because they could no longer locate the relevant contracts. This was not a surprise, given that those contracts were often decades old by this point. However, it was surprising to discover that in some cases their publishers also could not produce those contracts.

Some participants were also not sure what their book's print status was, and thus whether they were entitled to initiate the reversion process. As we saw above, out-of-print clauses are often drafted in ways that make this difficult to ascertain, and since the contracts rarely oblige publishers to report print status to their authors, they generally don't do so. Some participants further reported that their publishers resisted their attempts to reclaim their rights, despite no indications that the publishers would seek to re-publish those out-of-print works.

One of the biggest surprises was the discovery that sometimes books can disappear entirely through the gaps that can emerge when publishers are acquired, or their catalogues sold. In one instance, for example, the author could not reliably determine which publisher, if any, owned the rights, which made it difficult to verify the chain of ownership for reversion and republication purposes. The team made the call to proceed on the basis that the rights were effectively reverted, but was struck by the way careless recordkeeping could effectively disappear culturally valuable books without their authors even knowing.

As these results show, the process of actually enforcing contractual reversion rights can be far from smooth. While it was not surprising to discover that participants could not locate their original contracts, the sheer range of other obstacles they encountered in the course of exercising their rights *was* surprising.

## 5.3 KEY PROBLEMS WITH CONTRACTS SIMPLY CANNOT BE FIXED

Combined, our empirical investigations into publishing contracts and their real-world enforcement identify serious deficiencies arising from the use of contracts to safeguard authors' reversion rights. Many of these problems echo those of the statutory regimes we evaluated in Chapters 2 to 4, including poor design, outdatedness, inconsistency, uncertainty and undermining by rightsholders.

Our conclusions are of course most directly applicable to the English-language book publishing contexts in which these studies were conducted, and would be helpfully supplemented by further research into the experiences of creators in other fields and jurisdictions. But (a) the prevalence of the access and reward problems we identified in Chapter 1 across different creative industries and countries, (b) the vigour with which creators and representative organisations across the board have for decades campaigned for stronger statutory reversion mechanisms, and (c) the fact that most countries around the world have such protections all strongly suggest a widespread acceptance (beyond English-language book publishing industries) by creators and lawmakers that contracts are not enough when it comes to providing reversion rights for creators.

However, rightsholders, having a very strong preference for leaving author rights to be determined by their contracts, may argue that if contractual and statutory interventions result in similar deficiencies, there's no reason for statutory rights at all. While existing approaches have indeed resulted in similar problems, we argue that these would be far harder to rectify in the context of contracts than statutes. In other words, while statutory and contractual approaches currently both do a poor job of securing appropriate reversion rights to creators, contracts have certain structural features that make them *incapable* of doing it well. We identify these below.

### 5.3.1 *Individual Bargaining Exacerbates Power Imbalances*

In Chapter 4, we noted concerns that some of Europe's statutory rights were not being enforced because creators were afraid of retaliation from rightsholders, including the possibility of being 'blackballed' from future opportunities.[73] Such fears are a natural consequence of the structure of most creative labour markets, characterised as they are by an oversupply of workers willing to work at a discount, the small number of potential buyers for most cultural goods, and the fact that nobody knows what most works are worth at the time the contract is signed.[74]

The same fears also undermine creator enforcement of their contractual rights – and indeed, as Day documented in her comprehensive 2023 study of publishing practice, can be well founded. She recounts how one publisher proudly told her how they retaliated against an author who told them they wanted to take their books elsewhere to get a better deal. '[I]mmediately we stopped putting focus on her backlist because we've got plenty of other authors who we're going to give a backlist revamp and promotion to.'[75]

Such power imbalances don't just affect enforcement: they also cause creators to hold back from requesting changes to the offered terms for fear of 'jeopardis[ing] . . . the negotiation altogether'.[76] These realities are comprehensively evidenced by Day's study as well, which draws upon survey responses from 71 authors across various English-speaking territories.[77] Twenty-one per cent were unsatisfied or very unsatisfied with the negotiations over their publishing contracts.[78] These authors felt

[73] See Chapter 4, Section 4.3.1.4.

[74] See further Europe Economics, Lucie Guibault, Olivia Salamanca and Stef van Gompel, *Remuneration of Authors and Performers for the Use of Their Works and the Fixations of Their Performances* (2015) 138–9, 145 <https://op.europa.eu/en/publication-detail/-/publication/c022cd3c-9a52-11e5-b3b7–01aa75ed71a1>.

[75] Day (n 49) 107.

[76] Ibid 42, 45.

[77] Ibid 50.

[78] Ibid 55. The total number of the remainder is not clear from figure 4.9 (55), although it appears around 63 per cent of the total authors surveyed. The findings don't tell us whether the satisfied

the terms of those deals were generally non-negotiable,[79] with one describing publishers as 'mostly unwilling to budge'. Another described their publisher as having 'tried to bulldoze [them] ... into accepting terms that favoured [the publisher] ... rather than [the author]', while yet another reported their publisher was 'unhappy ... [they] got guidance on the contract from a friend who is also a literary agent'.[80]

However, most dissatisfied authors reported that they agreed to problematic terms despite their concerns.[81] This makes sense given the vast mismatch between the number of authors keen to be published, and capacity of publishers to do so, but suggests we should not be leaving such important rights to be determined by contracts. While statutorily mandated rights can also suffer from undermining by rightsholders, creators collectively advocating for appropriate rights as part of public lawmaking processes necessarily have substantially more bargaining power than individuals negotiating alone.

### 5.3.2 *Legal Advice Is Expensive*

Rub and Clark argue any imbalances in the creator-exploiter dynamic can be addressed by authors using agents or lawyers when negotiating their contracts,[82] but we see two critical problems with this.

First, representation is expensive. Given how little authors already make from their writing,[83] it will rarely be feasible for them to have their contracts reviewed. In a 2022 study of UK author incomes, for example, 79 per cent of authors reported signing publishing or production contracts without the benefit of expert advice in the year prior.[84]

authors *were* able to negotiate changes to their contracts. They may have been happy just to receive a contract: see, e.g., Don E Tomlinson, 'Everything That Glitters Is Not Gold: Songwriter-Music Publisher Agreements and Disagreements' (1995) 18(1) *Hastings Communications and Entertainment Law Journal* 85, 176 in relation to music publishing contracts.

79 Day (n 49) 55–6.

80 Ibid 56.

81 Ibid 59–60, figure 4.13.

82 Guy A Rub, 'Stronger than Kryptonite? Inalienable Profit-Sharing Schemes in Copyright Law' (2013) 27(1) *Harvard Journal of Law & Technology* 49, 85; see also Clark (n 42) 25 (claiming that most published authors in general trade publishing in the US and UK have agents); see also Copyright Law Revision Part 4 (US Government Printing Office, 1964) 275: 'Today an author is generally represented by a literary agent, by an attorney trained in the field of literary property and by tax counsel.'

83 See Chapter 1, Section 1.1.4.3.

84 Amy Thomas, Michele Battisti and Martin Kretschmer, 'UK Authors' Earnings and Contracts: A Survey of 60,000 Writers', *CREATe* (2022) 55. Samples reported in this study may display self-selection bias, but their findings still usefully highlight trends in the publishing industry: see further Rebecca Giblin, 'A New Copyright Bargain? Reclaiming Lost Culture and Getting Authors Paid' (2018) 41(3) *Columbia Journal of Law & the Arts* 369, 394.

Second, given the number of very similar creator contracts that are formed every day, it would be highly inefficient to rely on reversion rights being negotiated separately each time, even if it *was* economically feasible to do so. The high transaction costs of such an approach would shift even more of the profits from creative labour away from workers. For industries such as book publishing, where well-developed reversion norms already exist (even if they're not always well complied with), a shared set of clear, uniform, baseline rights makes particular sense.

### 5.3.3 *Investors Aren't Always Equipped to Draft Contracts Well*

We've seen that contracts can be ambiguous and poorly drafted, making it more expensive and time-consuming for authors to understand and enforce their rights. Our research unearthed examples of publishers imposing terms without understanding their legal significance, author entitlements we couldn't make sense of, core terms that were missing altogether, and unreconcilable inconsistencies. There were clear signs that at least some of these problems were caused by drafters not having the resources or expertise to do it well.

As we've seen, the same problems can afflict statutory provisions governing reversion – but in that context, they can be fixed via well-informed and thoughtful reform processes that learn from the flaws we identify within this book, combined with skilful legislative drafting. It would be exceedingly unrealistic to expect each individual publisher to achieve a similar result, especially given their decades of poor results, and highly inefficient to do so, given the potentially high costs of legal advice and drafting. Given how difficult it has proved to get right a finite number of statutory rights, it's not difficult to imagine how much harder it would be to achieve an appropriate standard across thousands of individual contracts.

### 5.3.4 *Contracts Evolve Too Slowly*

Our analysis showed that publishing contracts can be inordinately slow to evolve in response to changing industry norms. Most strikingly, although author organisations have consistently advocated for the use of objective criteria to determine print status from as early as the 1960s, nearly all the contracts we analysed with out-of-print clauses still used outdated formulae based on technical availability criteria, and almost none provided for the return of other unused rights. Assuming motivated policymakers and functional governments (which we do acknowledge are not always present), statutory reform is a much faster way of ensuring creator rights reflect best practice.

### 5.3.5 *Contracts Last Too Long*

Even if best practice reversion rights were routinely included in contracts, the sheer length of those deals still makes them an inappropriate repository. Depending on the author's age at signing, these agreements may bind the parties for a century or more. These inordinate durations cause two big problems.

First, as time passes, the risk increases that nobody will be able to find the contract to ascertain what the rights actually are.[85] The Untapped team experienced this reality with participants, who were at times unable to locate the documents enshrining their rights. It was startling to discover that sometimes even their publishers cannot do so. By contrast, nobody can lose rights enshrined in statute.

Second, not even the most prescient publishers, authors or agents will be able to predict the social, technological, economic and environmental realities of the 2100s. By making contracts the source of author rights, however, that's effectively what we're asking them to do. Consider how out-of-date contracts from the 1980s are today. In the four decades since, we've seen the advent of digital technologies and the internet and seismic shifts in the technological and economic realities of publishing. What will the next six decades bring? Without knowing, it's a hopeless task to try to predict so far in advance the circumstances in which authors should be able to reclaim their rights.

The statutory reversion rights we've examined in this book are, admittedly, as static as their contractual counterparts – but they don't need to be. In Chapter 6, we discuss possibilities for creating rights that can evolve over time in response to changing realities, which we think is well worth considering for situations involving decades-long terms.

### 5.3.6 *The Public Interest Isn't Represented in Contractual Bargains*

Since creators and investors are the only parties to these deals, there is nobody at the negotiating table to represent the public interest. That's important. When books, songs, video games and other types of works become unavailable because their rights are locked up with rightsholders who are not interested in exploiting them, it doesn't only affect authors: the public interest in access is injured too.

Creators do largely share that interest, but we've seen that their power, information and resource asymmetries relative to investors makes it difficult for them to negotiate terms that appropriately promote it. They have enough on their plates during contract negotiations in trying to protect their individual interests – it's not their responsibility to also concern themselves with the collateral damage that results from so many rights being locked up in the vaults of uninterested owners. That's not the concern of cultural investors, either: the winner-takes-all nature of most culture markets understandably put their focus on taking maximally broad rights 'just in case' rather than thinking about how best to provide for the return of those they

85 E.g., Brianna Schofield, 'Joseph Nye: A Rights Reversion Success Story', *Authors Alliance* (Web Page, 22 January 2016) <https://perma.cc/D2YK-Q3RX>.

don't exploit.[86] However, the public interest in access does need to be safeguarded *somehow*, and public lawmaking processes can ensure that it is.

### 5.3.7 *Public Rights Are the Path to Reform*

The structural realities we describe above may well have contributed to the World Intellectual Property Organization ('WIPO') convening a multi-continental working group to build model provisions to supplement contracts in the mid-1980s.[87] The group generated detailed draft provisions dealing with termination for works going out of print and publishers going into liquidation, including requirements for written notice and preservation of existing sub-licences. These provisions were supposed to form part of a 'Model Law on Copyright', but the initiative was abandoned around 1990. However, the fact that stakeholders from three continents managed to propose agreed principles for reversion of publishing rights suggests the issues are global: wherever books are published in the world (and *especially* in the developing world,[88] this initiative recognised the importance of authors having the ability, *independently of their contracts*), to regain their rights if books went out of print or publishers went out of business. More generally, given publishing market dynamics are broadly reflected in other creative industries,[89] this global lawmaking initiative further highlights the *importance* of going beyond contracts to best protect creators' reversionary interests.

For all the reasons identified above, we agree. If we are to have any hope of achieving reversion rights that meaningfully promote copyright's access and reward goals, it will not be via contracts.

While we're largely agnostic about what is used instead, we need mechanisms that are clear, identifiable, easier to update, not reliant upon individual legal advice and negotiation, and less subject to massive disparities of bargaining power. This all suggests publicly mandated rights would be most appropriate, whether in the form of statute, regulations, binding codes of practice or some other instrument. Chapter 6 draws upon the key lessons generated earlier in the book to provide a set of best practice principles to inform future reform discussions about how such public interventions could most effectively take advantage of reversion's unmet potential to reclaim lost culture and get artists paid.

86 See Chapter 1, Section 1.1.4.2.

87 This paragraph adapts material from Joshua Yuvaraj, 'Back to the Start: Re-envisioning the Role of Copyright Reversion in Australia and Other Common Law Countries' (PhD Thesis, Monash University, 2021) 78–82.

88 See World Intellectual Property Organization, 'Working Group on Model Provisions for National Laws on Publishing Contracts for Literary Works (Geneva, June 18 to 22, 1984)' (1984) 9 Copyright: Monthly Review of the World Intellectual Property Organization (WIPO) 307, 315 [11].

89 See Section 5.3.6.

# 6

# Best-Practice Principles for Copyright Reversion Mechanisms

## INTRODUCTION

In this book we have argued that copyright reversion has enormous potential to better secure economic rewards to creators and promote access to knowledge and culture, driven particularly by the new possibilities for creative production and distribution brought about by digital technologies and the internet. That potential has not yet been tapped, though movements towards reform over the last half decade exhibit growing appetite from creators and policymakers to do so.

This will be difficult to achieve. Current approaches to copyright have allowed a small number of firms to become extremely powerful. The fact that they control such vast catalogues of rights, for such long durations, gives major record labels, film studios and book and music publishers outsized power to control the future of those industries, and a strong vested interest in keeping it that way. The money and power at stake ensures that any meaningful attempt to shift the playing field in favour of creative workers will be resisted – something we've seen play out time after time in the context of reversion reform.

However, anything that cannot go on forever will eventually end.[1] As we explained in this book's Introduction, when systems reach crisis point there will be a need to urgently press new solutions into service. It is our hope that, if and when that time comes for copyright, and meaningful reforms shifting power back to creators become politically feasible, the lessons from this book will help inform discussions about how reversion's potential may be harnessed to do so. With that optimistic end in mind, this chapter sets out eight principles synthesising the most important considerations.

[1] This truism originates from the economist Herb Stein's famous observation that 'if something cannot go on forever, it will stop'. <https://www.cepweb.org/if-something-cannot-go-on-forever-it-will-stop/>.

We express these lessons in the form of principles rather than more specific recommendations in recognition of the widely varying legal systems, infrastructure and creator dynamics that exist around the world. Those differences ensure the mechanisms for best giving effect to these principles will also be different across nations. However, the global nature of many creative markets and fact that so much of copyright's framework is harmonised worldwide via international treaties suggests these lessons *can* usefully inform reversion reform debates around the globe.

In Chapter 5 we explained that contract-based reversion rights are much harder to improve than public interventions. For those reasons, these principles apply mainly to the latter.

They address ways in which both time and use-based reversion models can help copyright laws do a better job of achieving their aims. The two models have different but complementary strengths. Time-based reversion rights have particular potential for helping creators share fairly in the rewards of their work. Since most exploitation contracts are struck before anyone knows what the work is worth, term-length durations can make it difficult for creators to secure an appropriate share upfront – as *Superman*'s creators so painfully discovered. Time limits incentivise rightsholders to share their profits with creative workers, since not doing so could provoke them into taking rights elsewhere once they have the chance. Consider how different the economics of the recorded music market would be if performers had the option of taking their rights elsewhere after a fixed period of say 10 or 20 years. The heritage recording artists who signed on to 4 per cent royalty rates in the 1970s would have had an opportunity to re-negotiate them to the prevailing market rates – around 12 per cent in the 1990s, and at least 25 per cent today[2] – ensuring that they shared in the windfall that flowed from the shift to streaming.

Time-based reversion rights can also help further copyright's access aims, even for works that are still being actively exploited: if rights to existing works were to semi-regularly return to market, it could encourage bids from potential partners who believe they can do a better job of reaching audiences, thus encouraging fresh investments.

Use-based models also have the potential to secure greater rewards to creators, though these may be more modest since often rights are unexploited because there isn't a sufficient commercial market for them. As we've seen, however, that doesn't mean there's no market at all, and emerging low-cost digital and AI-driven production and distribution options in particular make feasible a great many more exploitation opportunities than was the case in the past. If there were better mechanisms to free up unused rights in order to facilitate such uses, some creators may well be interested in exploiting unused rights themselves – for example, by licensing digital versions for sale online. The existence of stronger reversion rights could also

[2] Cory Doctorow and Rebecca Giblin, *Chokepoint Capitalism* (Scribe Publications, 2022) 59, 222.

encourage new or existing investors to develop markets to assist in their exploitation, analogous to those we've already seen for re-publishing out-of-print books.

Thus, appropriately drawn use-it-or-lose-it rights can also play a pivotal role in satisfying creators' interests in ensuring their works continue to be available to the public, as well as promoting the broader public interest in access to knowledge and culture.

After setting out our eight principles for designing reversion rights to best achieve these aims, we conclude the book by provocatively sketching out an example of how taking a radical approach to reversion rights could very directly support public access while simultaneously generating new revenue to support creators.

## 6.1 BEST-PRACTICE REVERSION PRINCIPLES

### 6.1.1 *Principle 1: Reversion Mechanisms Should Be Calibrated to Maintain Investment Incentives*

Copyright has three core aims, and it's important not to lose sight of the first (amply incentivising initial production) in order to do a better job of securing the second (incentivising ongoing access to knowledge and culture) and third (recognising and rewarding creators). Thus, reversion mechanisms should be calibrated to ensure they do not disincentivise necessary investments in works' initial creation.

This is, obviously, a balancing exercise. On the one hand, the longer and broader an assignment or license of exclusive rights, the greater the collateral damage to the public (in terms of the unavailability of works) and creators (the inability to share in the rewards that might result from revitalisation). On the other hand, if assignments or licences can be ended too quickly (via too-short time-based mechanisms, or use-based mechanisms that don't give investors appropriate opportunity to exploit their rights), investors may be put off investing in that critical initial production. The key is to ensure a balance between these interests, avoiding undesirable collateral damage while maintaining investment incentives, promoting ongoing access, and helping to secure a fair share to creators. The UK's 'Terms of Trade' approach to the regulation of contracts between public broadcasters and independent film producers provides real world evidence that this is possible, given its success in maintaining the incentives necessary for initial production whilst simultaneously increasing public access and creator rewards.[3]

The appropriate balance of investment interests will be different depending on the relevant works and creative markets (see further Principle 2). Crucially, though, that balance is empirically calculable, based on inputs such as cultural depreciation rates and present value discounting as discussed in Chapter 1.[4] In the context of

[3] See Chapter 2, Section 2.6.3.

[4] See Chapter 1, Section 1.1.4.1.

recording copyrights, for example, in 2021 the UK House of Commons select committee proposed that rights ought to revert after 20 years, being the period after which record labels typically write off bad debt.[5] While the proposal has not yet passed, it is an example of lawmakers developing a time-based reversion mechanism with a trigger calibrated to benefit artists without deterring incentives for initial investment.

Importantly, implementing appropriate restrictions on exploitation contracts should not diminish the role investors play, or their opportunity to benefit fairly from investments in creative works. They should still have ample opportunity to compete to partner with creators, and, if they're doing a good job exploiting the rights of their existing stable, would be well placed to retain them.

Regularising the return of rights to the market would also create new investment opportunities. We saw one example of this with the Untapped project. To license books to libraries for e-lending, it's necessary to work with e-lending aggregators such as OverDrive. Before that collaboration, Untapped's publishing partner Ligature Press was too small for this to be worth their while, which meant there was no way for its small collection of a few dozen already reverted books to reach library readers. As a result of this substantial reversion project, however, it has become known as one of Australia's largest 'Classics' publishers, and provides the infrastructure for culturally important out-of-print books to be brought to libraries ongoing. If it became normal practice for rights to works to regularly return to market, it would similarly encourage the emergence of new business models and facilities to exploit them.

### 6.1.2 *Principle 2: Reversion Mechanisms Should Be Industry Specific*

Above, we recognised that cultural depreciation rates can differ across creative industries. They can have different investment models and reversion norms as well.

These differences can make it very difficult for lawmakers to formulate appropriate reversion triggers. Law reform processes for determining the scope of 'umbrella' provisions that apply universally across a wide range of creative industries (such as the US time-based termination right, or the EU's use-it-or-lose-it right) necessarily end up catering to the lowest common denominator. By that we mean whichever industry successfully pleads the need for broadest rights in order to maintain its investment or distribution incentives will effectively determine the fate of creators in quite distinct fields. In the context of time-based rights, if there are compelling reasons why one form of cultural output (say sound recordings) should not revert until 20 years after transfer, that might result in the same limit being set for other forms that depreciate much more quickly (e.g. news articles), rendering rights to reclaim the latter all but valueless. Such special pleading might potentially explain

[5] See Chapter 2, Section 2.6.3.2.

why the EU DSM's use-it-or-lose-it right was given a strict 'no exploitation' rather than broader 'inadequate exploitation' trigger.

By contrast, sector-specific provisions (such as the detailed French use-it-or-lose-it provisions applying to book publishing, or the Spanish and Italian time limits that apply in that same context) can grant rights with much more effective and useful triggers without threatening any industry's viability.

For these reasons, we recommend that rights be tailored to the specificities of key creative industries, perhaps in the form of binding codes of conduct, with umbrella provisions simply providing a supplementary catch-all where necessary.

### 6.1.3 *Principle 3: To Achieve Their Ends, Reversion Mechanisms Need Appropriate Triggers*

Reversion rights can only further copyright's aims if their triggers allow them to do so – and as this book's review of existing rights has demonstrated, that is rarely the case. We've argued that is partly explainable by the use of 'umbrella' rights that cover a wide variety of creative sectors rather than industry-specific approaches. Assuming industry-specific rights are adopted instead, we recommend thought also be given to the following considerations.

#### 6.1.3.1 Take Advantage of Opportunities Created by Technological Developments

When Samuel Clemens (aka Mark Twain) lobbied the US Congress for longer copyright terms in 1906, his claim wasn't based on the value of books, but their *lack* of value. Pointing out that 'only one book in 1000 ... can outlive the [existing] forty-two-year limit', he argued that when copyrights expired those few valuable books continued to be published, and the valueless continued not to be: the only difference was in whether or not their publishers would be obliged to continue sharing the profits with authors or their heirs. In those circumstances, there was no downside in granting long terms to every single work: it would enable authors of the few with lasting value to share in those benefits, and the rest would be lost to obscurity regardless.[6]

At the time, he was correct: high marginal costs of copying and distribution meant that only the most popular and valuable works could be made enduringly available. But that is no longer the case. Not only has the popularisation of the internet and digital technologies driven the marginal cost of copying and global distribution, for many kinds of work, to almost nothing, but technological developments such as

6 A Bill to Amend and Consolidate the Acts Respecting Copyright: Hearing on S. 6330 and H.R. 19853 Before the H. and S. Comms. on Patents, 59th Cong (1906) (statement of Samuel L Clemens [Mark Twain]), in James Boyle and Jennifer Jenkins (eds), *Intellectual Property: Law & The Information Society* (Center for the Study of the Public Domain, 3rd ed, 2016) 286–9.

generative AI are also massively reducing the costs of making derivatives and translations. As demonstrated in Chapter 1, the mere fact that a cultural investor holds those rights doesn't mean they'll have any interest in exploiting them. Unlike in Clemens' day, however, that can now have real costs.

In response to these changed realities, it's important that creators be able to appropriately reclaim unused rights *even where* some rights are being used. The approach of Spain and Lithuania to allow authors to revert rights over unused languages are good examples of this, as is the French publishing law that permits authors to revert digital rights even where the print rights are being sufficiently handled, and vice versa. By contrast, the EU's approach to Article 22, which appears to permit rightsholders to retain all rights so long as they are doing anything to exploit any one of them, wastefully throws away potential access for the public and rewards for creators.

#### 6.1.3.2 Maintain the Traditional Copyright Bargain

As we have seen, works' continued availability in the analogue era relied upon rightsholders being willing to make substantial investments, for example via new print runs, marketing to retail outlets, physical distribution, and the handling of unsold product and returns. Where they were no longer willing to do so, the work would become unavailable, with the consequence that neither the creator nor the rightsholder would continue to benefit.

However, the shift to digital distribution means that, in many cases, the rightsholder can keep works available ongoing without anything like the commitment previously required to do so – a shift encapsulated by HarperCollins CEO Brian Murray's recent description of publishers' growing backlist revenue as 'almost like an annuity'.[7] This changes the bargain in favour of rightsholders, allowing them to capture a bigger share than what is justified by their investments – and helping explain why the largest trade publishers with their huge backlists have much fatter profits than smaller competitors. Giving authors an opportunity to reclaim rights where their investment partners aren't doing enough to actively promote their works would give them an opportunity to renegotiate their deals to more fairly reflect the rightsholder's risk and investment, or perhaps shift them to one willing to take a more active approach.

### 6.1.4 *Principle 4: Reversion Mechanisms Should Be Kept Fit for Purpose*

This book's review of statutory and contractual reversion rights demonstrated how quickly they can become outdated, reducing their ability to achieve their aims.

7 Guy LeCharles Gonzalez, 'Marketing Math: Penguin Random Hour's 2 Percent Gambit', *The Hot Sheet* (Web Page, 14 September 2022) <https://mailchi.mp/hotsheetpub/publishing-math#mctoc3>.

The breakneck pace of economic, technological, environmental and political change necessitates careful consideration about how to ensure any reversion rights remain fit for purpose.

#### 6.1.4.1 Consider Making Reversion Rights 'Living Rights'

One appealing option is to make them what we call 'living rights', akin to the book publishing scheme contained in the French Intellectual Property Code. That code entitles authors to terminate book publishing contracts where their publisher fails to ensure permanent and continuous exploitation in print or digital form.[8] It also provides for the making of binding collective agreements to deal with prescribed issues, including the question of what amounts to permanent and continuous exploitation, with the Council of State able to determine those matters by decree in the absence of such an agreement.[9]

In 2014, the first collective agreement under this scheme was made binding, setting out a detailed set of requirements including what is necessary for publishers to ensure 'permanent and continuous exploitation'. That requires publishers to 'ensure the active distribution of the work to give it every chance of success with the public'.[10] It goes on to include specific mandates of what this involves: '[p]resent [ing] the work as available in at least one of the major interprofessional databases of commercially available works' (for printed editions) and '[m]ak[ing] . . . it available in a technical format that can be used, taking into account the usual formats on the market and their evolution, and in at least one non-proprietary format' (for digital editions).[11]

The agreement applies indefinitely, but the parties must consider revisions at five-yearly intervals in order 'to anticipate the changes brought about by digital technologies, to adapt to changes in professional practices or to resolve any difficulty arising from the application of the agreement'.[12] Any revised agreements will become mandatory too. Under this scheme, authors have an ongoing 'static' right to revert for failure to ensure permanent and continuous exploitation, but the

[8] Code de la propriété intellectuelle 1992 (Intellectual Property Code 1992 (France)) art L132–17-2.

[9] Ibid art L132–17-8(III).

[10] Arrêté du 10 décembre 2014 pris en application de l'article L. 132-17-8 du code de la propriété intellectuelle et portant extension de l'accord du 1er décembre 2014 entre le Conseil permanent des écrivains et le Syndicat national de l'édition sur le contrat d'édition dans le secteur du livre (Order of December 10, 2014 taken pursuant to article L. 132-17-8 of the intellectual property code and extending the agreement of December 1, 2014, between the Permanent Council of Writers and the National Publishing Union on the publishing contract in the book sector) (France) ('**PCW-NPU Agreement**', Microsoft Edge translation) cl 4 <https://www.legifrance.gouv.fr/jorf/id/JORFTEXT000029966188>.

[11] Ibid cl 4.1 and 4.2.

[12] Ibid Preamble.

*content* of that right is 'alive', able to evolve alongside the book industry's changing realities.

By applying updated rights to existing contracts, this model not only helps rights remain fit for purpose, but ensures all creators benefit when amendments are made to clarify any ambiguities that emerge – a desirable attribute, given the importance of certainty to the effectiveness of rights (discussed further at Principle 5). A 2017 Code of Good Practices for the Publication of Musical Works provides similar detail on how the publishing contract provisions will apply to music publishing,[13] demonstrating this model's capacity to scale to works other than books.

Using collective agreements to determine the scope and evolution of rights relies upon creator representatives having sufficient resources and bargaining strength, but where such conditions exist, it's an attractive way of ensuring the particularities of specific industries are adequately reflected.

#### 6.1.4.2 Time-Limited Licences May also Help

The importance of actively ensuring rights remain fit for purpose is heightened by the inordinate terms copyright transfers can often last for under current approaches – sometimes a century or more. If those contracts were to be wholly or partly subject to stricter time limits, enabling fresh bargains to be regularly restruck, the need for 'living' rights becomes less urgent.

In this regard the UK's 'Terms of Trade' regulating the agreements between public broadcasters and independent producers (discussed in Chapter 2) may provide inspiration. While they don't specify how independent producers can regain their rights, they do regulate what can be given away, and by imposing relatively short time limits they require investors to renegotiate deals rather than taking rights initially without a reflection of the changing value of the work across the copyright term.[14] The requirement for those terms to be sanctioned by an independent regulator further helps safeguard creator interests.

### 6.1.5 *Principle 5: Reversion Mechanisms Should Be Designed to Maximise Clarity and Certainty*

Regulation may take the form of standards (which are flexible, but correspondingly harder to apply to any given fact scenario) or rules (more precise and thus easier to predict how they will apply, but have less flexibility).[15]

[13] *Code of Good Practices for the Publication of Musical Works* (4 October 2017) <https://www.snac.fr/site/wp-content/uploads/2017/10/Code-of-Good-Practices-for-the-Publication-of-Musical-Works.pdf>. At the time of writing we could not confirm that this Code had been made binding like the book publishing code.

[14] See Chapter 2, Section 2.6.3.1.

[15] See, e.g., Vincy Fon and Francesco Parisi, 'On the Optimal Specificity of Legal Rules' (2007) 3(2) *Journal of Institutional Economics* 147.

#### 6.1.5.1 Reversion Rights Should Be Enhanced by Rules

In our view, reversion rights need to be at least accompanied by rules in order to achieve a desirable level of certainty. This is feasible only where there is some degree of industry-specificity (as argued for in Principle 2), since the rules that are most appropriate to book publishing don't apply as aptly to music publishing or recording.

The French example referenced above illustrates how rules can supplement standards to promote certainty. The entitlement for authors to reclaim rights in the absence of 'permanent and continuous exploitation' is a standard, while the industry codes that give it more precise meaning in the context of books and music are rules. They are specific enough to enable publishers and creators to each get a sufficiently clear understanding of their rights and responsibilities, and how to enforce them. And, because they are agreed collectively by creators and publishers after a formal bargaining process, they're much less likely to contain the kind of ambiguities and uncertainties that our research has found in individual contracts.[16]

Another benefit of having a single set of rules to regulate the reversion rights of an entire industry is that creators and their representatives (including unions, agents, lawyers and so on) can become deeply familiar with them, ensuring greater consistency of interpretation whilst simultaneously reducing the costs of determining and enforcing rights. Since high transaction costs would rule out most potential-but-not-particularly-lucrative uses, keeping them low would help further copyright's access and rewards aims.

#### 6.1.5.2 There Should Be Mechanisms for Resolving Uncertainties

Of course, as this book's analysis of the US termination law demonstrated, it's possible to have bad rules that are simultaneously inflexible and uncertain. That analysis also demonstrated the deleterious effects uncertainty can have on creators seeking to enforce their rights. Key uncertainties (such as whether and when sound recording transfers can be terminated) remain unresolved after more than half a century on the statute books, and those few creators who have pockets deep enough to challenge their contracting partners are quietened by confidential settlements to keep it that way. It is undesirable for reversion's public policy aims to be undermined by such uncertainties.

France's system of living rights, described above, is one potential solution to the certainty problem. Indeed, one of the express purposes of the five yearly reviews of France's collective agreements is 'to resolve any difficulty arising from the application of the agreement'.[17] Since updated rights apply to existing as well as future deals, all creators covered by the scheme benefit from any clarifications that are made.

[16] See generally Chapter 5.

[17] PCW-NPU Agreement, n 11, Preamble.

Alternative options for promoting certainty include requiring regulators to sign off on terms (as per the UK Terms of Trade model) or funding test cases in legal systems where that is appropriate.

Certainty may also be improved through the adoption and use of guidelines. This suggestion is inspired by a project that created guidelines to help documentary filmmakers navigate the US 'fair use' standard, markedly improving both their understanding of the law and their confidence actually exercising those rights.[18]

Industry guidelines could reduce uncertainty by helping parties determine the parameters of reversion mechanisms (e.g. around what types of works are typically considered works for hire, collective works, joint works, derivative works). They would not need to be prescriptive – the goal could simply be to inform creators of how reversion mechanisms have been operationalised in different industries, to improve certainty about what might happen if they try to rely on or enforce those mechanisms in a particular way.

### 6.1.6 *Principle 6: Reversion Mechanisms Must Be Protected against Contractual Subversion*

Above, we warned against allowing rightsholders to use uncertainty to undermine the author-protective intent of reversion rights. Additional care is necessary to prevent contracts from being used to achieve the same end. Throughout this book we have shown that rightsholders have consistently sought to use their superior bargaining power to require that creators effectively give up the benefit of statutory reversion rights. Sometimes this is explicit, as when rightsholders in the UK and US asserted they were taking both the initial and reversionary terms upfront. In other cases it is implicit, as when choice of law or choice of forum clauses are used to subvert one nation's author-protective laws. Since such practices can diminish or even obliterate the intended benefits, reversion mechanisms must be appropriately insulated against contractual subversion.

#### 6.1.6.1 Appropriate Prohibitions on Contracting Out

In the domestic context, this should primarily be achieved by appropriate prohibitions on contracting out, effectively limiting the alienability of the relevant rights.

[18] See, e.g., Association of Independent Video and Filmmakers, Independent Feature Project, International Documentary Association, National Alliance for Media Arts and Culture, and Women in Film and Video, Washington D.C., Chapter, *Documentary Filmmakers' Statement of Best Practices in Fair Use* (18 November 2005) <https://cmsimpact.org/wp-content/uploads/2016/01/Documentary-Filmmakers.pdf>. Regarding the success of those guidelines at promoting certainty, see Pat Aufderheide and Aram Sinnreich, *Documentarians, Fair Use, and Best Practices* (Summer 2014) <https://cmsimpact.org/resource/documentarians-fair-use-and-best-practices/>.

Such prohibitions already have strong precedents in the UK, US and EU for both time-based and use-based rights. In determining what is 'appropriate', slightly different considerations apply to time- and use-based rights given the different ends they seek to achieve.

6.1.6.1.1 LIMITING USE-BASED RIGHTS. There may be circumstances where a blanket prohibition on contracting out of use-based rights could problematically interfere with the certainty required for rightsholders to make their initial investments in works – something Principle 1 emphasised the importance of maintaining.

In that discussion, we flagged the importance of investors having appropriate opportunity to exploit the rights that do have value – and that can take some time to emerge. Use-it-or-lose-it rights should always be framed in ways that reasonably permit that to occur, and the industry-tailored rules we recommend provide scope to do so.

If greater certainty is required, however, consideration may be given to an approach like that of Austria and Hungary. As we saw in Chapter 4, those countries permit creators to waive their general use-it-or-lose-it rights for three and five years, respectively, effectively providing a guaranteed window for the rightsholder to determine which rights it is interested in exploiting. However, we caution against the approach taken by Denmark with its equivalent right, which prohibits contracting out but does allow the relevant time limits (including the period before which reversion can be enforced) to be altered by contract. The risk is that rightsholders could use their superior bargaining power to extend them to a length that could eliminate the right's value to its intended beneficiaries.[19]

Another approach that might be considered is to permit contracting out of specific reversion rights as part of collectively bargained agreements, as per the EU Parliament's original draft of what became Article 22 of the DSM Directive.[20] This could improve flexibility, which is especially important in cases where rights are framed to apply universally, rather than being tailored to different creative industries.

The appropriateness of such an approach depends on creator unions or equivalent bodies that are sufficiently strong and well-resourced to reach fair and informed deals. However, even where such conditions are present, additional safeguards against subversion would likely be needed. These are especially important given the public interest in ongoing access to knowledge and culture since the public would not usually be represented in negotiations for a collective bargain. One possible safeguard is to require that collective agreements contain some equivalent protection of the reversionary interest. EU lawmakers did something analogous in Article 20 of the DSM Directive by giving creators a legal right to seek adjustment of

[19] See Chapter 4, Section 4.2.2.3.
[20] See Chapter 4, Section 4.4.1.

a disproportionate exploitation contract if there was no equivalent mechanism in a collective agreement.[21]

6.1.6.1.2 LIMITING TIME-BASED RIGHTS. A central advantage of time-based reversion rights is that they can allow creators to negotiate fresh deals once the value of their work is better known, enabling them to more fairly share in the resulting rewards. That potential is subverted where rightsholders are permitted to procure the post-reversion period of rights via the initial contract, as we saw in the context of the UK and US rights. Similar attempts at undermining have been documented in Spain, where publishers have allegedly tried to get around the statutory 15-year limit on publishing contracts via the inclusion of automatic renewal clauses.[22]

Such blatant attempts to avoid reversion's author-protective intent should obviously be prohibited. However, care should be taken not to be too rigid lest that interfere with investments in fresh exploitations. For example, an inalienable right to reclaim rights 20 years after transfer could potentially deter rightsholders from making new investments near the end of the term. Such undesirable consequences can be avoided by simply allowing the parties to terminate the original contract by mutual agreement, replacing it with a new one that restarts the time clock. These are precisely the kind of renegotiations that stronger reversion rights should seek to achieve: those that will elicit revisions that incentivise new investments of the kind that will promote access and enable the original creator to share fairly in their work's value. So long as those fresh deals also contain time limits to appropriately provoke further renegotiations, they should be encouraged.

6.1.6.1.3 ALIENABILITY POST-DEATH. Since copyright lasts long after death, measures restricting alienability raise questions about how to determine the disposition of those rights once the author has passed. There are two main approaches. The first permits the creator to decide who inherits, creating an exception to the inalienability of those rights in order to respect their testamentary freedom. The second enshrines inalienability by prescribing those who inherit independent of the creator's testamentary wishes.

The US termination scheme has adopted the second approach, prescribing statutory heirs of the termination rights. As we saw in Chapter 3, where the testamentary heirs of the copyright are different to the statutory heirs of the termination right, disputes sometimes emerge. Do renegotiated deals that re-start the termination clock undermine the inalienability of those rights?[23]

The issue remains unsettled at US law, but in our view the more important question is *who* should have the right to decide who will benefit from reversion rights that don't accrue until after an author's death. Since reversion rights are

[21] EU DSM Directive, art 20(1).
[22] See Chapter 4, Section 4.2.2.3.
[23] See Chapter 3, Section 3.2.3.

predominantly about protecting the interests of creators, we see no reason why they should not be able to choose the beneficiary of their reversion rights in the same way as they can choose the beneficiary of their copyright rights. Any concern that this could lead to undermining (by, for example, rightsholders obliging artists to will reversionary interests to them or a related entity) could be addressed via statutory provision for testamentary dispositions to be set aside where there is evidence of subversionary intent.

#### 6.1.6.2 Protections against International Subversion

6.1.6.2.1 CHOICE OF LAW AND CHOICE OF FORUM CLAUSES MAY DEPRIVE CREATORS OF RIGHTS. The cross-jurisdictional nature of many creative markets (e.g. recordings, music publishing, books) means exploitation contracts will often cover many jurisdictions and specify the laws that will govern those contracts (choice of law), as well as where any resulting disputes will be adjudicated (choice of forum).

Rightsholders can use, and have used such clauses to avoid the operation of one country's reversion rights elsewhere. The *Gloucester Place Music v Le Bon* case pitting Duran Duran against its music publisher is the most famous example. As we saw in Chapter 3, the contract at issue involved a worldwide assignment of song rights, and specified it was to be governed by English law and adjudicated by English courts. The music publisher secured a finding that Duran Duran's exercise of statutory US termination rights would be a breach of English contract law.[24]

Allowing such clauses to dictate the applicable law can deprive creators of the benefits lawmakers intended them to have when crafting domestic reversion provisions. It can also exacerbate existing inequalities between the parties if the contract is governed by the laws of a country the author is unfamiliar with, as they may struggle to understand the language, legal system, and/or engage effective representation.

Unfortunately, this case was decided without the parties putting the choice of law question into controversy – a different outcome may have resulted if it had been.[25] Choice-of-law and choice of forum clauses are not always definitive. Courts may apply private international law rules to say the governing law is other than what the contract says. Private international law rules provide that if an issue relates to copyright law, it will be dealt with under the laws of the country where the work is exploited (*lex protectionis*).[26] But if it relates to the law of contract (*lex contractus*),

[24] See Chapter 3, Section 3.2.3.3.2.

[25] See Richard Arnold and Jane C Ginsburg, 'Foreign Contracts and U.S. Copyright Termination Rights: What Law Applies?' (2020) 43 *Columbia Journal of Law & the Arts* 437, 449.

[26] Jane C Ginsburg and Pierre Sirinelli, *Private International Law Aspects of Authors' Contracts: The Dutch and French Examples* (2015) 39 *Columbia Journal of Law & the Arts* 171, 177; Jane C Ginsburg, 'The Author as Revenue Sharer: Lecture in Memory of William R. Cornish' (2023) 18(11) *Journal of Intellectual Property Law & Practice* 787, 791.

it is dealt with either under the law of the country set out in the contract, or 'the law of the country in which the contractual relationship is localized.'[27] This means the contract between Duran Duran and Gloucester Place Music might have said it was governed under the laws of England, but a court may still have applied US law if they characterised the termination issue to be one about copyright.

It is not always clear when an issue stops being about copyright and starts being about contract.[28] Ginsburg and Sirinelli have expressed concern that rightsholders may incorporate choice-of-forum clauses for disputes to be heard by courts in jurisdictions most likely to characterise those disputes as being about the contract.[29] That would make choice-of-law clauses likelier to prevail, allowing rightsholders to rely on them to subvert domestic reversion mechanisms.

6.1.6.2.2 EXPLICIT GUARDING AGAINST INTERNATIONAL UNDERMINING. There are various ways to design reversion mechanisms against international subversion. This includes via explicit reference to such intention, which might influence interpretations of foreign courts. For example, the DSM Directive requires Articles 19–21 (though not Article 22) to be made mandatory, and for contractual clauses designating as applicable the law of a state other than that Member State to 'not prejudice the application' of those provisions.[30] The Netherlands has applied this protection to reversion as well, however, explicitly asserting that its domestic use-it-or-lose-it right will apply even if a choice-of-law clause exists in an exploitation contract applying the law of another jurisdiction to the dispute.[31] The requirement for this protection is that the contract would have been governed by Dutch law in the absence of that clause, or the exploitation does, or should, take place 'predominantly' or entirely in the Netherlands.[32]

6.1.6.2.3 USE DOMESTIC LAW TO LIMIT THE POTENTIAL SCOPE OF ASSIGNMENTS. Another way to minimise the risk of subversion is to design rights in ways that make it clear that creators *cannot* assign certain reversionary interests via contracts. In Chapter 3, we saw an example of this in the Second Circuit's interpretation of the existing US termination law in the *Morricone* case, involving a licence agreement the parties had agreed was governed by Italian law.[33] While the music publishing rights at issue had been transferred for the maximum permissible duration in each country worldwide, the Second Circuit ruled that the scope of the US grant was subject to the termination right, and thus did not include any copyright

27 Ginsburg and Sirinelli (n 26) 177; Ginsburg (n 26) 791.
28 Ginsburg and Sirinelli (n 26) 177–8.
29 Ibid 178.
30 EU DSM Directive, recital 81; see art 23(1).
31 *Copyright Contract Act* (the Netherlands) art 25h(2).
32 Ibid.
33 See Chapter 3, Section 3.2.3.3.3.

that would revert to the creator after exercising them.[34] Effectively, Morricone could not license any more than 35 years of protection, because that was all US law gave him to give.

This suggests that policymakers could minimise subversion by clarifying that copyright assignments or licences under the relevant domestic law do *not* include reversionary interests. They could also specify, to the extent possible in domestic law, that their statutory reversion mechanisms are 'overriding mandatory provisions' which other domestic courts must give effect to under the Rome I Regulation (an international treaty governing choice of law among other contract law issues).[35]

6.1.6.2.4 INTERNATIONAL TREATY REFORM. While the above tactics could help counter the threat of international subversion of domestic reversion mechanisms, there are limits to what any one country can do to influence the application of foreign law, or adjudications by foreign courts. Given the limits of domestic policy-making, in the event that international subversion of domestic reversion rights were to become prevalent, it may be appropriate to deal with it via international treaty.

### 6.1.7 *Principle 7: Reversion Mechanisms Should Incorporate Appropriate Carveouts*

Rights reversion isn't appropriate for all works, or all circumstances. While it's important to prevent rights from being subverted, it's equally important to ensure that those rights are appropriately scoped in the first place. This exercise can be tricky. Overbroad carveouts can remove much of the value a reversion right could generate (as we saw from the US's disastrously broad and uncertain work-for-hire exceptions), but framing them too narrowly can result in collateral damage too – for example, if that prospect would make it unfeasible to invest in works being created at all. This makes deciding on appropriate carveouts one of the most important aspects of reversion mechanism design. What's appropriate will differ by jurisdiction and context, but here we flag the carveouts that have proved most controversial in the jurisdictions we've focused on in our research: those covering works made in the course of employment, derivative works and collective works.

[34] Ibid.

[35] See further Graeme W Austin, 'Authors' Human Rights and Copyright Policy' (2017) 40(4) *Columbia Journal of Law & the Arts* 405, 425–9; Arnold and Ginsburg (n 25) 450; Regulation (EC) No 593/2008 of the European Parliament and of the council of 17 June 2008 on the law applicable to contractual obligations (Rome I). This would only be possible for contracts executed after 17 December 2009: art 28. According to art 9(1): 'Overriding mandatory provisions are provisions the respect for which is regarded as crucial by a country for safeguarding its public interests, such as its political, social or economic organisation, to such an extent that they are applicable to any situation falling within their scope, irrespective of the law otherwise applicable to the contract under this Regulation.'

### 6.1.7.1 Works Made in the Course of Employment

In what circumstances should works made in the course of their employment revert back to employees? The US termination law says the answer is none – and indeed, designates the employer as the legal author of its employees' works.[36] Canada's approach is slightly different, as Heald points out: 'only works created by people who look like employees are ineligible for reversion'.[37] And European nations, as we saw in Chapter 4, take a variety of approaches, including sometimes allowing employees to reclaim rights unless their employment contracts explicitly provide elsewise.[38]

While these three examples sit at varying points on the spectrum, they all recognise the importance of allowing employers to hold onto the rights of works created by employees in the course of their employment.

There are several justifications for this special treatment. Employee-created copyrighted material is made in exchange for salary and other benefits, commonly at the direction of their managers, which shows its originators have less claim to an ongoing interest than creators who develop work on their own behalf (and bear the risk that it won't pay off). Additionally, if employees could reclaim their rights, it could lead to similar problems to those affecting derivative works and collective works (discussed below), in terms of holdups, uncertainty and increased transaction costs. The risk of reversion might make it unfeasible for the business to invest in the initial creation of that work in the first place.

These arguments have merit. We note, however, that it's vital to frame employment carveouts in ways that don't leave them open to unfair manipulations by rightsholders – like the practice of US record labels to designate artists as employees exclusively for the purpose of the copyright ownership clause, without giving them the pay or conditions that usually accompany that status.[39]

In recognition of the ongoing link that can exist between creators and their outputs, we suggest that policymakers also consider including provisions that could allow employee creators to claim at least some rights, in appropriate cases. In this context, a partial reversion might sometimes be sufficient to achieve the desired ends while striking an appropriate balance of interests – for example, by granting the employee a right to a non-exclusive licence over uses that do not undermine the business purpose.

[36] 17 USC § 101.

[37] Paul J Heald, 'The Impact of Implementing a 25-Year Reversion/Termination Right in Canada' (2021) 28(1) *Journal of Intellectual Property Law* 63, 91.

[38] See Chapter 4, Section 4.2.2.2.3.

[39] Donald C Farber (ed), *Entertainment Industry Contracts: Negotiating and Drafting Guide* (LexisNexis, 2024) form 159-3, cl 4; see also Alexander Lindey and Michael Landau, *Lindey on Entertainment, Publishing and the Arts* (Thomson Reuters, 2024-1 ed) § 9:39, cl 5(c) ('employer for hire').

Works that are specially commissioned may also be inappropriate subjects of reversion even outside the employment context, particularly where the commissioner has exercised a high degree of control over the output, a particularly personal connection (as may be the case for wedding photographs, for example), or where the possibility of reversion would unjustifiably undermine the purpose of the commission. Yuvaraj has argued elsewhere that it may be appropriate to exclude such works from reversion *if* the rightsholder exercises discretion and control over the final product in a way that mirrors the employment relationship *and* the creator has been appropriately compensated for their labour.[40]

#### 6.1.7.2 Derivative Works

Works derived from existing copyrighted works (called 'derivative works' in the US context) need particularly careful treatment – Heald describes 'the question of how to treat the status of a properly licensed derivative work after reversion' as '[o]ne of the most bedeviling problems associated with any rights reversion system'.[41] Consider *The Witcher*, for example. This was originally a series of books and short stories written by the Polish author Andrzej Sapkowski; that source material has now been translated into 37 languages, been the subject of one film and two television adaptations, and spawned both a comic book series and a wildly successful video game.[42] That's a lot of new creativity derived from Sapkowski's original work!

If Sapkowski had an untrammelled ability to reclaim his rights over the source material, there is a risk that he might 'hold-up' those subsequent licensees for an unreasonable share of revenue, potentially making it impossible for the creators of that subsequent creativity to continue to benefit from it, as well as blocking continued public access. That risk could disincentivise investment in the creation of such derivative works in the first place, with similarly deleterious impacts.[43]

The US responded to these risks by carving derivative works out of its termination law entirely – no new derivative works can be made post-termination, but existing ones can continue to be exploited. However, that risks harming the original creator, who might as a result never be able to renegotiate their original contract, no matter how unbalanced that may have been.

We recommend that policymakers consider more nuanced approaches in order to more appropriately balance the interests of creators of 'base' works (to be able to renegotiate grants in order to more fairly share in the value created by their work),

40 Joshua Yuvaraj, 'Back to the Start: Re-envisioning the Role of Copyright Reversion in Australia and Other Common Law Countries' (PhD Thesis, Monash University, 2021) 161–3.

41 Heald (n 37) 88.

42 'The Witcher', *Wikipedia* <https://en.wikipedia.org/wiki/The_Witcher>.

43 Jill I Prater, 'When Museums Act like Gift Shops: The Discordant Derivative Works Exception to the Termination Clause' (1996) 17 *Loyola of Los Angeles Entertainment Law Review* 97, 105–6.

creators of derivative works (to encourage investments in their creation, and share in the associated rewards), and the public (to enjoy ongoing access).

One way of doing so might be to couple any exception permitting the post-reversion use of derivative works with robust fair remuneration rights.[44] This would eliminate the possibility of destructive and wasteful hold-ups, whilst enabling original creators to renegotiate their royalties where it's appropriate to do so.

#### 6.1.7.3 Collective Works

The final controversial carveout we flag concerns application of reversion rights to collective works, by which we mean works that incorporate distinct works by multiple different authors.

The individual contributions that make up collective works often have their own copyrights, but there can additionally be a copyright in the compilation itself, first owned by whoever selected and arranged the material. The critical question is whether individual contributors should be able to withdraw their rights to contributions to larger projects.

This was one of the major controversies during development of the US termination law, as we saw in Chapter 3. Encyclopaedia and textbook publishers were particularly vocal in arguing against their having any ability to do so, and their arguments had merit. Such works can have contributions from a vast number of authors at different points in time, and the prospect of having to untangle and replace them might threaten the viability of the overall work. Permitting authors to withdraw such contributions could create the same kind of hold-ups as are feared in the context of derivative works. That could harm all three of copyright's core aims, by threatening necessary to elicit the initial investment, but also risk public access and put into doubt the ability of other contributors to ongoing rewards for the other contributors.

Carveouts need to be crafted in ways that guard against that kind of collateral damage. However, the US experience also warns policymakers to cabin them carefully, lest exceptions designed to protect against the circumstances described above get co-opted by rightsholders to exclude works that have no such considerations – such as the record labels who try to prevent artists from reclaiming rights to albums, by characterising them as compilations. As discussed in Chapter 3, the carveouts from the US termination right introduced a number of uncertainties and ambiguities, including around collective works, that have had the practical effect of

[44] See, e.g., EU DSM Directive, art 20. 'Bestseller' clauses and fair remuneration are also important elements in the battle against copyright's broken bargain, but they are beyond the scope of this book to discuss. For further research on these types of clauses, see, e.g., Dirk JG Visser, 'Dutch Copyright Contract Law' in Simon Geiregat and Hendrik Vanhees (eds), *Copyright Contracts Tomorrow* (LeA Uitgevers, 2023) 31–3; Anikó Grad-Gyenge, 'The Renewed Bestseller Clause of the Copyright Act' (2022) 18(1) *European Integration Studies* 93.

stripping away much of the law's intended value for creators. Designing rights with an emphasis on certainty (Principle 5) and ensuring they're readily updatable in case any ambiguities nonetheless come to light (Principle 4) would help safeguard against such problems.

### 6.1.8 *Principle 8: Reversion Mechanisms Should Promote Enforceability*

The value of any right depends on its ability to be enforced. As we've seen, creators face particular challenges enforcing rights against their investment partners, with high costs and fears about retribution both acting as significant deterrents. These issues need to be taken seriously: even the most carefully scoped reversion rights cannot achieve their potential if enforcement barriers keep their intended benefits theoretical, rather than actual.

#### 6.1.8.1 Reversion Should Be Available at the Lowest Possible Cost

We've seen that most works depreciate quickly, and that even where rights continue to have commercial value, it might not be substantial. Thus, for a reversion regime to successfully promote the exploitation of such rights, it needs to free them up as cheaply as possible.

In this regard the US once again provides an example of what not to do: the complexity and uncertainty of its regime makes it difficult to navigate without professional advice, which can be costly, and the high fees charged on top of that put it out of reach of many creators. The latter can be particularly problematic for fields such as photography and music, where creators may generate high numbers of works.

Of course, the exercise of rights does need to follow some appropriate procedure – for example, requiring some form of notice containing necessary details identifying the creator, rightsholder, work and the entitlement to revert – but this does not have to be expensive. It's possible to create fair, clear rules that can be applied at a low cost, particularly where these are developed for specific industries rather than attempting to fit all potential cases. The US is an outlier in making reversion subject to any fee at all, and it could be avoided via procedures that either bypass any central registry or provide for the costs of any such service to be covered from other sources.

The adoption of updatable 'living rights', discussed at Principle 4, can further aid enforcement by providing a mechanism for clarifying uncertainties, and ensuring those updated rules apply even to pre-existing contracts. That's attractive, given the extent to which uncertainty can interfere with creators' ability to actually exercise their rights (discussed at Principle 5). By ensuring all agreements within a particular industry were governed by the same rules, such an approach could also welcomely reduce the cost of expert advice.

European nations have created their own disincentives to enforcement, notably via mechanisms that require judicial intervention for reversion to take place.[45] Such approaches unnecessarily raise costs whilst also exacerbating creator fears of retaliation (discussed further below), and should be avoided. Third party interventions should be required only where there is some dispute between the parties, for example as to whether the reversion trigger has been met in a given case.

Where disputes do arise, consideration should be given to providing creators with low-cost enforcement options for resolving them. That's important because traditional litigation's high costs and potential liability for the other party's costs put it out of reach for most.[46] The EU went some way towards recognising that reality via Article 21 of the DSM Directive, which requires Member States to provide 'voluntary' alternative dispute resolution ('ADR') procedures for disagreements concerning Article 19's transparency right and Article 20's right for creators to obtain additional remuneration should existing arrangements not reflect the subsequent success of their work. While they did not mandate availability of ADR for disputes arising from the Article 22 reversion right, it's easy to see how it might help. For example, should it *really* be necessary for there to be some independent imprimatur before rights revert, perhaps because a rightsholder disagrees that the trigger is satisfied, ADR processes could provide an appropriately low-cost way of getting it.

The ADR processes giving effect to Article 21 vary by nation. For instance, some EU Member States have simply said this can be a mediator or arbitrator as regulated in their national law,[47] while others have used existing general or IP-specific alternative dispute resolution mechanisms.[48] That is another reminder of the importance of tailoring rights to their specific legal and cultural context. Having

[45] See Chapter 4, Section 4.3.1.4.

[46] For discussions of the time and cost of litigation, see, e.g., Tania Sourdin and Naomi Burstyner, 'Justice Delayed Is Justice Denied' (2014) 4(1) *Victoria University Law and Justice Journal* 46; Charles Silver, 'Does Civil Justice Cost Too Much?' (2002) 80(7) *Texas Law Review* 2073; Satu Saarensola, 'The Risk of Legal Costs and Its Effects on Access to Court' in Laura Ervo and Anna Nylund (eds), *The Future of Civil Litigation: Access to Courts and Court-annexed Mediation in the Nordic Countries* (Springer, 2014); Noel Semple, 'The Cost of Seeking Civil Justice in Canada' (2015) 93(3) *Canadian Bar Review* 639. The existence and impact of costs provisions varies widely by country, but see, e.g., Erik S Knutsen, 'The Cost of Costs: The Unfortunate Deterrence of Everyday Civil Litigation in Canada' (2010) 36(1) *Queen's Law Journal* 113.

[47] European Union (Copyright and Related Rights in the Digital Single Market) Regulations 2021, rr 27(9); 28(5) (Ireland); 180–1, Legea nr. 8 din 14 martie 1996 privind dreptul de autor şi drepturile conexe Publicat în Monitorul Oficial nr. 489 din 14 iunie 2018 (Law no 8 of 14 March 1996 on copyright and related rights (Romania)) art 48; Ula Furgal, 'Creator Contracts: Report on the Implementation of Chapter 3 of the Directive on Copyright in the Digital Single Market', Report for the European Composer & Songwriter Alliance (June 2022) 19 <https://composeralliance.org/media/721-creator-contracts-report-on-the-implementation-of-chapter-3-of-the-directi.pdf>.

[48] Furgal (n 47).

said that, however, there are a few principles that policymakers everywhere may find useful to take into account in order to help achieve the desired outcomes.

For one thing, consideration should be given to ensuring those procedures have open justice, rather than confidentiality. Doing so upholds the integrity of the process and lets others learn from past decisions, thus promoting 'certainty and predictability'[49] and potentially reducing the enforcement costs for future cases. Consideration should also be given to offering ADR to creators as an option, not a mandate, allowing them to pursue recourse via courts should they wish to do so.[50]

Increasing the scope of ADR powers beyond resolving disputes could also be considered as a way of improving the creator-investor balance. For example, ADR bodies could be granted the power to ban certain terms in exploitation contracts or declare them unenforceable, as courts in Australia and New Zealand can do for unfair standard form contract terms.[51] Such powers could trigger meaningful change across entire creative industries at relatively little cost – and the very fact of their existence could potentially discipline rightsholders against abuses.

#### 6.1.8.2 Reversion Frameworks Should Reduce Retaliatory Potential

The bigger enforcement challenge is to design reversion rights in ways that ameliorate creator fears that exercising their rights could lead to retaliation.

As explained previously, such concerns are greatest in relation to rights that are intended to benefit creators within their working lives, since that's when potential loss of deals or support will cut deepest. Those (well-founded![52]) concerns are created by the same factors that make it difficult for creators to negotiate fair terms in the first place, including the oversupply and desirability of creative labour and the lack of potential buyers that comes from excessive market concentration.

There are any number of ways of reducing the risk of retaliation, and what's most appropriate will of course differ by industry and jurisdiction. However, we offer the following ideas by way of inspiration.

Retaliation is less likely where there is widespread acceptance of the legitimacy and fairness of rights, as well as awareness of their existence and scope. One way of promoting this is by using collective agreements to determine them in the first place,

49 Sundaresh Menon, 'Arbitration's Blade: International Arbitration and the Rule of Law' (2021) 38(1) *Journal of International Arbitration* 1, 11.

50 EU DSM Directive, recital 79. Arbitration agreements can attempt to bar parties' rights to seek recourse via the court system, though courts may also find such provisions invalid: see, e.g., *Heller v Uber Technologies* 2020 SCC 16, discussed in Jodi Gardner, 'Being Conscious of Unconscionability in Modern Times: *Heller v Uber Technologies*' (2021) 84(4) *Modern Law Review* 874.

51 See, e.g., *Competition and Consumer Act 2010* (Cth) Schedule 2, ss 23–28A; *Fair Trading Act 1986* (NZ) ss 26A–26E.

52 See Chapter 5, Section 5.3.1.

as per the French example. Express prohibitions on retaliatory practices would also help.

Giving creator representatives such as unions the right to take enforcement action could also help achieve the desired outcomes with less risk to individual authors. This may have been the inspiration for the mandate in Article 21 of the DSM Directive that representative organisations be able to initiate proceedings on behalf of authors and performers. Such intermediaries don't have the same vulnerabilities as individuals, so allowing them to take the driver's seat on enforcement reduces the scope for retaliation, particularly if they are given the power to challenge practices on behalf of a class rather than specific individuals.

Policymakers can also help by introducing measures aimed at normalising reversion. As the practice grows more common, it follows that retaliation would become increasingly administratively costly and less well tolerated. New markets would also likely emerge to exploit freed-up rights, giving creators additional options and greater confidence that it's safe to exercise their rights. Accompanying reversion rights with investments intended to encourage such markets – for example, in the form of public initiatives to fund republication of culturally important works, analogous to the Untapped project but on a larger scale – could welcomely accelerate this process. Awareness-raising campaigns could also assist, though the extent to which they'll successfully reach creators depends on the degree to which rights are likely to provide them with any meaningful benefit.

Another option is to make reversion automatic, rather than creator-initiated, thereby ensuring no individual has done anything for which they would need to fear retaliation. However, care must be taken to ensure that automatic reversion does not interfere with copyright's aim of promoting ongoing access – something that may easily occur if authors or their heirs are not aware that they now control the rights, or if they are unwilling or unable to appropriately exploit them. Canada's law automatically reverting rights to heirs 25 years after the author's death has been validly criticised for leading to precisely such outcomes, as has the prospective South African law that will automatically revert rights 25 years after transfer.[53]

This does not mean automatic reversion should be ruled out – simply that any such mechanisms need to be accompanied by appropriate safeguards. In the following section, we sketch one radical proposal for a time-based reversion right that would not only avoid the potential for orphaning, but generate additional rewards to support new creativity in the process.

## 6.2 A FINAL PROVOCATION

The best practice principles set out above are intended to act as prompts to help guide policymakers and advocates in their thinking about how they might craft

[53] See Chapter 2, Section 2.6.2.

bespoke reversion mechanisms that are well suited to their local conditions and which re-write the copyright bargain to benefit creators, investors and the public alike.

As we bring this book to a close, though, we wanted to leave you with a more detailed and provocative vision of what a reversion mechanism implementing some of these principles might actually look like – a radical upending of traditional thinking around copyright ownership that would maintain incentives for initial investment, improve access to knowledge and culture *and* generate new income for creators, all within the existing treaty framework. It is drawn from Giblin's previous theoretical work, and those interested in diving deeper can find all the eye-watering detail there.[54] In these final pages though, we provide just an outline, with the intent of encouraging you to dream about the kind of system we *could* have if we got serious about designing copyright to better achieve its aims.

### 6.2.1 *Revert Rights Automatically after 25 Years*

Imagine if rights over most works – think books, music, sound recordings and visual art – boomeranged back to their creators automatically, after a specific period of time. As described above, the most appropriate time period would differ by industry, but empirical modelling clearly demonstrates that 25 years at the outside would amply incentivise even the most lavish investments in initial production and distribution.[55]

At that point rights would return to the market, giving creators the opportunity to re-negotiate deals with the original investors or seek new exploitation avenues. That could spur the original rightsholder to give works a fresh promotional push, or propose a new royalty split that reflects its lower level of investment. Since the rights for so many works would be potentially up for grabs, it would encourage investors to develop with new business models to serve them.

Where works still had meaningful value by this time, such a mechanism would give creators an opportunity to ensure they share fairly in it. The recording artists signed to 4 per cent royalty rates in the 1970s would have been able to re-negotiate rates above 10 per cent after the first 25 years, and to at least 25 per cent the next renegotiation after that, consistent with the deals new acts were securing at those times. That would have translated to the biggest labels having less of a profit edge, giving them less capacity to buy up distressed competitors, and less to spend on rent-seeking. It would also have created the conditions for greater competition: new investors could compete for valuable catalogue by demonstrating their ability

[54] Rebecca Giblin, 'A New Copyright Bargain? Reclaiming Lost Culture and Getting Authors Paid' (2018) 41(3) *Columbia Journal of Law & the Arts* 369; Rebecca Giblin, 'A Future of International Copyright? Berne and the Front Door Out' in Megan Richardson et al (eds), *Across Intellectual Property* (Cambridge University Press, 2020).

[55] See Chapter 1, Section 1.1.4.1. See also more detailed analysis in Giblin (n 54) 374–7.

to do a better job. Even before the termination took place, the knowledge that it was *coming* could do much to discipline rightsholders into treating their artists fairly, so they would want to sign for another term. All this would promote a healthier balance of power between creators and the investors they rely upon to get their works to market.

### 6.2.2 *Getting Creators Paid* by *Promoting Access to Culture*

Making reversion automatic would turbocharge the pace of change, and reduce creator fears that taking action to reclaim their rights could provoke retaliation. But it creates the risk of actually becoming less available to the public, which could easily happen if rights went to authors or heirs without their knowledge, or to those who weren't willing and able to exploit them. Safeguards are necessary to prevent that from happening.

Throughout this book we've been focused on two core failings of copyright: the fact that despite having used the moral claims of authors to justify its expansion for decades, it doesn't do a very good job of getting them paid; and second, that current approaches very often cause cultural value to be lost. This latter is partly driven by a collective action problem: the threshold for copyright is so low that the overwhelming majority of works are not individually valuable enough for their owners to exploit, but cumulatively the lost value to society from copyrights that outlast their owners' interest is enormous. In other words then, there's not enough money, and there's money being left on the table. What if we used one problem to help solve the other?

This framing evokes Victor Hugo's idea of a domaine public payant. Hugo argued that publishers should have an obligation to share revenues from out-of-copyright books with authors' heirs. Interestingly though, he didn't think they should go to an authors' blood heirs (at least not beyond a single generation), but rather their 'heirs of the spirit' – new generations of writers who needed support to write and get established.[56] Some of the proceeds from their own works could then, in turn, nourish future generations of writers.

What if we were to take inspiration from Hugo, and design reversion rights in a way that not only eliminated the potential for orphaning, but generated new revenue to directly support authors at the same time?

We could achieve this by asking creators to register ongoing interest in their copyrights as the time for reversion comes near (see Giblin's work elsewhere for a detailed analysis of how this can be achieved while complying with international treaty prohibitions on formalities[57]). If they didn't do so, the rights could be held on

[56] See Victor Hugo, *Actes et Paroles Depuis L'exil 1876–1880* (J Hetzel and Cie – Maison Quantin eds, 1889) 99–104.

[57] Giblin (n 54).

trust by a cultural steward, tasked with the dual mission of generating revenues while also promoting widespread availability and access.

What kind of access might be enabled by such a system? Books could be bulk-licensed to universities, schools and libraries. New investments could be made into making them available in digital and audiobook formats. Museums and galleries could open up access to swathes of art and culture. Lost video games could be made available again. Creators could license forgotten songs, news snippets and postcards to remix them into new forms of creativity. Documentary filmmakers would have new troves of material to draw upon. And recordings of culturally iconic sporting moments might no longer be locked away in broadcaster archives: they could be re-released and re-marketed to stimulate youth participation in those sports.[58]

But the real beauty of such a scheme is that it would generate new revenue that is currently being left untapped, which could be used to benefit authors generally – Hugo's 'heirs of the spirit'. It could be distributed via initiatives such as fellowships, grants, pensions and prizes, securing more rewards to creators and providing the resources to fund new creativity. Of course (as Giblin elaborates elsewhere[59]) it would be vital to get the governance right, and there would need to be mechanisms permitting creators to appropriately reclaim rights they'd previously not registered. Assuming appropriate attention is given to such logistics, however, this provocation shows how a much more radical approach to reversion could help get creators paid *by* reclaiming lost cultural value.

## 6.3 REVERSION, RE-ENVISIONED

Our goal with this book has been to raise awareness of reversion's potential to help copyright better achieve its aims, and identify the considerations key to designing rights that can succeed in doing so. The automatic time-based approach presented above is just one way reversion could help recover lost culture and secure greater rewards for creators. If it excites you, we encourage you to dream even bigger by thinking about how such a system could be tailored to different industries, cultures and legal systems, and how time-based rights might be supplemented by similarly bold use-it-or-lose-it rights to help creators and the public get more of what they need.

Our Western bias means the lessons in this book are most readily applicable to jurisdictions such as the US, UK, EU and Australia. But they can also be integrated more widely as long as policymakers appropriately contextualise them to address the issues they face in their own countries.

58 As a devoted Australian rugby fan, Yuvaraj dreams of the day historical Wallabies content is freely and fully available on streaming platforms to encourage greater youth participation and public interest in 'the game they play in heaven'.

59 See Giblin (n 54) 396–411 for a much more detailed exploration of the mechanics such a scheme might involve.

Further research would help to ensure that any new rights have the best chance of achieving their aims. We would particularly welcome new empirical evaluations comparing the effects of 'no exploitation' vs 'inadequate exploitation' thresholds for EU use-based reversion laws, as well as investigations exploring creator perspectives about how to make reversion rights maximally useful (in terms of development process, scope and enforcement) across different creative sectors. If we are correct in our hypothesis that the DSM Directive's Article 22 will do little to shift the needle in favour of creators, such work would usefully inform the planned 2026 review of the DSM Directive, giving lawmakers a fresh opportunity to get it right.[60]

We are also intrigued by the potential for using rights reversion as a tool for improving enforceability of other creator-protective rights. Recall that the EU Parliament's initial proposal for the DSM Directive would have allowed authors and performers to reclaim rights for failure to comply with the transparency obligation that became Article 19.[61] While this was deleted for reasons that weren't made public,[62] it could have provided a powerful incentive for rightsholders to comply with those obligations. Transparency is just one of the additional triggers that could be considered: the Industry, Research and Energy Committee of the European Parliament recommended including others, too, such as a lack of reporting, inadequate promotion and non-payment.[63] While making the case for any specific trigger is outside this book's scope, we encourage consideration of how rights reversion could incentivise rightsholders to comply with their broader contractual and statutory obligations to creators as well.

Anything that cannot last forever must eventually end. When we finally reach the tipping point, and are ready to demand that the copyright bargain be rebalanced to give creators and the public more of what they need, reversion gives us pathways to do so.

60 EU DSM Directive, art 30(1).
61 See Chapter 4, Section 4.4.1.
62 See Chapter 4, Section 4.4.3.
63 Ibid.

# Index

**Titles in the Series (formerly known as Cambridge Studies in Intellectual Property Rights)**

Graeme W. Austin, Andrew F. Christie, Andrew T. Kenyon and Megan Richardson
*Across Intellectual Property: Essays in Honour of Sam Ricketson*

Brad Sherman and Lionel Bently
*The Making of Modern Intellectual Property Law*

Irini A. Stamatoudi
*Copyright and Multimedia Products: A Comparative Analysis*

Pascal Kamina
*Film Copyright in the European Union*

Huw Beverley-Smith
*The Commercial Appropriation of Personality*

Mark J. Davison
*The Legal Protection of Databases*

Robert Burrell and Allison Coleman
*Copyright Exceptions: The Digital Impact*

Huw Beverley-Smith, Ansgar Ohly and Agnès Lucas-Schloetter
*Privacy, Property and Personality: Civil Law Perspectives on Commercial Appropriation*

Catherine Seville
*The Internationalisation of Copyright Law: Books, Buccaneers and the Black Flag in the Nineteenth Century*

Philip Leith
*Software and Patents in Europe*

Geertrui van Overwalle
*Gene Patents and Clearing Models: Patent Pools, Clearinghouses, Open Source Models and Liability Regimes*

Lionel Bently, Jennifer Davis and Jane C. Ginsburg
*Trade Marks and Brands: An Interdisciplinary Critique*

Jonathan Curci
*The Protection of Biodiversity and Traditional Knowledge in International Law of Intellectual Property*

Lionel Bently, Jennifer Davis and Jane C. Ginsburg
*Copyright and Piracy: An Interdisciplinary Critique*

Megan Richardson and Julian Thomas
*Fashioning Intellectual Property: Exhibition, Advertising and the Press, 1789–1918*

Dev Gangjee
*Relocating the Law of Geographical Indications*

Andrew Kenyon, Megan Richardson and Ng-Loy Wee-Loon
*The Law of Reputation and Brands in the Asia Pacific*

Edson Beas Rodrigues Jr
*The General Exception Clauses of the TRIPS Agreement: Promoting Sustainable Development*

Annabelle Lever
*New Frontiers in the Philosophy of Intellectual Property*

Sigrid Sterckx and Julian Cockbain
*Exclusions from Patentability: How Far Has the European Patent Office Eroded Boundaries?*

Sebastian Haunss
*Conflicts in the Knowledge Society: The Contentious Politics of Intellectual Property*

Helena R. Howe and Jonathan Griffiths
*Concepts of Property in Intellectual Property Law*

Rochelle Cooper Dreyfuss and Jane C. Ginsburg
*Intellectual Property at the Edge: The Contested Contours of IP*

Normann Witzleb, David Lindsay, Moira Paterson and Sharon Rodrick
*Emerging Challenges in Privacy Law: Comparative Perspectives*

Paul Bernal
*Internet Privacy Rights: Rights to Protect Autonomy*

Peter Drahos
*Intellectual Property, Indigenous People and their Knowledge*

Susy Frankel and Daniel Gervais
*The Evolution and Equilibrium of Copyright in the Digital Age*

Edited by Kathy Bowrey and Michael Handler
*Law and Creativity in the Age of the Entertainment Franchise*

Sean Bottomley
*The British Patent System during the Industrial Revolution 1700–1852: From Privilege to Property*

Susy Frankel
*Test Tubes for Global Intellectual Property Issues: Small Market Economies*

Jan Oster
*Media Freedom As a Fundamental Right*

Sara Bannerman
*International Copyright and Access to Knowledge*

Edited by Andrew T. Kenyon
*Comparative Defamation and Privacy Law*

Pascal Kamina
*Film Copyright in the European Union* (second edition)

Tim W. Dornis
*Trademark and Unfair Competition Conflicts: Historical-Comparative, Doctrinal, and Economic Perspectives*

Ge Chen
*Copyright and International Negotiations: An Engine of Free Expression in China?*

David Tan
*The Commercial Appropriation of Fame: A Cultural Analysis of the Right of Publicity and Passing Off*

Jay Sanderson
*Plants, People and Practices: The Nature and History of the UPOV Convention*

Daniel Benoliel
*Patent Intensity and Economic Growth*

Jeffrey A. Maine and Xuan-Thao Nguyen
*The Intellectual Property Holding Company: Tax Use and Abuse from Victoria's Secret to Apple*

Megan Richardson
*The Right to Privacy: Origins and Influence of a Nineteenth-Century Idea*

Martin Husovec
*Injunctions against Intermediaries in the European Union: Accountable but Not Liable?*

Estelle Derclaye
*The Copyright/Design Interface: Past, Present and Future*

Magdalena Kolasa
*Trade Secrets and Employee Mobility: In Search of an Equilibrium*

Péter Mezei
*Copyright Exhaustion: Law and Policy in the United States and the European Union*

Graham Greenleaf and David Lindsay
*Public Rights: Copyright's Public Domains*

Ole-Andreas Rognstad
*Property Aspects of Intellectual Property*

Elena Cooper
*Art and Modern Copyright: The Contested Image*

Paul Bernal
*The Internet, Warts and All: Free Speech, Privacy and Truth*

Sebastian Felix Schwemer
*Licensing and Access to Content in the European Union: Regulation between Copyright and Competition Law*

Daniela Simone
*Copyright and Collective Authorship: Locating the Authors of Collaborative Work*

Emily Hudson
*Drafting Copyright Exceptions: From the Law in Books to the Law in Action*

Graeme Gooday and Steven Wilf
*Patent Cultures: Diversity and Harmonization in Historical Perspective*

Mark Burdon
*Digital Data Collection and Information Privacy Law*

Tanya Aplin and Lionel Bently
*Global Mandatory Fair Use: The Nature and Scope of the Right to Quote Copyright Works*

Edited by Niklas Bruun, Graeme B. Dinwoodie, Marianne Levin and Ansgar Ohly
*Transition and Coherence in Intellectual Property Law: Essays in Honour of Annette Kur*

Alexander Peukert
*A Critique of the Ontology of Intellectual Property Law*

Brent Salter
*Negotiating Copyright in the American Theatre: 1856–1951*

Patrick R. Goold
*IP Accidents: Negligence Liability in Intellectual Property*

Péter Mezei
*Copyright Exhaustion: Law and Policy in the United States and the European Union* (second edition)

Jose Bellido and Kathy Bowrey
*Adventures in Childhood*

Henning Grosse Ruse-Khan and Axel Metzger
*Intellectual Property Ordering Beyond Borders*

Brad Sherman
*Intangible Intangibles: Patent Law's Engagement with Dematerialised Subject Matter*

Joshua Yuvaraj and Rebecca Giblin
*Copyright Reversion: Reclaiming Lost Culture and Getting Creators Paid*

For EU product safety concerns, contact us at Calle de José Abascal, 56–1°, 28003 Madrid, Spain or eugpsr@cambridge.org.

www.ingramcontent.com/pod-product-compliance
Lightning Source LLC
Chambersburg PA
CBHW050745291025
34551CB00048B/169
* 9 7 8 1 0 0 9 3 3 4 8 2 2 *